Houghton Mifflin

EXPLORE

LITERACY ACTIVITY BOOK

Senior Authors
J. David Cooper
John J. Pikulski

Authors
Kathryn H. Au
Margarita Calderón
Jacqueline C. Comas
Marjorie Y. Lipson
J. Sabrina Mims
Susan E. Page
Sheila W. Valencia
MaryEllen Vogt

Consultants
Dolores Malcolm
Tina Saldivar
Shane Templeton

Houghton Mifflin Company • Boston

Atlanta • Dallas • Geneva, Illinois • Palo Alto • Princeton

Illustration Credits
Leo Abbett 247, 250; Susan Aiello Theme Icons, 7, 56, 83–84, 131; Andrea Barrett 179; Shirley Beckes 236, 240, 242; Karen Bell/Carolyn Potts & Associates 13; Paulette Bogan 211, 227; Chuck Brache/Steven Edsey & Sons 216; Cindy Brodie/Square Moon Productions 131; Ruth Brunke 19, 25, 28, 105, 121, 127, 152, 156, 157, 173–174, 186, 223, 237, 241, 243, 246, 252; Robert Burger/Deborah Wolfe 12, 15, 112, 124, 219; Jannine Cabossel 100; Tony Caldwell/Cornell & McCarthy 181, 274–275, 288; Dan Clifford 272–273, 278–279; Olivia Cole/Asciutto Art Reps 137, 199; Daniel Collins 188, 189, 192; Mike Dammer/Steven Edsey & Sons 198, 202; Ruta Daugavietis 63, 132, 149, 153, 230, 231; Anna Dewdney 268–269, 283; Shelly Dieterichs-Morrison 39; Tom Duckworth 54, 69, 72, 79, 85, 95, 108, 114, 122, 141, 166, 207, 251, 253, 256; George Eisner/Steven Edsey & Sons 73, 76, 95; Kate Flanagan/Cornell & McCarthy 192, 194–195, 262; Bryan Friel/Steven Edsey & Sons 101; Dave Garbot iv, 2, 203, 224; Steve Gillig 235; Susan Greenstein 144, 146; Gary Hamilton 104, 175, 177, 193, 196; Paul Hoffman 123; Robin Hotchkiss/Deborah Wolfe 232; Bob Lange 32, 38, 40, 59, 63, 96, 162, 169, 227, 228; Jared D. Lee 103; Judy Love 291–298; Bert Mayse 49, 51, 110, 139, 178, 183, 190, 204, 234; Lori Mitchell 45, 50, 53; Paul Moch 4, 34, 36, 55, 64, 130, 150; Andy Myer/Deborah Wolfe 213, 215, 218; Carol O'Malia 233, 239; Hank Parker/Steven Edsey & Sons 191, 196–197; Mike Quon 232; Lauren Scheuer 265, 270–271, 276–277, 286–287; Stephen Schudlich/Ceci Bartels Associates 135, 136, 160; Jack Scott 96; Neil Shigley/Carol Chislovsky 151, 155; Scott Snow/Creative Freelancers 19, 86, 93; Mike Sobey/Steven Edsey & Sons 168, 217, 221; Darren Thompson 3, 5, 43–44, 71, 75, 201, 205; George Thompson iii, 87, 147, 238; George Ulrich/HK Portfolio 17–18, 46, 97, 111, 116, 137, 180; Quentin Webb/Creative Freelancers 61–62, 100, 226, 229; Linda Wielblad 259–261; Dave Winter 23, 52, 77, 91, 109, 194, 220, 222, 254.

Photo Credits
©Alfred M. Bailey from National Audubon Society/Photo Researchers, Inc., 17; ©BPS Ltd./H. Armstrong Roberts, Inc., 143; ©Allan D. Cruickshank from National Audubon Society/Photo Researchers, Inc., 202; ©Tomas del Amo/H. Armstrong Roberts, Inc., iii, top left, 20; ©Tony Freeman/PhotoEdit, 203, top right; ©Francois Gohier/Photo Researchers, Inc., 206; ©A. Gurmankin/Unicorn Stock Photos, 114; ©H. Armstrong Roberts, Inc., 221, inset; ©Hella Hammio/Photo Researchers, Inc., 167; ©Ed Harp/Unicorn Stock Photos, 47, top left; ©Hoeoeck/Mauritius/H. Armstrong Roberts, Inc., 208, top; ©Image Club Graphics, Inc., 141, 230; ©Gary Irving/Tony Stone Images, 129; ©1971 Karl H. Maslowski/Photo Researchers, Inc., 16; ©Tom McHugh/Photo Researchers, Inc., 151; ©Will & Deni McIntyre/Photo Researchers, Inc., 155; ©NASA, 33, top left, 164, 166, 171; ©NASA/Jupiter Productions, 33, all other, 35; ©Michael Newman/PhotoEdit, 140; ©Courtesy of the George C. Page Museum/Natural History Museum of Los Angeles County, 247, 248; ©PhotoDisc, 60, 76, 88, 92, 97, top, 102, 118, right, 126; ©Rod Planck/Tony Stone Images, 107; ©Maresa Pryor/Animals/Animals, 47, bottom right; ©Leonard Lee Rue III from National Audubon Society/Photo Researchers, Inc., 56; ©M. Schneiders/H. Armstrong Roberts, Inc., iv, 184; ©Jim Stamates/Tony Stone Images, 50; ©1986 Norm Thomas/Photo Researchers, Inc., 14; ©Rob Tringali Jr./Sports Chrome Inc., 119, top; ©David Young-Wolff/PhotoEdit, 144; All other photographs by Ralph J. Brunke.

2001 Impression

Printed in the U.S.A.

ISBN: 0-395-91498-1

10 11 12 13 14 15-WC-04 03 02 01

CONTENTS

CONTENTS

Name

My Reading Strategy Guide

✔ As I **Predict/Infer**, I . . .

- ❑ Look for important information.
- ❑ Look at illustrations.
- ❑ Think about what I know.
- ❑ Think about what will happen next.

✔ As I read, I **Self-Question** and . . .

- ❑ Ask questions to answer for myself as I go along.

✔ As I read and **Think About Words**, I . . .

- ❑ Figure out words by using context, sounds, and word parts.
- ❑ Think of similar words.
- ❑ Read to the end of the sentence or paragraph.
- ❑ Look at the illustrations.

✔ As I **Monitor** my reading, I ask . . .

- ❑ Does this make sense to me?
- ❑ Does it help me meet my purpose?

I try fix-ups:

- ❑ Reread.
- ❑ Read ahead.
- ❑ Look at illustrations.
- ❑ Ask for help.

✔ During and after reading, I **Summarize** and . . .

- ❑ For stories, I think about story elements.
- ❑ For informational texts, I think about main ideas and important details.

✔ As I read, I **Evaluate** and ask myself . . .

- ❑ How do I feel about what I read?
- ❑ Do I agree or disagree with it?
- ❑ How does this compare with similar types of writing that I've read?

Name ....

Are You Gasping for Words?

faint	wobbled
numb	staggered
huffed	collapsed

Use a vocabulary word to write a sentence that tells what is happening in each picture.

1 ______________________________

____

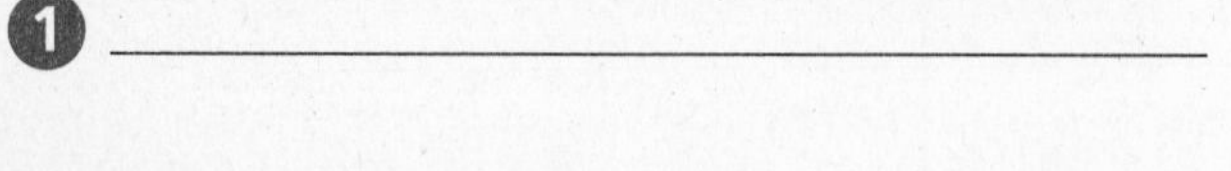

2 ______________________________

____

3 ______________________________

____

4 ______________________________

____

5 ______________________________

____

6 ______________________________

____

Name

Wayside School Days

Answer the questions about "A Package for Mrs. Jewls."

What was Louis doing when the truck drove up?

What happened to Louis on the fifteenth floor?

Why wasn't Miss Zarves in her classroom?

Why did Louis have to wait such a long time for someone to open the door to Mrs. Jewls's classroom?

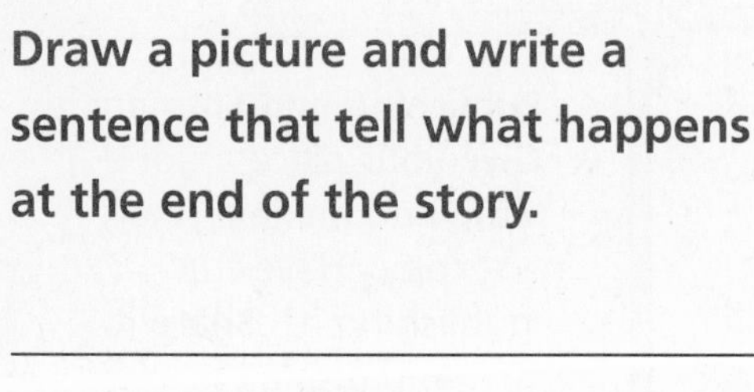

Draw a picture and write a sentence that tell what happens at the end of the story.

Name

The Writing Process

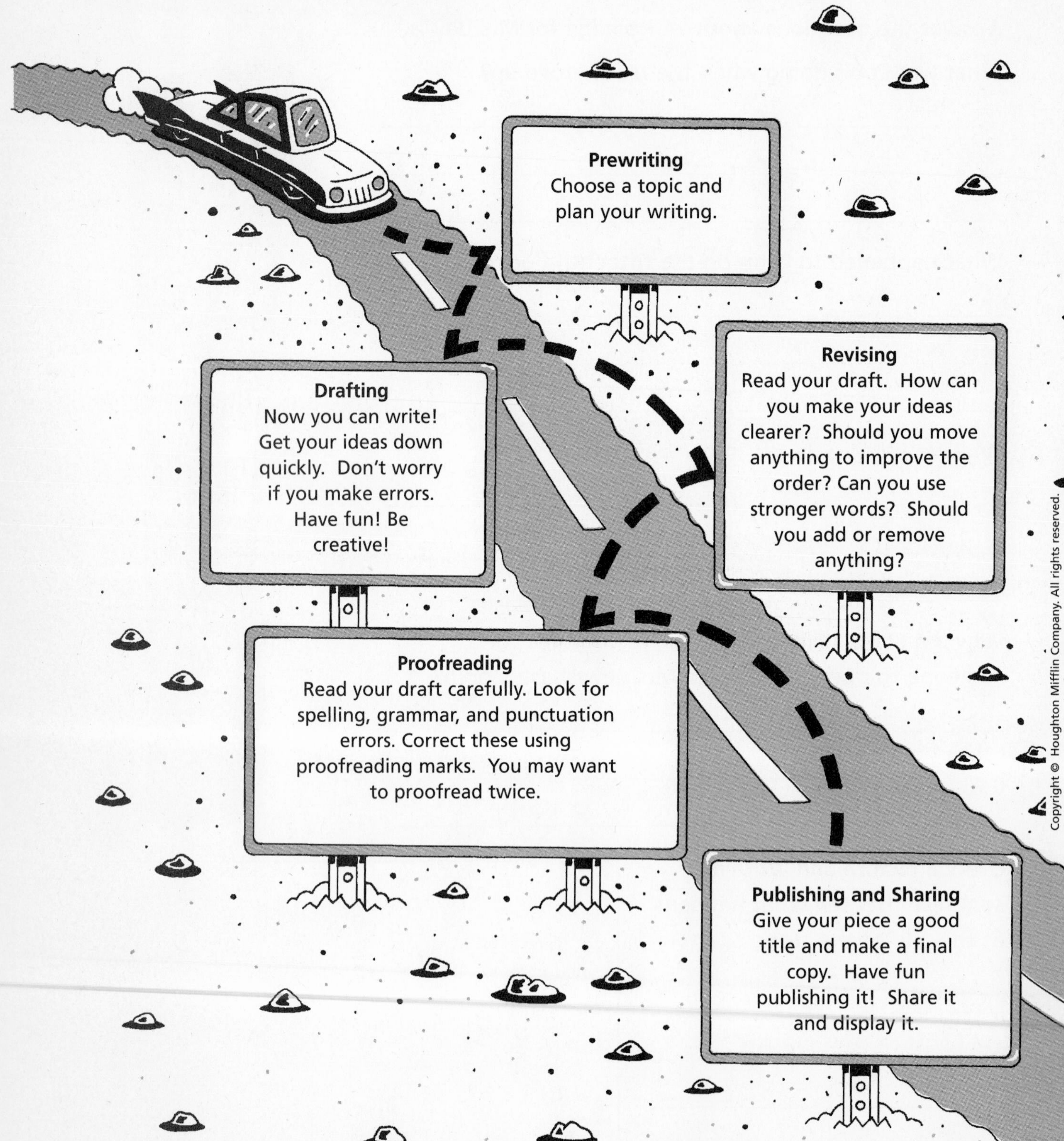

Name

Get Started!

Choose a Topic List three or four choices you might like to write about.

1 ________________
2 ________________
3 ________________
4 ________________

Plan Your Writing Write your topic on the box top. Then write a few sentences about the beginning, the middle, and the end of the incident in each panel.

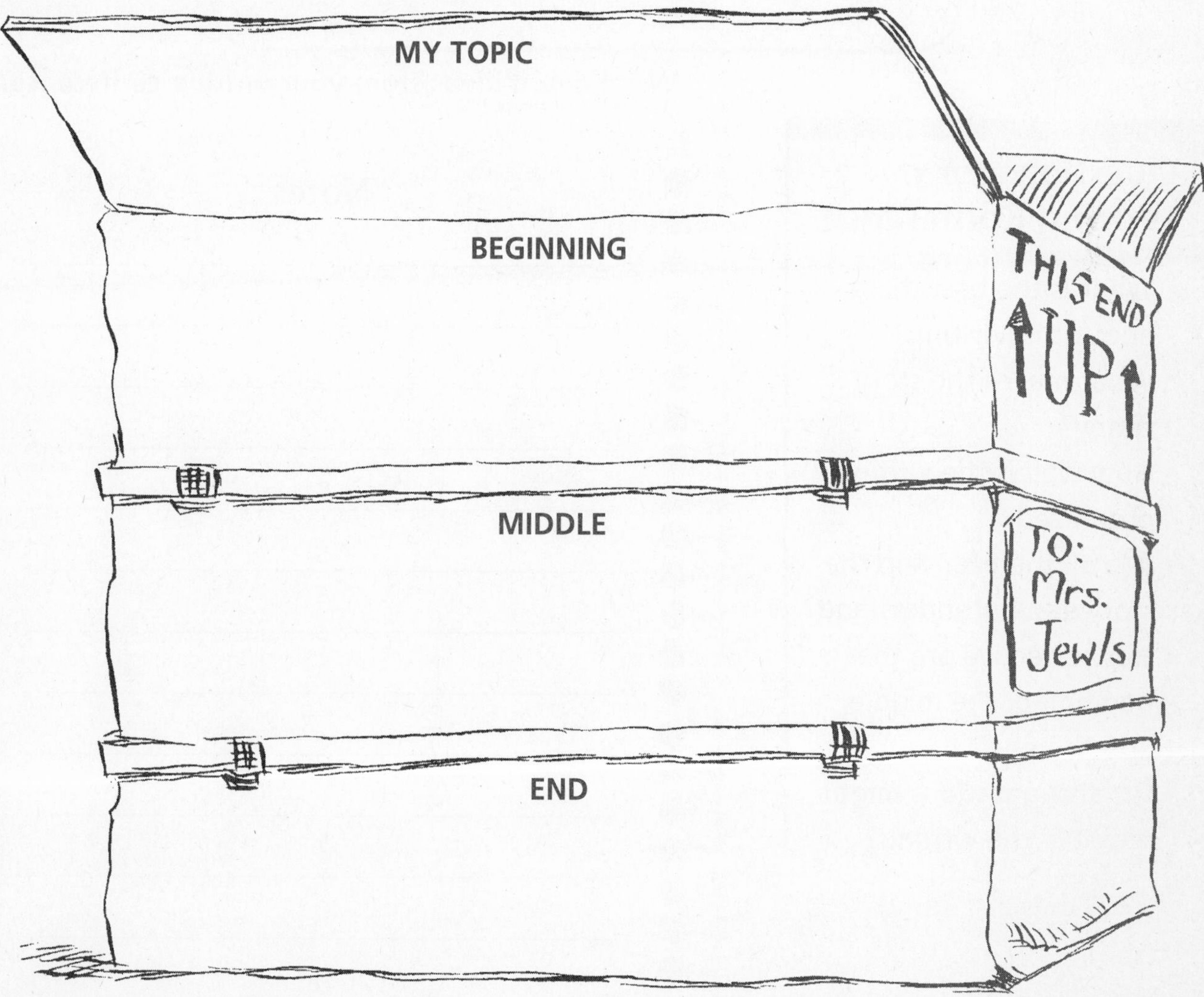

Name

Revising Your Writing

Reread and revise your story. Use the Revising Checklist as a guide. Then have a writing conference with a classmate. Use the Questions for a Writing Conference to guide the discussion.

Revising Checklist

- ❑ Is the writing easy to understand?
- ❑ Should I leave anything out?
- ❑ Do I need to add anything?
- ❑ Does the writing have a beginning, a middle, and an end?
- ❑ Do I need to replace uninteresting words?

Write down ideas from your writing conference.

Questions for a Writing Conference

- What is the best thing about this writing?
- What makes the story funny?
- How well is the writing organized?
- Are all the events in the story easy to understand?
- How effective are the beginning, the middle, and the end?
- What suggestions might improve the writing?

Notes

Name

Journey to Adventure!

After reading each selection, complete the chart below and on the next page to show what you discovered.

	What qualities do the adventurers in the selection have?	Where does the adventure take place?
James and the Giant Peach		
Arctic Explorer: The Story of Matthew Henson		
Voyager: An Adventure to the Edge of the Solar System		

Name

Journey to Adventure!

After reading each selection, complete the chart to show what you discovered.

	What risks or challenges do the adventurers in the selection face?	How do the adventurers overcome dangers and complete their adventure?
James and the Giant Peach		
Arctic Explorer: The Story of Matthew Henson		
Voyager: An Adventure to the Edge of the Solar System		

What have you learned in this theme about facing challenges and overcoming obstacles?

Name ______________________________

Dangerous Words

Use words from the box to complete the sentences and send the characters on a journey to adventure! At the end of each paragraph, add a sentence to the story.

pandemonium
exhorting
lunge
tethered
aghast

A storm was approaching. Pete and Gale had just ______________________ their boat to the dock when a giant wave hit. Suddenly the rope they had used to tie the boat to the dock snapped! ____

____

Pete and Gale made a ______________________ for the dock, but it was just out of reach. They began to drift out to sea. ______________________________________

____

They rowed their boat as fast as they could, ______________________ each other to row faster. However, the wind and waves were too strong. ______________

____

Sharks began to circle the boat. Pete and Gale were ______________________, shocked by what was happening. ______________________________________

____

The waves began to crash over the boat. Panic and ______________________ broke out. Just as they were about to give up hope, Gale had an idea. ______________

____

Describe a situation that would make you frantic.

____

____

____

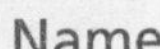

Name

Capture the Captions

These illustrations show some of the events in *James and the Giant Peach.* Write captions that describe the illustrations.

Name

Flying Peaches

James wanted to make a peach fly. The steps of his plan have been provided. Show the proper sequence by numbering them. The first step has been numbered for you.

How to Make a Peach Fly

___ The 502 seagulls will lift the peach out of the water and fly away with it.

___ Use the Earthworm to lure a seagull.

1 Get Miss Spider and the Silkworm to spin silk strings.

___ Repeat steps 1–4 until you catch 502 seagulls.

___ As a seagull dives for the Earthworm, capture it with a silk string. Make sure you pull the Earthworm out of danger in time.

___ Tie the silk string to the peach stem.

Name

Mystery Writing!

A friend was cutting out words to write a mystery note but fled before finishing. Find out what the friend was going to say. Add your own words to make each fragment into a complete sentence. Then put the sentences together and write your mystery note.

leaving on a trip

a million dollars

a tall man

Friday night at seven o'clock

the captain

a telephone booth

Name

What's the Ending?

For each word, write the base word and ending. Check a dictionary if you are unsure about the spelling of a base word.

	Base word	Ending
1 fatter		
2 hurling		
3 cruises		
4 tethered		
5 zaniest		

Write the word from the chart that best completes each sentence. (Hint: If you're not sure what the word means, the ending of the word will help you place it in the right sentence.)

6 When a shark is hungry, it ______________________ the waters in search of food.

7 The sharks kept ______________________ themselves at the peach.

8 James thought the Earthworm would make good bait because he was ______________________ than the others.

9 The Earthworm thought James's plan was the ______________________ idea he had ever heard.

10 James caught a seagull and ______________________ it to the peach stem.

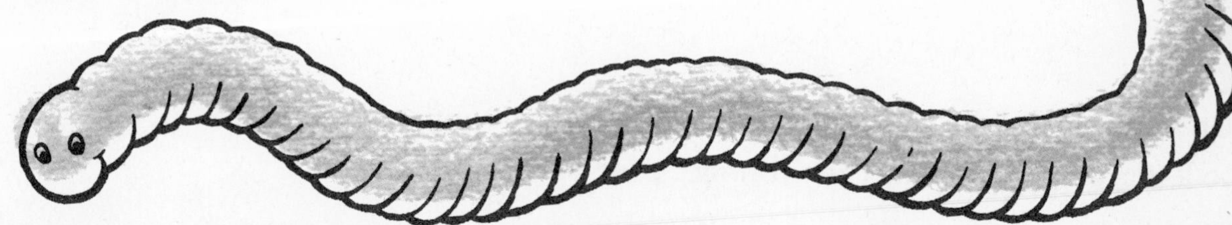

Name

Dangerous Word Rescue

Find a word outside the peach that has the same, or almost the same, meaning as a word inside the peach. Draw a line connecting the two words.

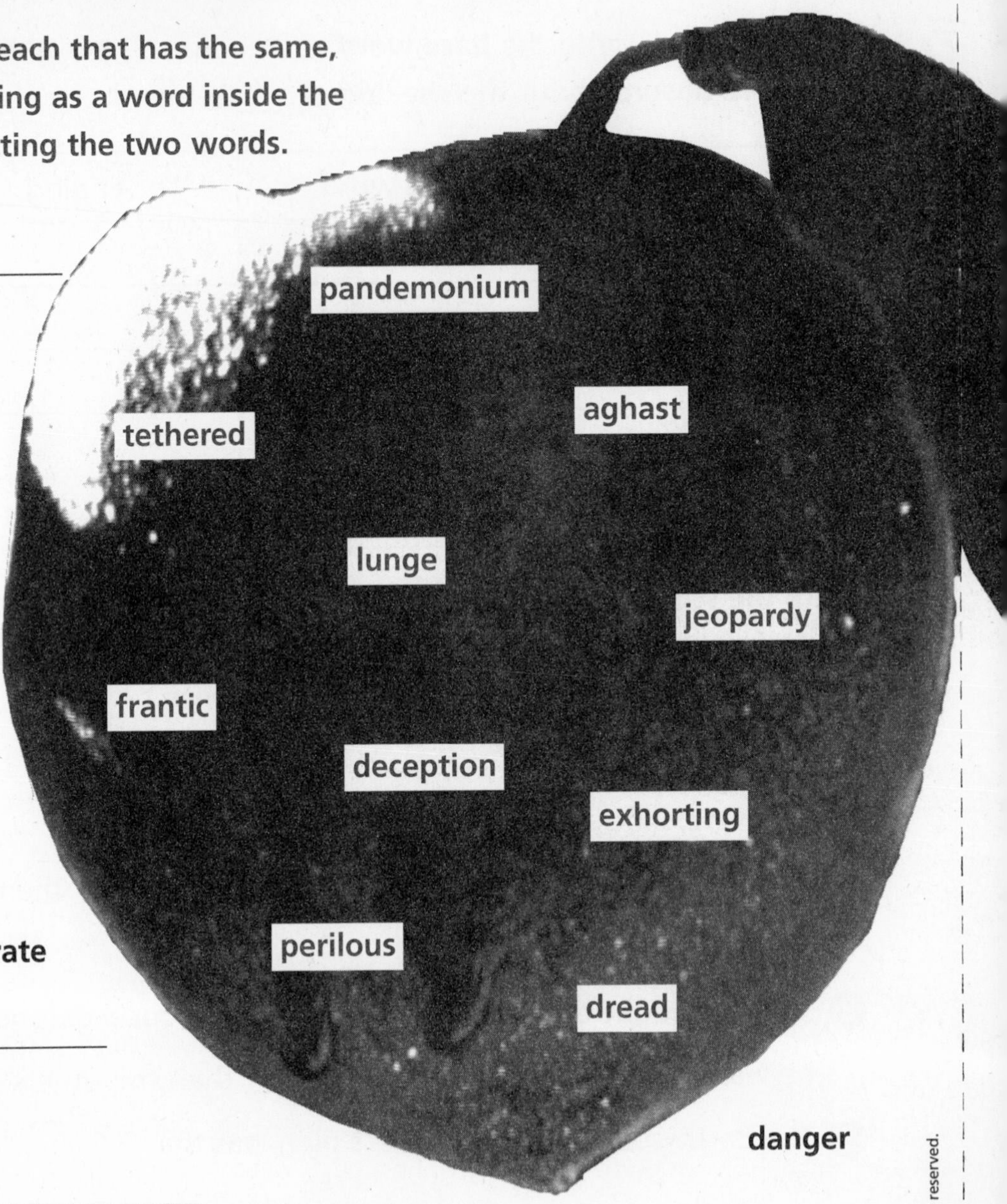

pandemonium

tethered

aghast

lunge

jeopardy

frantic

deception

exhorting

perilous

dread

uproar

dive

tied

stunned

lie

dangerous

desperate

fear

danger

pleading

On each blank line, write another word that has a meaning similar to a word in the peach. Then connect your new word to its synonym.

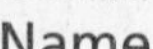

Name

Make Waves

Long *a* and Long *e* Some Spelling Words have the long ***a*** sound, shown as |ā|. The |ā| sound can be spelled with the pattern ***a***-consonant-***e***, ***ai***, or ***ay***.

|ā| wake bait sway

The other Spelling Words have the long ***e*** sound, shown as |ē|. The |ē| sound can be spelled with the pattern ***ea*** or ***ee***.

|ē| peach between

Spelling Words

1. peach
2. bait
3. beast
4. between
5. afraid
6. wake
7. sway
8. scale
9. speed
10. stray

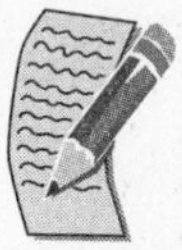

My Study List
What other words do you need to study for spelling? Add them to My Study List for *James and the Giant Peach* in the back of this book.

Write the Spelling Words that match the pattern for the long vowel sound shown on each wave.

|ā|
a*-consonant-*e

1. ______
2. ______

|ā|
ai

3. ______
4. ______

|ā|
ay

5. ______
6. ______

|ē|
ea

7. ______
8. ______

|ē|
ee

9. ______
10. ______

Name

Spelling Spree

Spelling Words

1. peach
2. bait
3. beast
4. between
5. afraid
6. wake
7. sway
8. scale
9. speed
10. stray

Proofreading Circle five misspelled Spelling Words in this poem by Miss Spider. Then write each word correctly.

We float on our peach betwen sky and sea,
So afrade when we start to swai.
And should a straye breeze
Make one of us sneeze,
A beest just might bite us today!

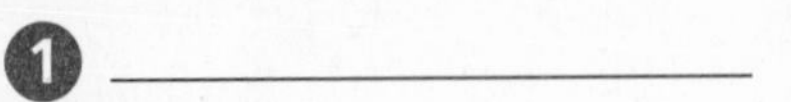

1 ____________ 3 ____________ 5 ____________

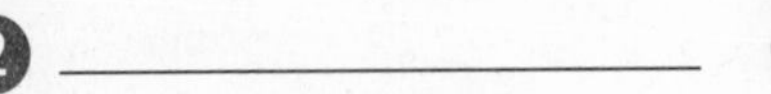

2 ____________ 4 ____________

Twisted Twisters Write a Spelling Word to complete each tongue twister.

6 Silkworm spun string with spectacular ____________.

7 Put the ____________ pit on the pink plate.

8 Bill bought ____________ at the boathouse on the bay.

9 Set the six silk spools on the silver ____________.

10 We'll ____________ the weary worm so he will work.

Peach Patrol Imagine that you are floating over the sea on a giant peach. What is the weather like? Is it windy? Rainy? On a separate piece of paper, write a short weather report. Tell what the day is like. Also describe how the weather conditions will affect your trip. Use Spelling Words from the list.

Name

Soar with Seagulls

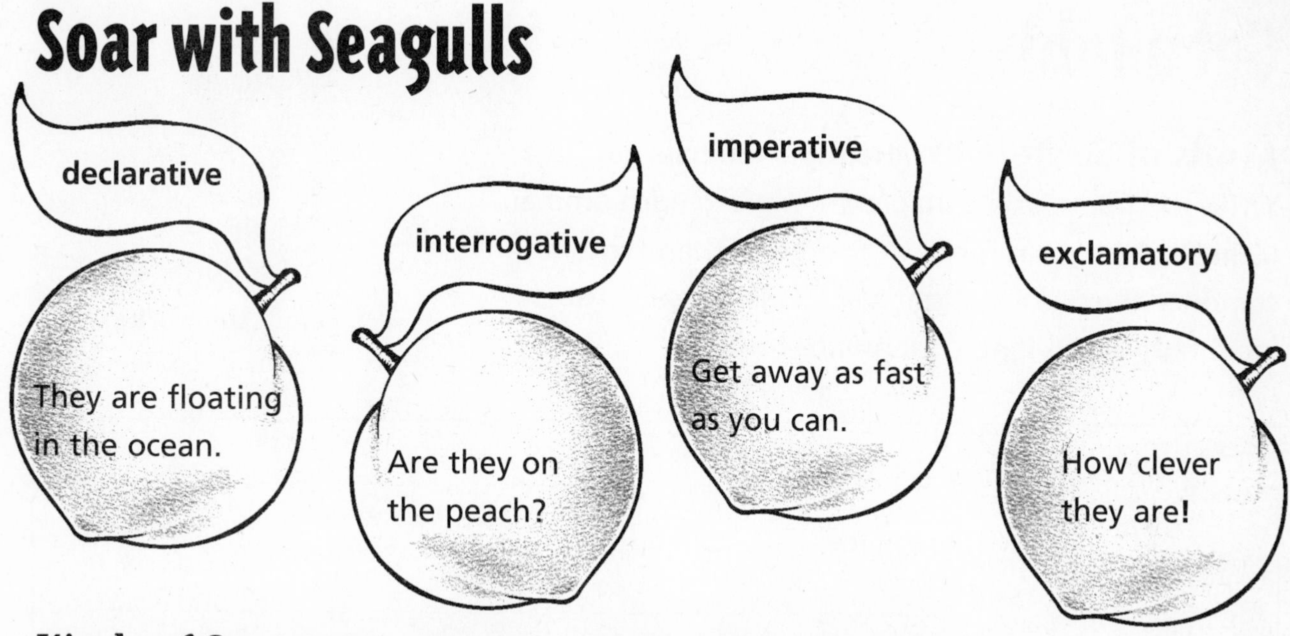

Kinds of Sentences **Read the seagulls' ads for their airline service. Write the correct end mark at the end of each sentence. Then name each sentence by writing *declarative, interrogative, imperative,* or *exclamatory* on each banner.**

. ? !

1. What a peachy ride you will have
____
2. Whistle when you are ready
____
3. We can take you anywhere
____
4. What are you waiting for
____
5. We promise a smooth flight
____

Name

Get a Job!

Kinds of Sentences Help the animals get jobs. Write the name of a suitable job next to each animal, using jobs listed in the box or others. Then write a sentence the animal might say to "sell" itself. The label tells which kind of sentence to write.

butcher
window washer
tennis player
carpenter
firefighter
postal worker

Animal	
	Job ______ Declarative ______ ______
	Job ______ Exclamatory ______ ______
	Job ______ Declarative ______ ______
	Job ______ Imperative ______ ______
	Job ______ Exclamatory ______ ______

Name

Rescue Diagram

Draw a diagram that shows

1. an explorer on one side of a wide lead
2. the rest of the expedition on the other side
3. some sledges and dog teams
4. an ice floe floating down the lead

How can the explorer use the ice floe to rejoin the expedition?

1. Add arrows to show the route the stranded explorer must take.
2. Add an interpreter translating your directions to the explorer. Write your directions in a speech balloon.
3. Then use the underlined words to label your diagram.

DIAGRAM

Name

Following in Henson's Footsteps

Answer each question. You may look back at the selection if you wish.

1. Why did Peary and Henson make six attempts to reach the North Pole? ______________________

2. What were some of Matt's responsibilities once the expedition arrived at Cape Sheridan? ______________________

3. What is an example of Henson using his survival skills to help himself or another person? ______________________

4. How did Matt feel when the expedition reached the North Pole? Why do you think he felt that way? ______________________

5. Which of Matthew Henson's qualities and abilities do you think were most important? Why? ______________________

Name

Pack It Up!

Pack your bags for a trip to the Arctic. In the box are all the names of items you'll need. Write each item name in the correct category. When you've used all the words, you'll have finished packing.

parka	bacon
mitten	pemmican
pickax	thermometer
shovel	walrus meat
bandages	compass

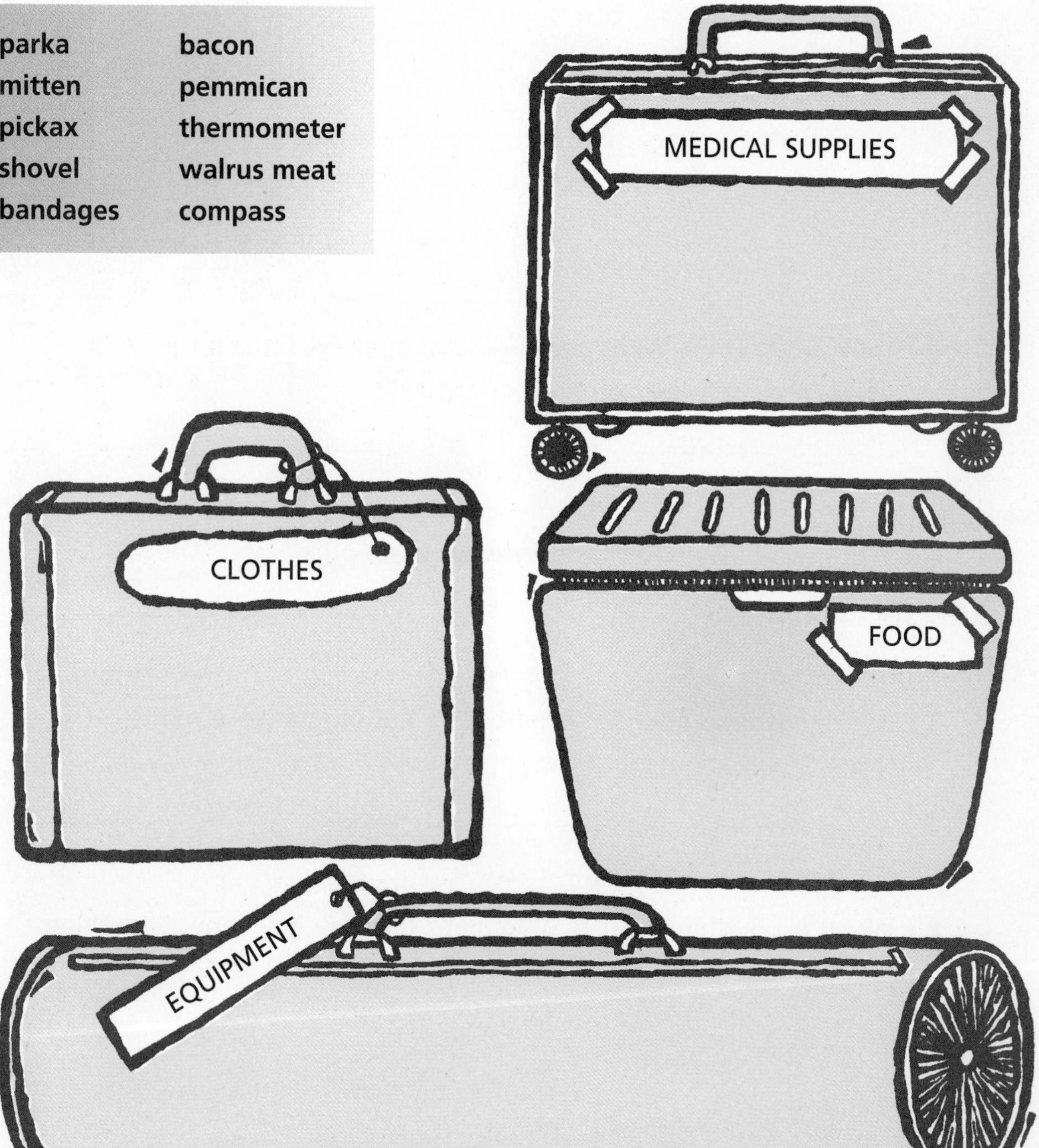

MEDICAL SUPPLIES

CLOTHES

FOOD

EQUIPMENT

Name

Keeping a Journal

Matt Henson kept a journal of events in his life. Answer these questions. Then use the answers to begin your own journal.

1. Have you wondered about something today but not asked anyone about it? Write your question.

___

___

2. Look around you. What object catches your eye? Name the object and list a few words to describe it.

___

___

3. Write two new words, facts, or ideas that you learned today.

___

___

4. Watch a stranger on the street or in a bus or in a store. Write three details about what the person does or says.

___

___

5. What do you think? List two opinions that you have about anything.

___

___

Name ....

Igloo Words

Matthew Henson's igloo has words on it. Circle each word with a suffix meaning "someone who." Then use those words to complete the sentences.

typist

number driver sailor sugar

list biologist commander accordian

assist under error

scholar musician author powder anchor

poor

burglar Italian cover twist fist under

1. Marco is an ______________________________ pilot from Rome.
2. The bus ______________________________ drops me off near my house.
3. We caught a ______________________________ climbing in the window.
4. The ______________________________ pulled up the ship's anchor.
5. The navy ______________________________ shouted orders.
6. The ______________________________ is conducting an experiment in the laboratory.
7. Who is the ______________________________ of that book?
8. She is the fastest ______________________________ in the office.
9. The ______________________________ is rehearsing with the orchestra.
10. Good study habits will make you a better ______________________________.

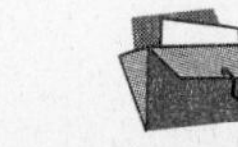

Name

Who Am I?

Make up riddles to ask your classmates! Write the job of your choice next to the question "Who am I?" Then choose a word from each list to complete the clue sentences. Each sentence should give a clue about the job.

TIP: When you share your riddles, read only the clues. Don't read the answer to the question "Who am I?"

1. Who am I? ______________________
   Clue: I am part of a(n) ______________________.
   Clue: I travel by ______________________.
   Clue: I work near a(n) ______________________.
   Who am I?
2. Who am I? ______________________
   Clue: I belong to a(n) ______________________.
   Clue: I take (a) ______________________ to work.
   Clue: I see a(n) ______________________ where I work.
   Who am I?

Write your own clues!

3. Who am I? ______________________
   Clue: ______________________
   Clue: ______________________
   Clue: ______________________
   Who am I?

Jobs
interpreter
explorer
sailor
doctor

Teams
expedition
crew
medical practice
staff

Transportation
sledges
ship
airplane
train

Surroundings
ice floe
lead
office
playground

Name ....

Safe Crossing

Long *i* and Long *o* Some Spelling Words have the long *i* sound, shown as |ī|. The |ī| sound is often spelled with the pattern ***i***-consonant-***e*** or ***igh***.

|ī| drive sight

The other Spelling Words have the long ***o*** sound, shown as |ō|. The |ō| sound is often spelled with the pattern ***o***-consonant-***e***, ***oa***, or ***ow***.

|ō| froze goal snow

Spelling Words

1. **snow**
2. **goal**
3. **froze**
4. **sight**
5. **drive**
6. **wrote**
7. **load**
8. **midnight**
9. **prize**
10. **narrow**

My Study List
What other words do you need to study for spelling? Add them to My Study List for *Arctic Explorer: The Story of Matthew Henson* in the back of this book.

Help Matt cross the ice to return to the ship. Write the Spelling Words that match the spelling pattern shown on each block of ice.

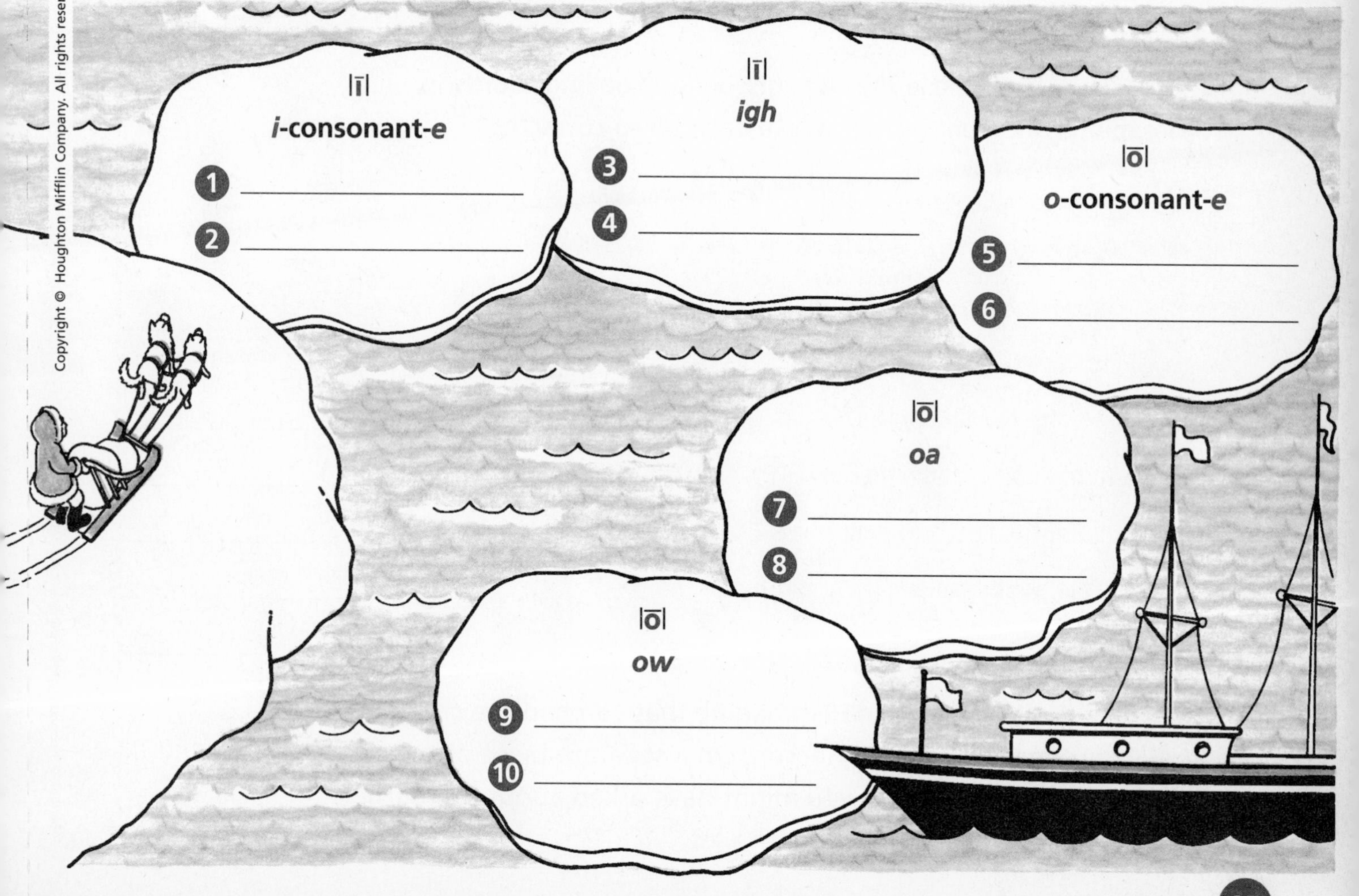

|ī| ***i*-consonant-*e***

1. ____________________
2. ____________________

|ī| ***igh***

3. ____________________
4. ____________________

|ō| ***o*-consonant-*e***

5. ____________________
6. ____________________

|ō| ***oa***

7. ____________________
8. ____________________

|ō| ***ow***

9. ____________________
10. ____________________

Name

Spelling Spree

Spelling Words

1. snow
2. goal
3. froze
4. sight
5. drive
6. wrote
7. load
8. midnight
9. prize
10. narrow

Analogies

An **analogy** compares two pairs of words. The words in the first pair are related to each other in the same way as the words in the second pair. Write a Spelling Word to complete each analogy.

Example: Water is to ice as rain is to snow.

1. Morning is to evening as noon is to ______.
2. Present is to gift as award is to ______.
3. Plane is to fly as car is to ______.
4. Highway is to wide as path is to ______.
5. Suitcase is to pack as moving van is to ______.

Proofreading

Circle the five misspelled Spelling Words in this explorer's log entry. Then write each word correctly.

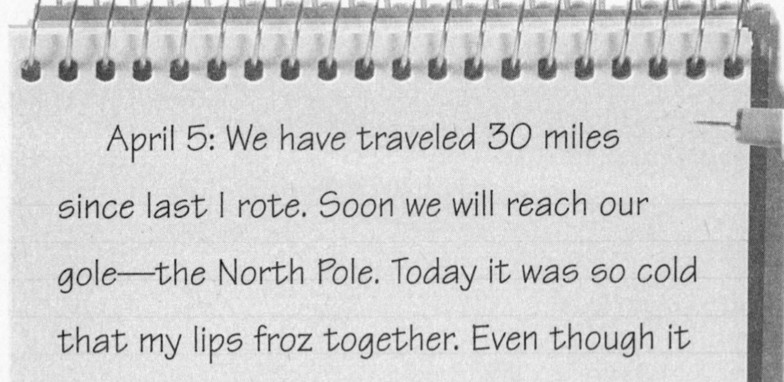

April 5: We have traveled 30 miles since last I rote. Soon we will reach our gole—the North Pole. Today it was so cold that my lips froz together. Even though it is midnight, the sun still shines brightly on the sno. What an amazing sighte!

6. ______
7. ______
8. ______
9. ______
10. ______

Ask the Explorer

Imagine that you had the chance to interview Matthew Henson. On a separate piece of paper, write five questions that you might have asked about his journey. Use Spelling Words from the list.

Name

Bold Explorers

Subjects and Predicates A computer mixed up the predicates in the following paragraph. In the left column, write the complete subjects. In the right column, write the complete predicate that goes with each subject.

A growing dampness sniffed. The women in the expedition raised his nose to the scent of the coming danger. The dogs, the sleds, and the ice were not aware of the change. Some of the dogs was making the cold air heavy. One were demanding all their attention.

SUBJECT	PREDICATE
1	
2	
3	
4	
5	

Name ....

Keep It Simple!

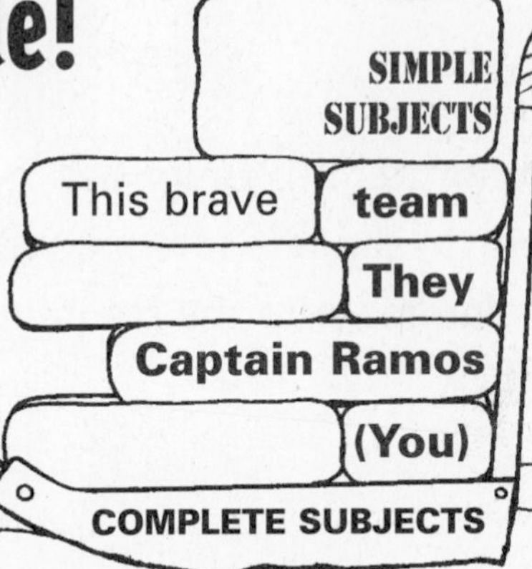

Subjects and Predicates **Underline the simple subjects and the simple predicates. If the subject is understood, circle the sentence.**

1. Matt Henson will plant a flag.
2. The ice split with a loud crack.
3. They sledged in sunlight at night.
4. Jump over the crack in the ice.
5. The brave team had been gone for days.
6. The route to the Pole is long, hard, and confusing.

Write the simple subjects to complete this puzzle. The numbers in the puzzle match the sentences.

Write the simple predicates to complete this puzzle. The numbers in the puzzle match the sentences

1. __ __ __ __ __ __ __ __ __ ◯
2. __ __ __ ◯ __
3. __ __ __ __ ◯ __ ◯
4. __ __ ◯ __

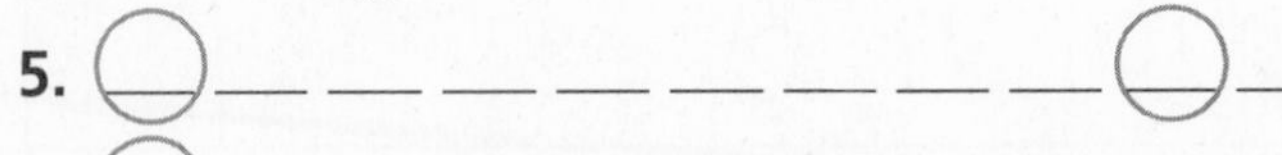

5. ◯ __ __ __ __ __ __ __ __ __ ◯ __

6. ◯ __

Unscramble the letters to tell when Peary and Henson often traveled.

The secret word is ____________________.

Name

In My Opinion

What do you have opinions about? Does one of these topics spark a reaction?

Topics for a Personal Essay

- Winning and Losing
- Clothing Fads
- Being Female/Male
- Fairness
- Eating
- Life in the City/Country
- Report Cards
- What's Important to Me
- My Favorite Holiday
- Rain
- What Makes Me Angry

My Personal Essay Topics

Write five topics that you have opinions about.

Think about each topic you wrote. Ask yourself these questions.

Would I enjoy writing about this?

Do I have enough to say?

Can I think of good examples to make my thoughts clear?

Circle the topic you will write about.

Name

Your Thoughts, Please

Complete the idea map to show your focus idea, the thoughts about it, and examples that you can use.

FOCUS IDEA:

THOUGHT 1:

THOUGHT 2:

THOUGHT 3:

EXAMPLE:

EXAMPLE:

EXAMPLE:

EXAMPLE:

EXAMPLE:

EXAMPLE:

Name

Making It Better

Reread your essay to yourself and make changes, using the Revising Checklist. Then use the Questions for a Writing Conference to help you discuss your essay with a classmate.

Revising Checklist

- ☐ Did I state my focus idea clearly?
- ☐ Do all my points, thoughts, and examples relate to my focus idea?
- ☐ Is each point or thought treated clearly and separately?
- ☐ Did I give an example to support each point or thought? Could I give better ones?

Questions for a Writing Conference

- What is the best part?
- Is the opening interesting?
- Is the focus idea clearly presented?
- Do all of the ideas keep to the focus?
- Are related thoughts and examples grouped together?
- Are more or different examples needed?
- What parts are unclear?
- Does the closing make the essay seem finished?

Write notes to remember ideas discussed in your writing conference.

My Notes

Name

Mission to Mars

Use these space words to complete the space log entry.

atmosphere gravity orbit meteorites comet particles

Stardate: December 1, 2053

Mission: To explore Mars

After months of traveling, we have finally spotted Mars. The planet is still a distance away, but already the spacecraft is being pulled by Mars's ______________. Within a few days we will begin our ______________ of the planet. We will circle Mars ten times before we land on its surface.

Once we land, we'll explore the planet. My first job is to collect rocks. With luck, I'll find some ______________. They are ______________ of rock that have fallen from outer space. My other job is to set up a telescope to view the glowing tail of a ______________ as it flies by Mars.

We'll have to wear space suits while we're walking on the planet. The ______________ of Mars has very little oxygen, and we wouldn't be able to breathe otherwise.

Name

Space Profiles

Complete these profiles of *Voyager* and the planets.

Voyager 1 and *Voyager 2* were launched in 1977 to study ____________________ ____________________ ____________________. *Voyager 1* visited and photographed ____________________ ____________________. *Voyager 2* traveled to Jupiter, Saturn, Uranus, and Neptune.

Saturn has thousands of rings made up of ____________________ ____________________. Saturn's largest moon is called ____________________.

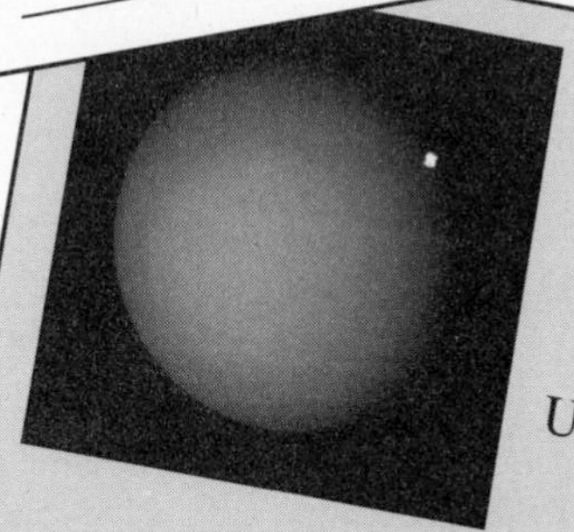

Uranus is ____________________ ____________________ in color. Scientists think that ____________________ ____________________ hold one of Uranus's rings together.

In size, Jupiter is the ____________________ of all the planets in the solar system. Jupiter has a mark on its surface called ____________________ ____________________.

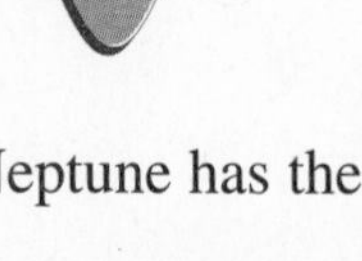

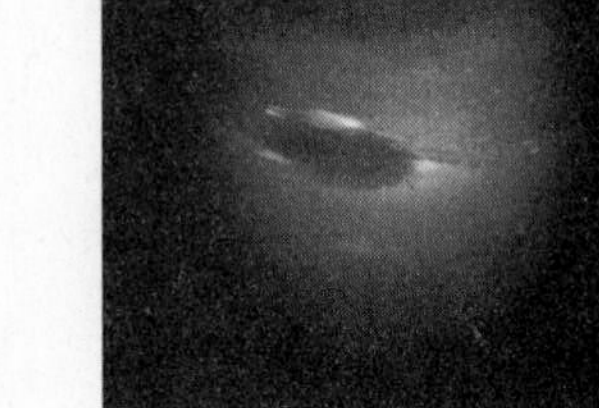

Neptune has the strongest ____________________ measured on any planet. Neptune's moon Triton has streaks on its icy surface. The streaks are caused by ____________________ ____________________.

Name

One Giant Leap!

Label each part of the article with a word from the box. Then answer the question.

- graphic aid
- heading
- caption
- introduction

On July 20, 1969, Neil A. Armstrong made history by being the first human to walk on the moon. As Armstrong stepped from his Apollo 11 *lunar module he said, "That's one small step for a man, one giant leap for mankind." This article will examine, in the order they happened, the many "baby" steps that were important for the success of the* Apollo 11 *mission.*

1 ______________________

Blast Off!

2 ______________________

The mission began on the morning of July 16, 1969. At 9:32 A.M. the earth shook as the *Apollo 11*'s Saturn 5 rocket ignited. More than seven million pounds of thrust heaved the spacecraft off the launch pad. In the command module atop the rocket, astronauts Neil A. Armstrong, Michael Collins, and Edwin E. Aldrin, Jr. nervously waited.

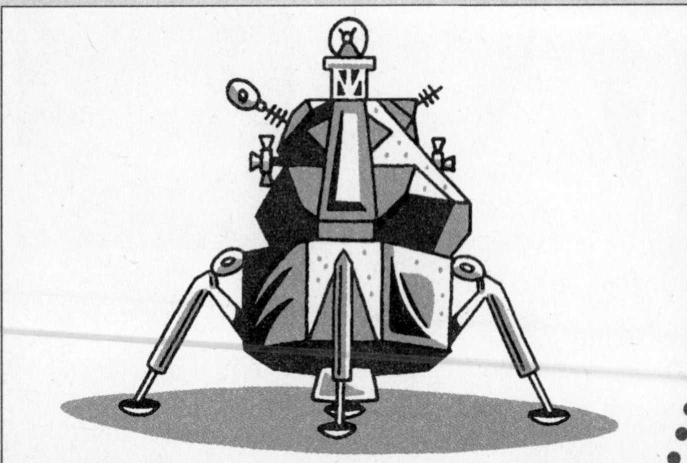

When the astronauts returned to Earth, the landing craft's descent stage was left on the moon.

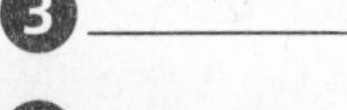

3 ______________________

4 ______________________

5 How does the introduction say the article is organized?

____

____

____

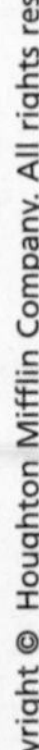

Name

Alike and Different

Use this graphic organizer to plan your paragraphs of comparison and contrast. Write the name of one of the objects you are comparing in one of the circles. Under each name, list the ways in which that object is different from the other one. In the space where the circles overlap, list the ways the objects are alike.

Object

Object

Name ....

Categorically Speaking

What category fits each list? Write the category names above the lists. Then add at least one more word to each list.

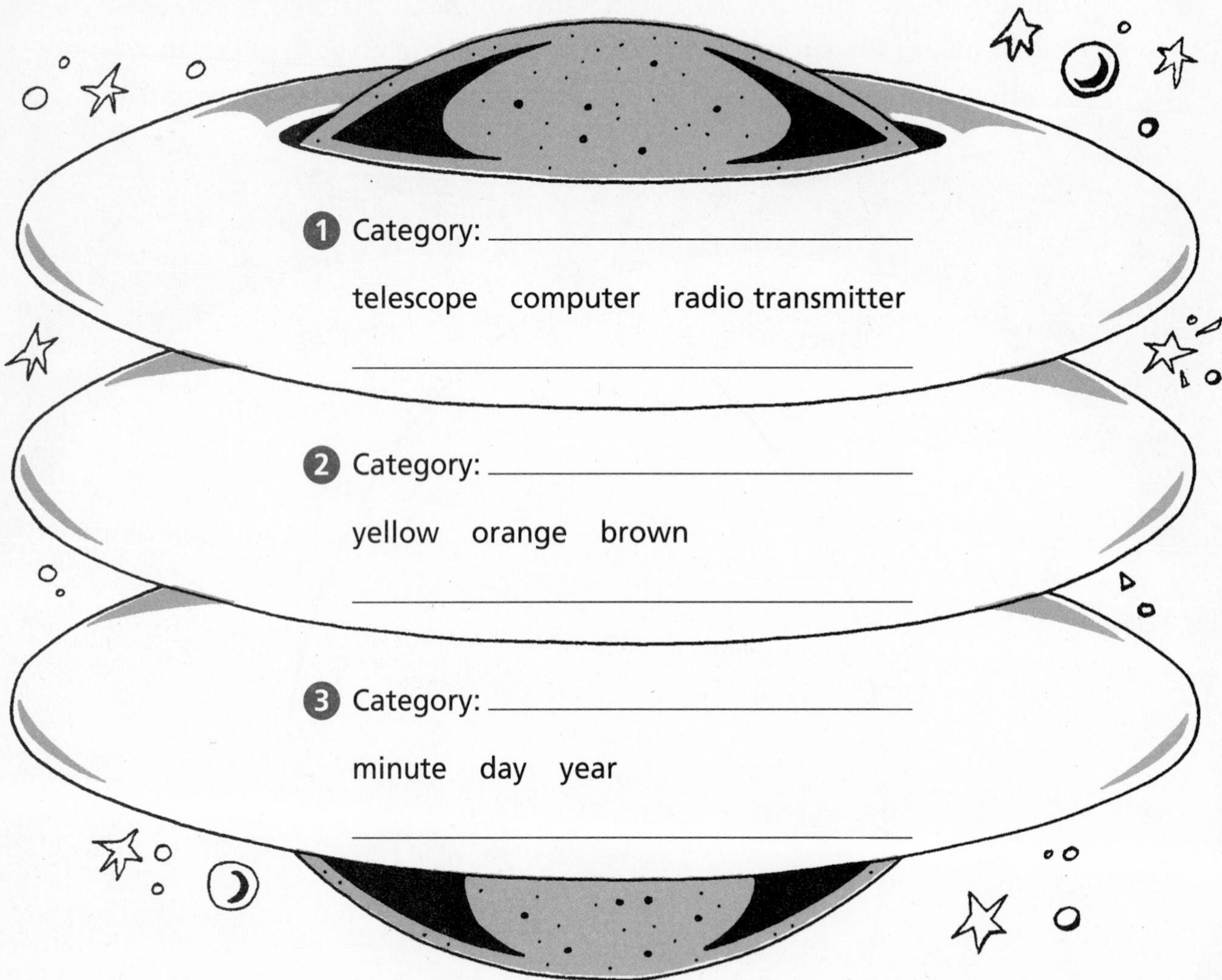

Circle the word that does not belong in each category. Then tell why it does not belong.

4 river mountain lake pond

____

5 Spain Australia California Mexico

____

Name

Blue (and Red and Green) Moons

Draw a picture of one moon that you've read about. Label some of the features of your drawing. Features might include **meteorites, craters, geysers,** and **volcanoes.**

Name of Moon: ______________________

Write a description of the moon. Use these words in your description: **gravity, atmosphere, orbit, particles, comet,** and **asteroid.**

____

____

____

____

____

Name

Voyage to the Stars

Long *u* Each Spelling Word has the long ***u*** sound. This sound can be said two ways, as in ***huge*** and ***blue.*** The long ***u*** sound you hear in ***huge*** is shown as |**yōō**|. The long ***u*** sound you hear in ***blue*** is shown as |**ōō**|. The |**yōō**| and |**ōō**| sounds are often spelled with the pattern ***u***-consonant-***e***, ***ue***, ***oo***, ***ui***, or ***ou***.

|yōō| or |ōō| huge blue smooth juice group

Spelling Words

1. **huge**
2. **blue**
3. **smooth**
4. **clue**
5. **ooze**
6. **group**
7. **juice**
8. **route**
9. **rude**
10. **bruise**

My Study List

What other words do you need to study for spelling? Add them to My Study List for *Voyager: An Adventure to the Edge of the Solar System* in the back of this book.

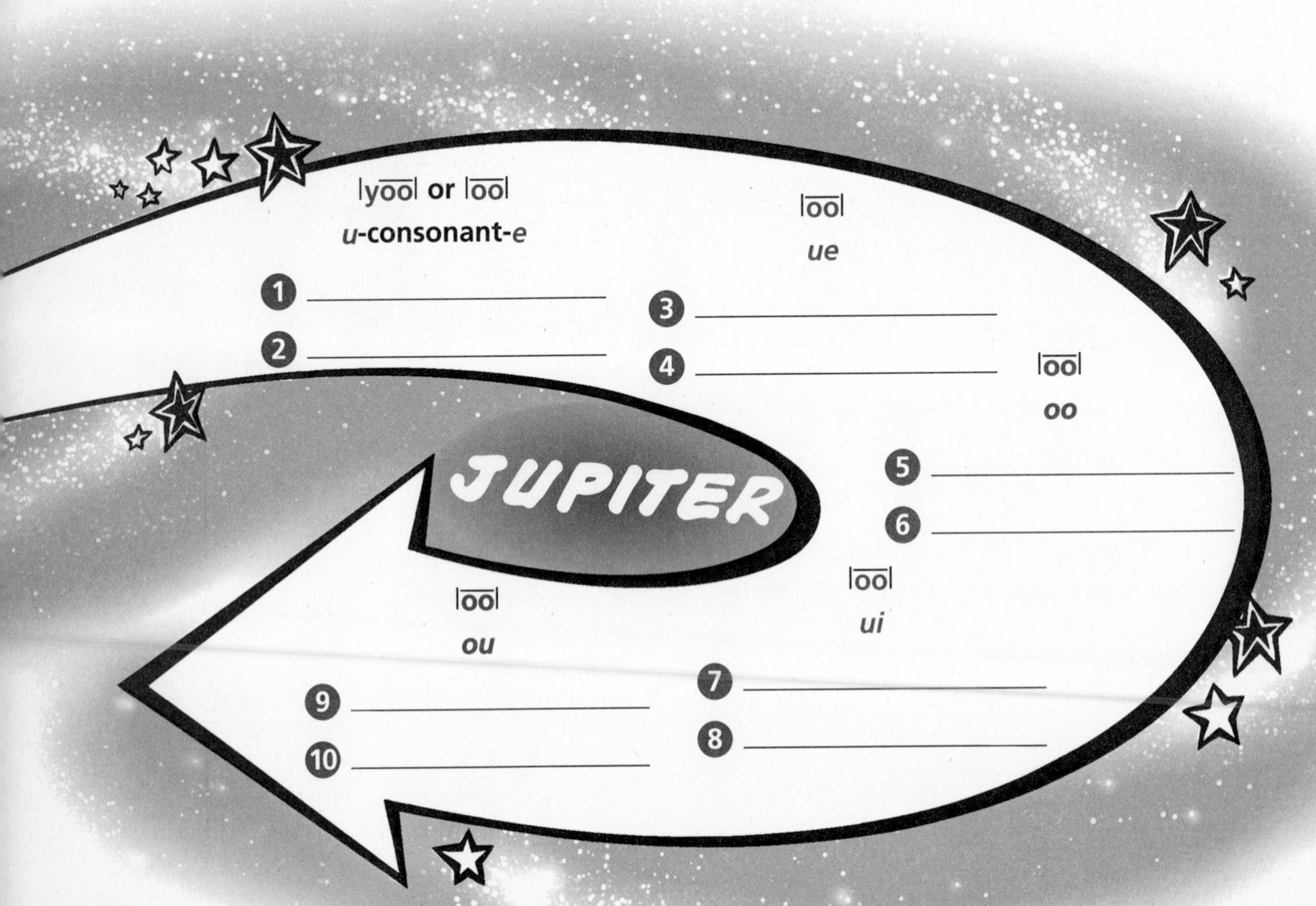

Write each Spelling Word beneath the matching pattern.

JUPITER

|yōō| or |ōō|
u*-consonant-*e

1. ____________
2. ____________

|ōō|
ue

3. ____________
4. ____________

|ōō|
oo

5. ____________
6. ____________

|ōō|
ui

7. ____________
8. ____________

|ōō|
ou

9. ____________
10. ____________

Name

Spelling Spree

Spelling Words

1. huge
2. blue
3. smooth
4. clue
5. ooze
6. group
7. juice
8. route
9. rude
10. bruise

Across the Universe

Write the Spelling Word that fits each clue.

Across

4. more than two people or things
5. what a detective looks for
6. not polite

Down

1. a black eye is one
2. what you squeeze from an orange
3. a color of the sky

Proofreading

Find and circle four misspelled Spelling Words in this description of a prize in the distant future. Then write each word correctly.

Here's what you've won—a trip to Jupiter! Follow the rute *Voyager I* took past the smoothe, blue surface of Europa, one of Jupiter's moons. Watch lava ooz over Io's surface. Then gasp as the gas giant itself comes into view, with its huje red spot and many colors. You'll live a lifetime of thrills in just one day!

7 ______________________

8 ______________________

9 ______________________

10 ______________________

Over and Out

Imagine that you are the pilot of the first mission to Neptune. You are seeing sights previously seen only by *Voyager*'s cameras. On a separate piece of paper, write a dialogue you might have with Mission Control. Describe where you are, what you are seeing, and how you feel. Use Spelling Words from the list.

Name

Robot Connections

Run-on:
Astronauts could not travel to Neptune a robot spacecraft could.

Correct:
Astronauts could not travel to Neptune. A robot spacecraft could.

Correct:
Astronauts could not travel to Neptune, but a robot spacecraft could.

Correcting Run-on Sentences

A robot spacecraft has beamed back information about newly discovered planets, but the robot uses run-on sentences. Write the run-on sentences correctly.

1. This planet has a huge red spot the spot seems fiery.

2. Moons circle this planet nine were identified.

3. This planet appears very stormy a closer look is needed.

4. Could this planet have forests there are many large, green areas.

5. What an amazing planet this is tiny lights sparkle all over it.

6. Does this planet have mountains with clouds overhead does it have erupting volcanoes?

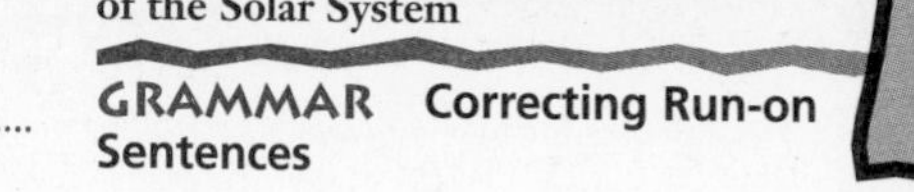

Name ______________________

Message from Space

Correcting Run-on Sentences This paragraph has been sent directly from space as one long run-on sentence. Help the scientist read it by writing it correctly.

United States scientists have sent several spacecraft to Mars in 1964 Mariner IV was launched it sent back the first pictures of the planet some Mariners flew by Mars one orbited the planet for about a year two Viking spacecraft actually landed on Mars in 1976 they studied the planet for over four years they collected information about its atmosphere and surface much has been learned about our neighboring planet there are still many unanswered questions.

____

____

____

____

____

____

____

____

____

____

____

____

____

____

Name

Planning an Expedition

Plan an expedition to one of the planets or moons described in *Voyager* to collect samples of what you find there.

Planet I will visit	
Special challenges I will face on this planet	
Equipment I will need to travel to and from the planet	
Equipment I will need for survival	
Equipment I will need to collect samples	

List six important stages or events in your expedition plan. Your list should include examples of these categories: Travel, Survival, and Collecting Samples.

1. ____________________
2. ____________________
3. ____________________
4. ____________________
5. ____________________
6. ____________________

Create drawings and descriptions showing each stage or event. Use your drawings to present your expedition plan to your classmates. Use the checklist to be sure you are ready to present your plan.

Checklist

- ❑ My drawings and presentation show how to meet the special challenges of this planet.
- ❑ My drawings show how I will travel, survive, and collect samples.
- ❑ My drawings are organized in the correct sequence.

Name

In the Wild

After reading each selection, complete the chart below and on the next page to show what you discovered.

	Wolves	The Midnight Fox	Adiós falcón/ Good-bye, Falcon
What kind of writing is the selection an example of?			
What do you think are the author's feelings about wildlife?			
What problems do the animals face? How are they resolved?			

Name

In the Wild

After reading each selection, complete the chart to show what you discovered.

	Wolves	The Midnight Fox	Adiós falcón/ Good-bye, Falcon
What ideas about wildlife preservation are raised in this selection?			
How do you feel about the animals in the selection?			

What have you learned in this theme about preserving wildlife?

Name

Tracking Down Definitions

Track down the definitions for the vocabulary words. Draw a line from each word to its definition.

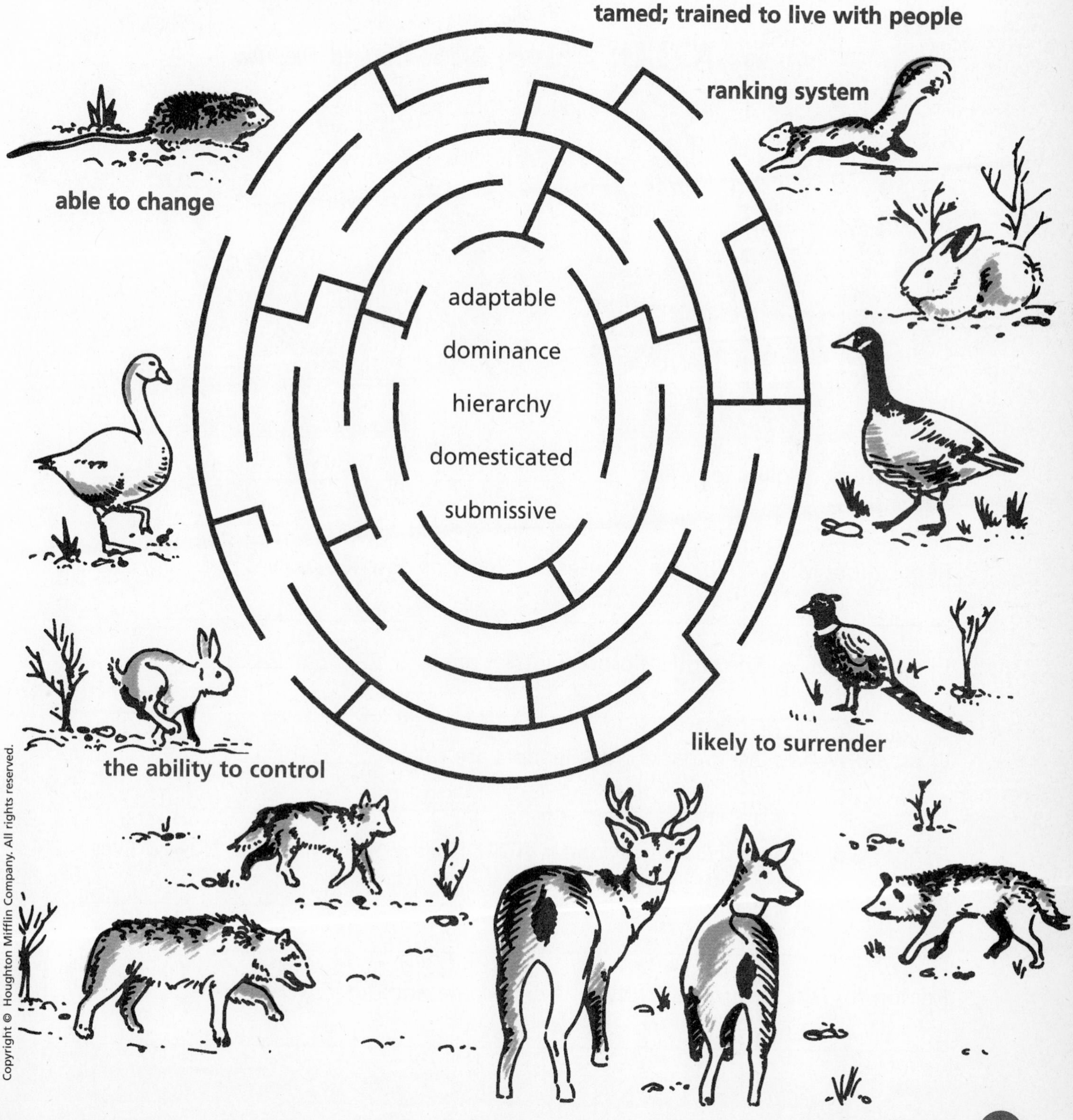

adaptable

dominance

hierarchy

domesticated

submissive

tamed; trained to live with people

ranking system

able to change

likely to surrender

the ability to control

Name

Wanted: More Wolves!

Use what you've learned about wolves to complete this "wanted" poster.

WANTED: Wolves, alias *Canis lupus*

Description: Wolves look like ______________________________

____

Reputation: Many frightening stories and legends describe wolves as being ______

____

Closest Relatives: The wolf's closest relatives are ______________________

____

Lifestyle: Wolves live in packs. Pack leaders are called ______________

____

Range: Wolves once lived across much of the Northern Hemisphere. Now wolves can be found mostly in ______________________________

____

Reason for Disappearance: Wolves have become endangered because ________

____

Name

Get the Facts

Decide whether the sentences in bold are statements of fact or statements expressing opinions. Then write F for fact or O for opinion on the lines.

The Key Deer

Just a few years ago, Big Pine Key was a rural crossroads with a population of only 1500. **But times have changed for the worse on these sunny islands off the southern tip of Florida.** ________ **Now Big Pine Key has a population of over 3000.** ________ A shopping mall and sprawling neighborhoods have replaced its beautiful pine forests and palm trees.

But Big Pine Key is in danger of losing some of its unique wildlife as well. **The islands are the last home of the endangered key deer.** ________ **Today there are fewer than 300 of the deer left.** ________ The deer, which grow no bigger than the average dog, need the shelter and food that the forests provide.

Wildlife is a precious resource. ________ Should we search for ways to protect our precious wildlife? **We must decide now.** ________ Soon there may be no key deer left.

What do you think is the writer's viewpoint?

____

____

____

____

____

Name

Plan Ahead

Use this page to plan your book report. Then write your report on a separate sheet of paper.

Title:

Author:

Fiction or Nonfiction:

Setting:

Main Character(s):

What is the book about?

What is your favorite part of the book?

Do you like this book? Why or why not?

Name ______________________________

Howl!

Match the correct definition to the boldface word. Then write the homophone pairs under the wolves.

____ **1.** The wolf followed the **scent** of the moose.

____ **2.** Wolves have long, bushy **tails.**

____ **3.** The gray wolf **won** the fight.

____ **4.** Water runs off wolf fur the **way** it runs off a raincoat.

____ **5.** That fuzzy pup is only **one** week old.

____ **6.** The sound of shots **sent** the wolves running.

____ **7.** How much does an average wolf **weigh?**

____ **8.** Baby wolves can't eat **meat** right away.

____ **9.** Many nursery **tales** describe wolves as being sly.

____ **10.** Would you be afraid to **meet** a wolf?

a. gained victory
b. animal flesh used as food
c. manner of doing something
d. to come in contact with
e. caused to move or go
f. parts of animals' bodies
g. the trail of a hunted animal
h. to have a particular heaviness
i. stories
j. the number before two

11 ______________________
____

13 ______________________
____

15 ______________________
____

12 ______________________

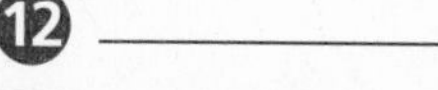

____

14 ______________________
____

Name

Track of the Wolf

Write the vocabulary word that completes each sentence. Then use the letters that the wolf tracks touch to complete the sentence describing wolves.

adaptable	domesticated	prey	dominance
traits	hybrid	hierarchy	submissive

1. Ranking of wolves in a pack is called ____. __ __ __ __ __ __ __ __ __
2. Lower-ranked wolves are ____ to higher-ranked wolves. __ __ __ __ __ __ __ __ __ __
3. Alpha wolves have ____ over the other wolves in the pack. __ __ __ __ __ __ __ __ __
4. Wolves make bad pets because they aren't ____. __ __ __ __ __ __ __ __ __ __ __ __
5. Wolves survive in different climates because they are ____. __ __ __ __ __ __ __ __ __
6. The red wolf might be a ____ of the wolf and the coyote. __ __ __ __ __ __
7. Wolves hunt in packs to catch larger ____ such as moose or elk. __ __ __ __
8. Wolves and dogs share many of the same ____. __ __ __ __ __ __

Wolves __ __ __ __ __ __ __ __ .

Name

Haunting Howls

Vowel + *r* Sounds Some Spelling Words have the vowel + *r* sounds that you hear in ***bare.*** These sounds, shown as /âr/, are close to the /ā/ sound. The /âr/ sounds are often spelled with the patterns ***are*** and ***air***.

/âr/ b**are** h**air**

The other Spelling Words have the vowel + *r* sounds that you hear in ***sharp***. These sounds, shown as /är/, are close to the /ä/ sound. The /är/ sounds are usually spelled with the pattern ***ar***.

/är/ sh**ar**p

Spelling Words

1. sharp
2. bark
3. hair
4. bare
5. startle
6. pair
7. care
8. share
9. apart
10. stare

My Study List
What other words do you need to study for spelling? Add them to My Study List for *Wolves* in the back of this book.

Write each Spelling Word under the wolf with the correct sounds and spelling pattern.

/âr/ **are**

1. ______
2. ______
3. ______
4. ______

/âr/ **air**

5. ______
6. ______

/är/ **ar**

7. ______
8. ______
9. ______
10. ______

Name

Spelling Spree

Spelling Words

1. sharp
2. bark
3. hair
4. bare
5. startle
6. pair
7. care
8. share
9. apart
10. stare

Wolf Words Write the Spelling Word that fits each clue.

1. surprise or alarm __ __ __ __ __ (__) __
2. set of two matched things, such as shoes __ __ (__) __
3. not together; in pieces __ __ __ __ (__)
4. gaze at steadily __ (__) __ __ __
5. give help or keep safe __ __ __ (__)
6. not dull __ __ __ (__) __

Now write the letters from the circles in order. This word names a group of wolf pups born at once to the same mother.

Mystery Word: __ __ __ __ __ __

Proofreading Find and circle four misspelled Spelling Words in this magazine article. Then write each word correctly.

My dog Shep and I have had our shar of adventures. Once we were hiking along a mountain trail. Suddenly, Shep began to barck. The hare on my neck stood up when Shep started to bair his teeth. Just then a pair of wolves began howling, not ten feet away! I sprinted for the car, but Shep beat me there by a mile!

7. __________
8. __________
9. __________
10. __________

Howling Hits As a songwriter, you hope to raise money to save the wolves. On separate paper, write the titles of four "wolf" songs to include on your next album. Use capital letters to begin the first, last, and each important word in the title. Use Spelling Words from the list.

Name

Plural Puzzle Play

Singular	pack	ranch	body	valley	silo	tomato	woman	elk
Plural	packs	ranches	bodies	valleys	silos	tomatoes	women	elk

Singular and Plural Nouns Complete the puzzle by writing the plural form of each singular noun. Use a dictionary if you need help.

Across

1. coyote
7. bush
8. trout
9. turkey
11. baby
14. foot
15. glass
16. hero
17. personality

Down

1. cage
2. year
3. trait
4. joy
5. path
6. wolf
7. birch
10. rodeo
12. arm
13. eye
15. goose

Name

Animal Park Plurals

Singular and Plural Nouns **Complete the signs by writing the plural form of each animal's name. Use a dictionary if you are unsure how to form the plural.**

1. wallaby
2. reindeer
3. dingo
4. ox
5. panda
6. ostrich
7. donkey/burro
8. penguin

How Do I Get There? On another sheet of paper, write instructions telling how to get from the front gate of the animal park to the food stand. Be exact. Be sure to include the names of all the animals you would walk by.

Name

Odd Word Out

Draw a line through the word that does not belong in each group. Write why the other three words belong together. The first one has been done for you.

urgent ~~cautious~~
desperate frantic

Example: All but cautious mean "insistent; demanding attention."

depressed gloomy
discouraged cheerful

1 ______________________________

dread terror
courage apprehension

2 ______________________________

calmly anxiously
worriedly uneasily

3 ______________________________

doomed condemned
fortunate ill-fated

4 ______________________________

despair hopelessness
glee powerlessness

5 ______________________________

Name

Foxy Falsehoods

Mark a T if the statement is true and an F if it is false. If the statement is false, correct it to make a true statement.

1. ______ Tom is spending the summer at Uncle Fred and Aunt Hazeline's farm.

   ____

2. ______ You can tell from reading the story that Uncle Fred probably has hunted foxes before.

   ____

3. ______ Tom wants Uncle Fred to find the den.

   ____

4. ______ Happ finds the fox's scent and leads Uncle Fred to the den.

   ____

5. ______ Tom is overjoyed when Uncle Fred finds the den.

   ____

Answer each question.

6. Why do you think Tom closes his eyes when Uncle Fred digs for the baby fox?______________________________

   ____

   ____

7. Why does Aunt Millie feel better by the end of the story?

   ____

   ____

   ____

Name

What Are They Like?

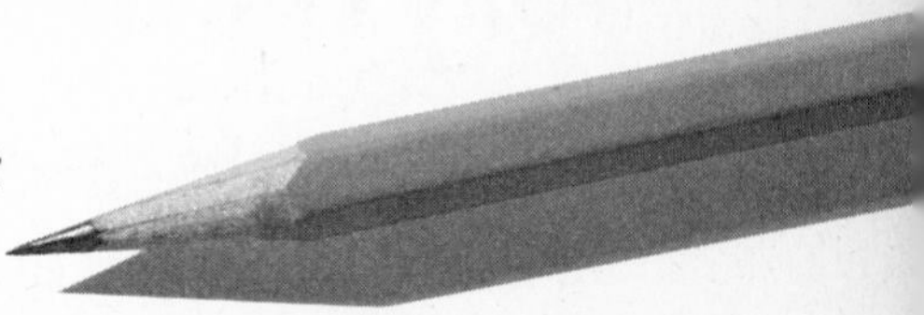

Complete the chart to tell what the characters in *The Midnight Fox* are like. You may look back at the selection if you wish.

Character	What character says, does, or thinks	What you can infer about the character
Uncle Fred	He tells Tom, "Don't be in too big a hurry. Let's look a bit."	
Tom	Inside he's screaming, "You're burning up."	
Aunt Millie	She tells Tom not to be too late. When she sees that his face is red, she asks him if he's all right. Then she says Hazeline can take the shovel to her dad.	
Tom	He closes his eyes and presses his hands against his eyelids when Uncle Fred begins digging.	

Name

Foxy Facts

Compound Sentences **Revise this report on foxes to combine and vary the length of the sentences. Use commas and conjunctions.**

Foxes live in farmlands and forests. Their dens may be underground. They may be in hollow trees. Foxes rely on their highly developed senses for survival. They watch for traps with their remarkable eyesight. Their keen hearing picks up a mouse squeak from over one hundred feet away! Baby foxes are called different names. They can be called pups. They can be called cubs. The size of a fox litter varies. Red foxes have from four to nine pups at a time. Gray foxes have from three to five pups. Foxes make farmers angry by eating their chickens. They help farmers by eating mice and rats.

Name ....

Hunting for Suffixes

Circle the words with the suffixes *-ful, -less,* and *-ly* in the fox trail. Use the circled words to complete the story.

hlewkrunadrojsitirexcitedlyetryetfearlesshortyphappeacefulovinyouthappilyellowhatskillfulighoppractigracefulivelicyeswiftlyearlinelihopelessadl

It was daybreak, and the forest was __________________. But not for long! A shot rang out. The sleeping fox woke up and began running __________________ through the forest. Hunting dogs smelled the fox and barked __________________. But the __________________ fox knew how to outsmart them! He made __________________ leaps into the air, backtracked, and ran through water to make them lose the scent. He wasn't at all afraid. He was __________________! The hunters knew it was __________________ and gave up the chase. The fox seemed to smile __________________ as he watched them go.

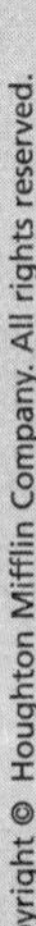

Name

Frantic Fox Frenzy

Read the sentences. If the underlined word is used correctly, color the egg. If not, use the correct word from the box to rewrite the sentence at the bottom.

hopelessness	feeble	discouraged	dread	desperate	ecstatic

1. Anne knew the fox was in the hen house, so she opened the door anxiously.
2. She was overjoyed when she saw that three of her favorite hens had disappeared.
3. When Anne noticed that five other hens were missing, she was filled with unconcern.
4. She was certain a fox was stealing the hens. Unless she could capture the fox, she knew the hopefulness of the situation.
5. When the frightened fox saw Anne, a satisfied look flashed across his eyes.
6. The fox had no way to escape—he knew he was doomed.

Name

Fox Trot

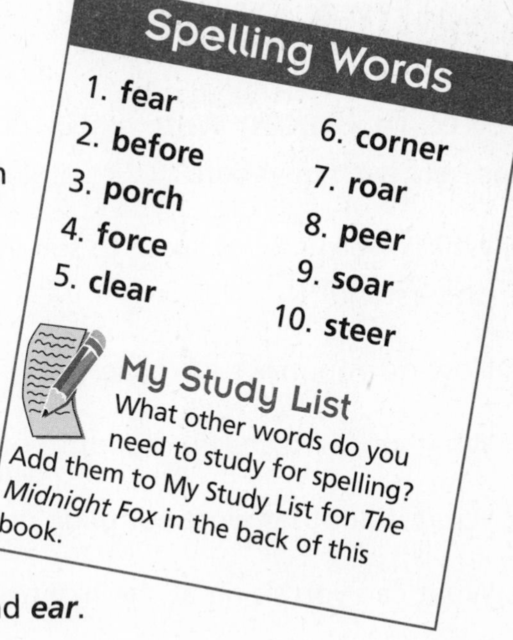

More Vowel + *r* Sounds Some Spelling Words have the vowel + *r* sounds that you hear in ***before***. These sounds, shown as |ôr|, are close to the |ō| sound. The |ôr| sounds are often spelled with the patterns ***or***, ***ore***, and ***oar***.

|ôr| porch before roar

The other Spelling Words have the vowel + *r* sounds that you hear in ***fear***. These sounds, shown as |îr|, are close to the |ē| sound. The |îr| sounds are often spelled with the patterns ***eer*** and ***ear***.

|îr| peer fear

Follow the fox. Write each Spelling Word next to the paw print with the correct sounds and spelling pattern.

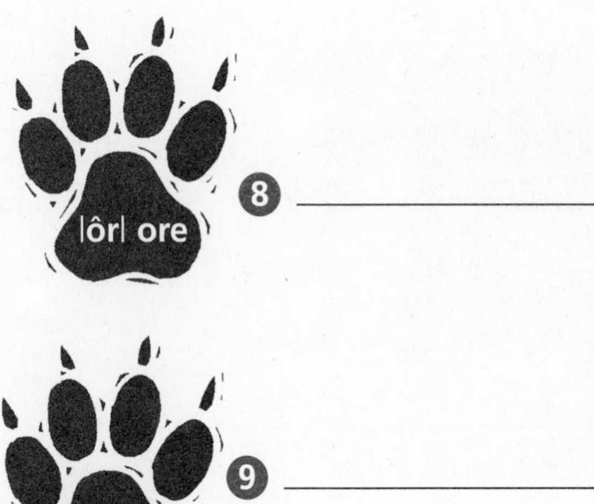

Name

Spelling Spree

Foxes in Boxes **Write the Spelling Word that answers each question.**

1. Which word means "easy to see, hear, or understand"?
2. How do you make a bicycle turn right or left?
3. What word means the opposite of *weakness?*
4. What is another word for *glide* or *fly high?*
5. What can you sit on at the front, side, or back of a house?
6. What sound does an angry lion make?

Proofreading **Find and circle four misspelled Spelling Words in these notes by a nature photographer. Then write each word correctly.**

7. Set up the camera on the cornor of the cabin porch, where the view is clear.
8. Get shots of fox babies as they pere out from under a bush.
9. Film them befour they eat; they often nap afterwards.
10. Do not shout or make sudden moves. Otherwise, they'll feer the camera.

7 ______________________ 9 ______________________

8 ______________________ 10 ______________________

Animal's Eye View Imagine that you are a wild animal. Are you a fox stealing chickens? A raccoon raiding garbage cans? A wolf hunting for food? How do you view people and the way they treat your kind? State your opinion in a brief paragraph. Include at least three reasons why you think as you do. Use Spelling Words from the list.

Name

Trail Guide

Singular Possessives | **Plural Possessives**

A man's hat is in front of the fox's den.

The men's hats are in front of the foxes' den.

home of a porcupine
den of the fox
tracks of a deer
lodge of the beavers
playground of the squirrels
cave of the bats
honks of the geese
cocoons of the butterflies
call of the chickadee

Possessive Nouns Use the trail guide to complete the sentences. For each stop on the trail, find the phrase in the box that tells what to see. Rewrite the phrase, using a possessive noun.

Example: The whole forest is the squirrels' playground.

1. Look for the ________________ just beyond the bramble bushes.
2. If you listen carefully, you might hear the ________________.
3. Notice the ________________ at the edge of the field.
4. Look across the marsh to see the ________________.
5. Listen for the ________________.
6. This hollow log is a ________________.
7. Keep your eyes open for ________________ on branches.
8. You may spot a ________________ near the pond.

1 2 3 4 5 6 7 8

Name

Creature Features

spots of a leopard
mane of a lion
wings of a bat
tusks of a walrus
antlers of two moose
hoofs of a horse
tails of two lizards
pouch of a kangaroo

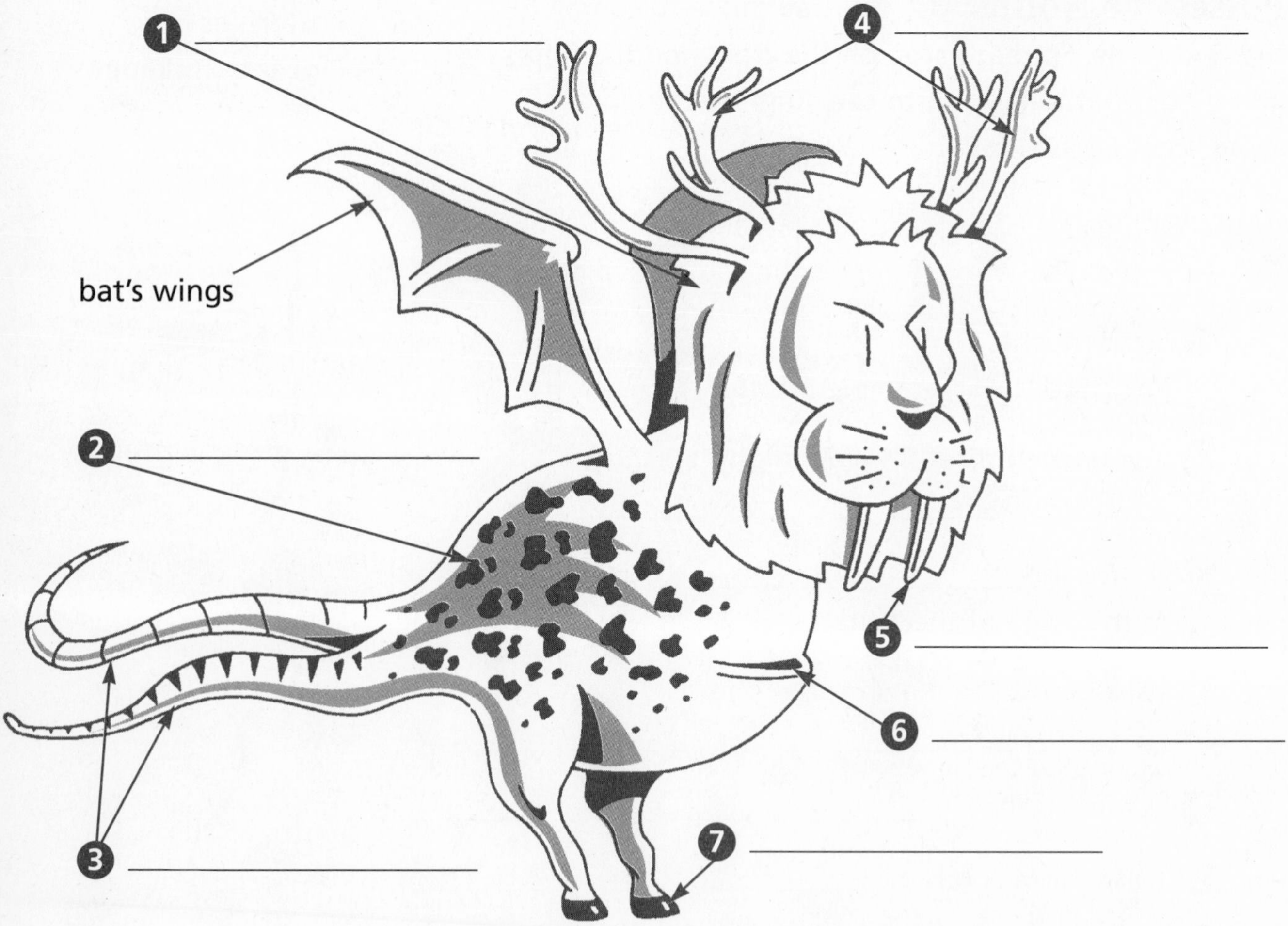

Possessive Nouns **What a strange animal you just saw in the woods! Match each phrase to its place on the animal. On the line next to the feature, rewrite the phrase, using a possessive noun. One label has been done. Draw one animal feature of your own on this creature and label it.**

1 ____________________

4 ____________________

bat's wings

2 ____________________

5 ____________________

6 ____________________

3 ____________________

7 ____________________

8 ____

Create Your Own Creature On a separate sheet of paper, draw another creature made of different animal parts. Write phrases using possessive nouns to describe its features. Have a classmate try to identify the parts.

Name

Be Persuasive

Does one of these topics get you thinking?

TOPIC IDEAS

Persuade the owner of a computer store to sponsor a computer club
Persuade an author to speak to the class
Persuade the owner of a movie theater to build a wheelchair ramp
Persuade other students to help with a charity fund-raising event
Persuade the town council to pass a leash law
Persuade the physical education teacher to start a girls' soccer team

Do I know enough about this?

Can I give strong reasons with facts and examples?

Do I feel strongly about this?

Can I reach an audience who can make this happen?

My Ideas

Write five ideas that you have for persuading someone to do something. Next to each idea, write the audience you need to persuade.

	Idea	Audience
1		
2		
3		
4		
5		

Ask yourself these questions about each idea. Then circle the topic that you will write about.

Name

Prepare to Persuade

Fill in the persuasion map. Write your opinion and your goal—what you want your audience to do. Then list your reasons and the supporting facts and examples that you will use.

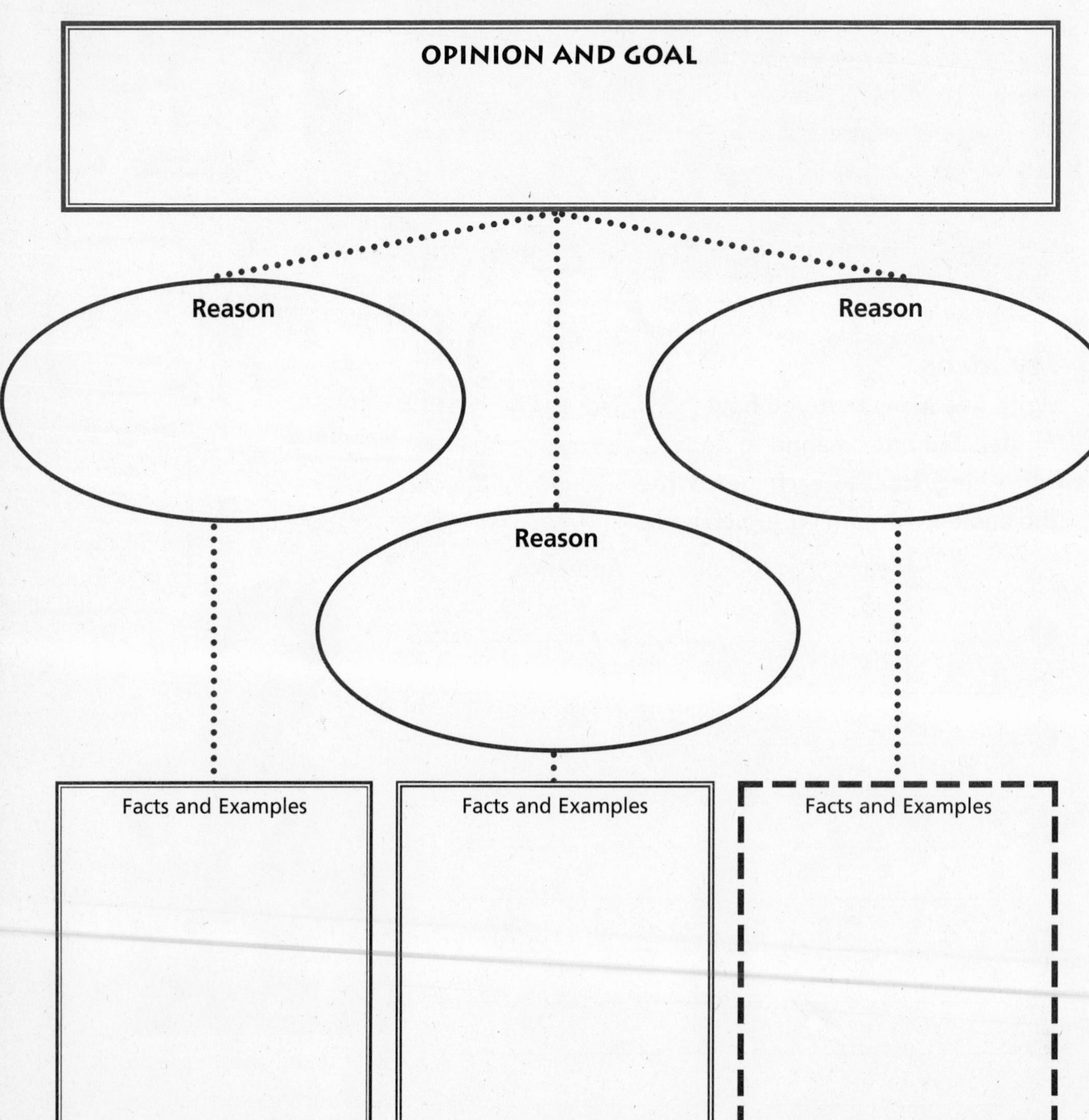

Name ______________________________

Perfect Persuasion

Reread and revise your persuasive argument, using the Revising Checklist. Then use the Questions for a Writing Conference to discuss your paper with a classmate.

Revising Checklist

- ❑ Did I state my opinion clearly?
- ❑ Did I use strong reasons?
- ❑ Did I treat each reason separately?
- ❑ Did I support each reason with facts and examples?
- ❑ Did I clearly state my goal?

Questions for a Writing Conference

- What do you like about this piece?
- Are the opinion and the goal clear?
- Will the reasons convince the audience? If not, why?
- Have possible objections been addressed?
- Are any parts unclear?

Write notes to remember ideas discussed in your writing conference.

My Notes

____

____

____

____

____

____

____

____

____

____

Name

Let the Falcon Fly!

Complete each sentence with a word from the box. Then cut out the falcon and its cage. Fold up the sides of the cage so the sentences are on the outside. Put the falcon in the cage and close the top of the cage. After you read each sentence on the outside of the cage, open that side of the cage. When you've read all four sentences, you'll have set the falcon free!

endure
captivity
liberty
warily
clashed

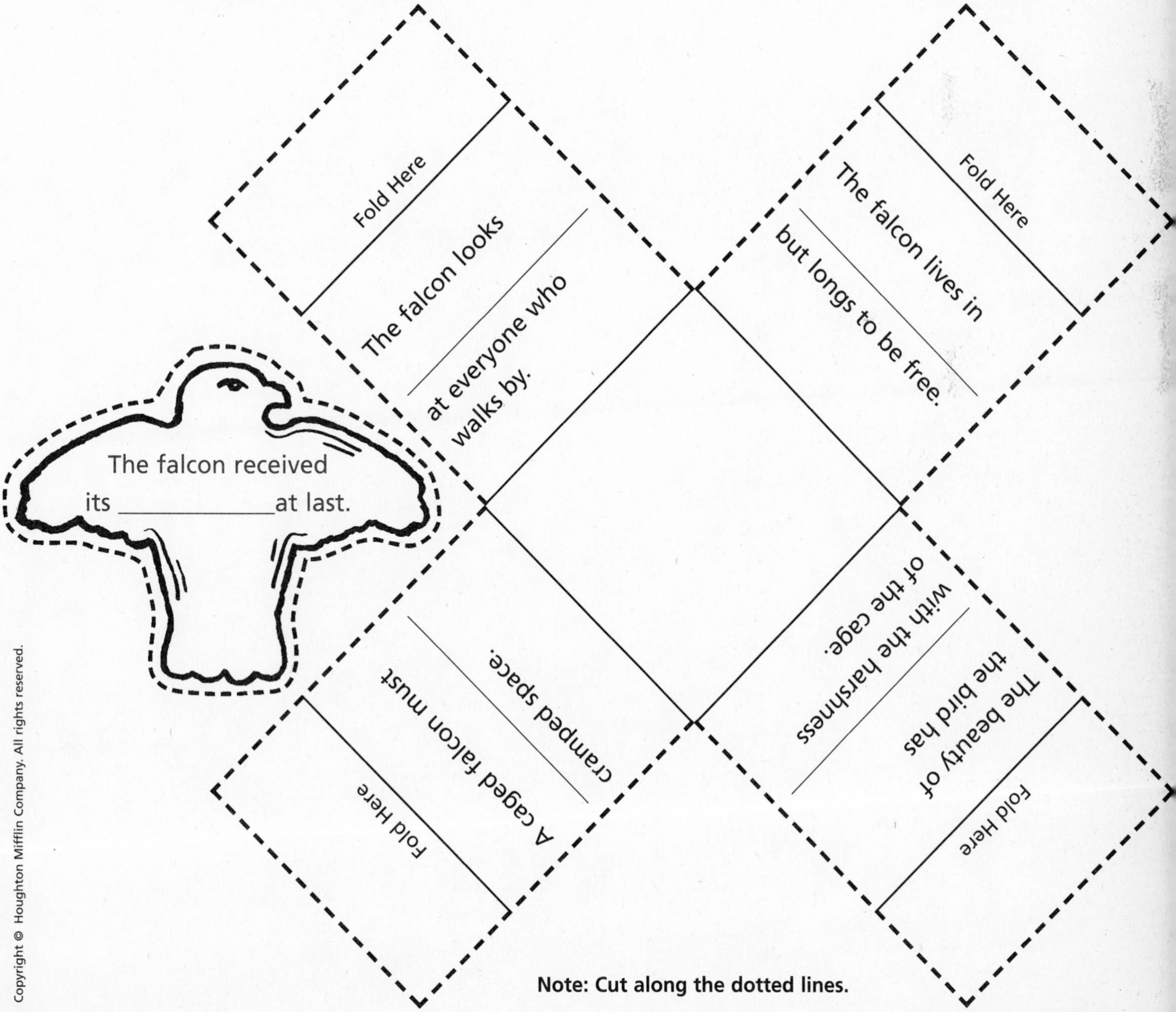

Fold Here

The falcon looks ____________ at everyone who walks by.

Fold Here

The falcon lives in ____________ but longs to be free.

The falcon received its ____________ at last.

A caged falcon must ____________ cramped space.

Fold Here

The beauty of the bird has ____________ with the harshness of the cage.

Fold Here

Note: Cut along the dotted lines.

Name

From Captivity to Freedom

The pictures show events from *Adiós falcón/Good-bye, Falcon*. Write a caption that tells what event the picture illustrates.

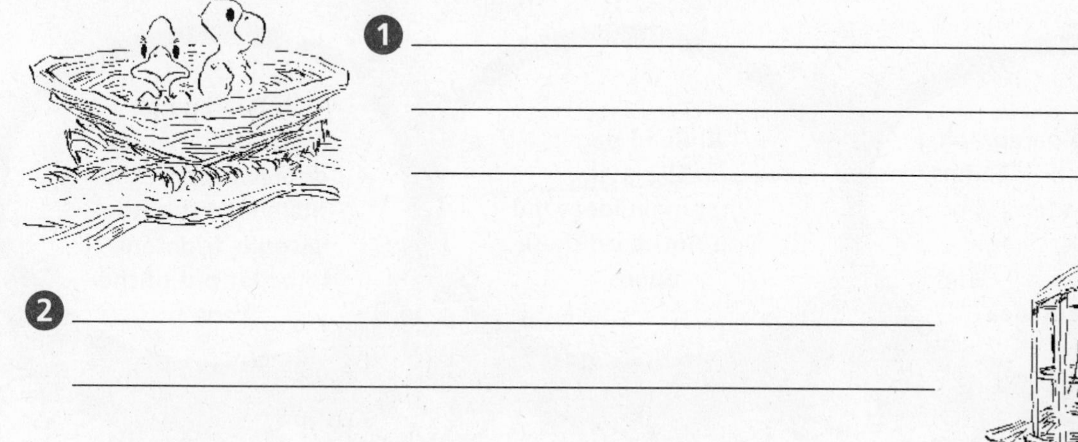

1 ______________________________

2 ______________________________

3 ______________________________

4 ______________________________

5 ______________________________

Name

Take Your Ideas and Fly

Read the pages referred to in the eggs. Then write your answers on the lines.

1. Read the paragraph on page 190 that begins, "Duranté todo . . ." or page 191 that begins, "For the rest . . ." What is the main idea?

2. Read pages 192–193. What main ideas did you notice on these pages?

3. Read pages 194–195. What details support the main idea that the falcon is frightened to be let out of the cage?

1 ______________________________

____

____

2 ______________________________

____

____

3 ______________________________

____

____

What was the topic of *Adiós falcón/Good-bye, Falcon*?

____

Write a summary of the selection on a separate sheet of paper. Use the answers you gave above to help you.

Name ______________________

The Wild Life

Imagine that you are the editor of a wildlife magazine. A writer has given you the following article, but you only have space for five sentences. Combine the ten sentences in the article into five.

Falconry has existed for over three thousand years. Falconry was an ancient Chinese and Persian sport. A falconer is a unique kind of hunter. A falconer uses falcons to hunt game. Falconers often use the peregrine falcon because it can dive after its victims at speeds close to two hundred miles per hour! The peregrine is a very fast bird of prey.

I spoke yesterday with Robert Vivez about training falcons. Mr. Vivez is a falcon owner and trainer. He explained that an eyas can be easily trained. A young falcon that has not learned to fly is called an eyas.

1 ____

____

____

2 ____

____

____

3 ____

____

____

4 ____

____

____

5 ____

____

____

Name

Free as a Bird

Read this diary page. Underline each word with a prefix and circle the prefix.

Prefix	Meaning
re-	again, back
un-	not, the opposite of
pre-	before, in advance

Letting the falcon go free wasn't a prearranged thing, but when I saw the unhappy look in his eyes, I knew it was time. I unlocked the cage. The falcon just sat there, and I began to reconsider. I'd miss my bird! But it would be unfair to think only of myself, so I did an unselfish thing—I helped him out and flung him in the air. The falcon flew unsteadily for a few seconds before landing on a tree branch. Once he'd regained his balance, he sat and looked down at me sadly.

Now it's nighttime, and I'm worried. My bird might be afraid and could even be in danger! Maybe I should have let him reenter his cage just for the first night, as a precaution. I hope he's okay!

Now write the words you underlined. Use the chart to write the meaning of each word.

1. ____________________
2. ____________________
3. ____________________
4. ____________________
5. ____________________
6. ____________________
7. ____________________
8. ____________________
9. ____________________
10. ____________________

Name ....

Captive in a Cage

Complete each phrase in the word web with a word from the box.

clashed	endure	captivity	warily	liberty
captured	cautiously	escape	liberate	captive

lives in ______ but longs to be free

looks ______ and ______ at everyone who walks by

must ______ a cramped space

longs for ______

immediately thought the cage ______ with the wide open skies

If the falcon in the story could talk, what would he say? Use the rest of the words in the box to write a paragraph that describes how the bird wins his freedom.

____

____

____

____

Name ....

Falcon Flight

Vowel + *r* Sounds in *bird* Each Spelling Word has the vowel + ***r*** sounds, shown as /ûr/, that you hear in ***bird***. The /ûr/ sounds are often spelled with the patterns ***er***, ***ir***, ***ur***, ***ear***, and ***or***.

/ûr/ perch bird return learn world

Write each Spelling Word under the matching spelling pattern for the /ûr/ sounds.

Spelling Words

1. bird
2. perch
3. return
4. learn
5. hurt
6. world
7. prefer
8. firm
9. worth
10. early

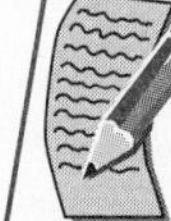

My Study List
What other words do you need to study for spelling? Add them to My Study List for *Adiós falcón/Good-bye, Falcon* in the back of this book.

/ûr/ er

1. ______________________
2. ______________________

/ûr/ ir

3. ______________________
4. ______________________

/ûr/ ur

5. ______________________
6. ______________________

/ûr/ ear

7. ______________________
8. ______________________

/ûr/ or

9. ______________________
10. ______________________

Name

Spelling Spree

Spelling Words

1. bird
2. perch
3. return
4. learn
5. hurt
6. world
7. prefer
8. firm
9. worth
10. early

Proofreading Find and circle six misspelled Spelling Words in this student's report. Then write each word correctly.

A falcon is a byrd of prey. Falcons purch their nests on steep cliffs. Their babies learn to fly and hunt at an erly age.

Once falcons could be found in many parts of the werlt, but later too many pesticides were used. They hirt the falcon eggs. The shells became less furm, so the eggs broke very easily. Falcons are much rarer now.

1 __________ 3 __________ 5 __________

2 __________ 4 __________ 6 __________

Goof Proof Professor Zoof often gets mixed up. Write a Spelling Word that means the opposite of each underlined word in his speech.

7. People can <u>teach</u> about nature by watching falcons.
8. Falcons <u>dislike</u> uncrowded areas with clean water and air.
9. We will not <u>go</u> to a place where food is hard to find.
10. The lessons falcons teach people show the <u>uselessness</u> of birdwatching!!

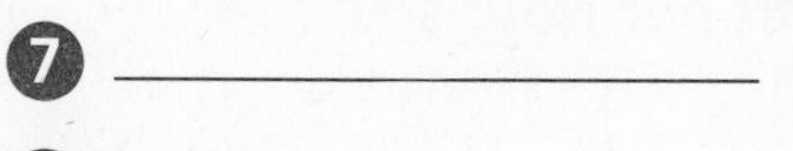

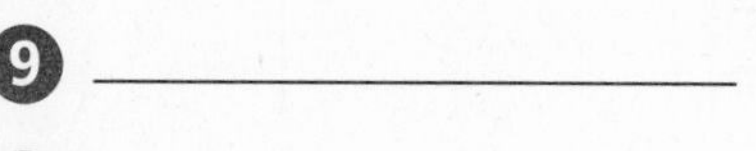

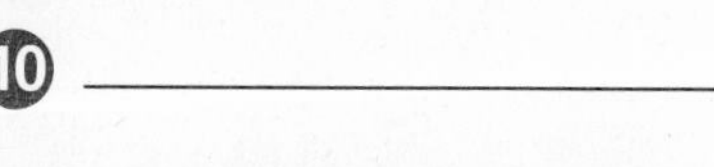

7 __________ 9 __________

8 __________ 10 __________

View of the Wild You cannot always study a real animal in the wild, but you can learn about it from a TV show. What would you want to see during a program on your favorite wild animal? On a separate sheet of paper, make a list of sentences that tell what details to include in the TV show. Use Spelling Words from the list.

Name

A Letter from Puerto Rico

Proofread this part of a letter written by a visitor to Puerto Rico. Use proofreading marks to correct the mistakes the writer made using common and proper nouns. Two corrections are shown.

Proofreading Marks

- / Make a letter small.
- ≡ Make a capital letter.

14 Calle marina

Playa De Ponce, Puerto Rico 00731

january 15, 1996

Dear andre,

Hello from an Island in the Caribbean sea! San juan, the Capital, is very interesting. On monday aunt Clara took the family to the beach and brought burritos and Bananas for lunch. The surf was great! Unfortunately, my Uncle could not come.

Now write each noun in the letter correctly in the chart.

Common Nouns		Proper Nouns	

Name

A Bird World

On a separate sheet of paper, create a tourist map for a bird refuge. Cut out each picture and glue it on your map to show where to find that item. Label each picture with a proper noun. Then complete the map key by writing a common noun to label each picture. Cut out the key and glue it to your map.

Example: Woodland Trail

hiking trail

Draw pictures for two ideas of your own.

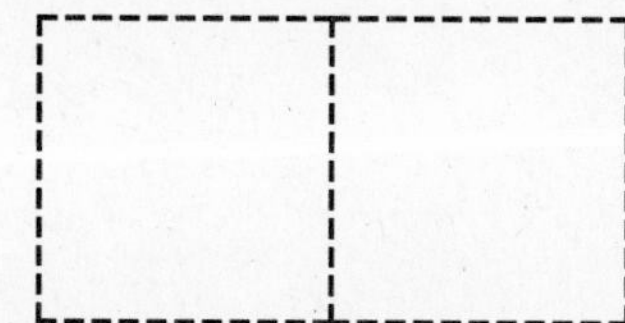

Write a name for your refuge. Then write a brief description of the refuge to interest tourists. Attach it to your map.

Name

Letter to the Editor

Write a Letter to the Editor that convinces readers of the importance of protecting a specific wild animal. Think of the ways humans affect this creature, such as by hunting or using pesticides. What points do you want to emphasize? How can readers change their behavior in order to protect this animal?

Your letter should have two or three main ideas that give your opinion of why it's important to protect this animal. Include factual details to support each main idea. Complete the chart to help you plan your letter.

Animal: ______________________________

Main Ideas (Opinions)	Supporting Details (Facts)
1.	a.
	b.
	c.
2.	a.
	b.
	c.
3.	a.
	b.
	c.

Your Letter to the Editor should show that you understand some ways in which human beings are responsible for the survival of the natural world. Use this checklist to check your work.

Checklist

- ❑ My letter tells readers how to protect the animal I have described.
- ❑ Each paragraph has one main idea and supporting details.
- ❑ I back up all my opinions with facts.

Name

Try to See It My Way

How do the characters in the stories see things in a new way? After reading each selection, answer the questions to complete the chart.

	In the Year of the Boar and Jackie Robinson	Like Jake and Me
Who are the main characters?		
What problems do the main characters have?		
What does one character discover about another character?		
What does a character learn or understand through another character or characters?		

Name

Try to See It My Way

How do the characters in the stories see things in a new way? After reading each selection, answer the questions to complete the chart.

	Me, Mop, and the Moondance Kid	Felita
Who are the main characters?		
What problems do the main characters have?		
What does one character discover about another character?		
What does a character learn or understand through another character or characters?		

What have you learned in this theme about there being more than one point of view to every story?

Name

Dear Diary

Use each word from the box to complete the sentences. Then answer the questions.

foreign	foreigner	ambassador
reputation	escapade	

Monday

I've been in the United States for two days now. The food seems so ______________________ to me! Sometimes it's hard being a ______________________ in a new country. Mother told me that I am an ______________________ for the Chinese people. If I behave well, we will all have a good ______________________.

Tuesday

My new friend and I were baby-sitting his little sister when all of a sudden she was gone! We were worried and looked all around the apartment for her. Finally, we found her sleeping behind the couch. What an ______________________!

1. What is an escapade a person could have?

____

2. What could a person do to get a good reputation?

____

3. What language would be foreign to you?

____

4. What question would you ask an ambassador?

____

5. What question might a foreigner ask you?

____

Name

Shirley's Eventful Day

Answer the questions about Shirley's first day of school.

What mistake does the principal make when she enrolls Shirley?

What strange foreign custom does Shirley learn about from watching the principal?

What adventure does Shirley have at lunchtime?

Why is Shirley worried when she comes back to her class?

Why does Mrs. Rappaport write that she thinks there is something wrong with Shirley's eyes?

Name

From Me to You

The envelope for a letter should include the name and address of the person receiving the letter and the name and address of the person sending the letter.

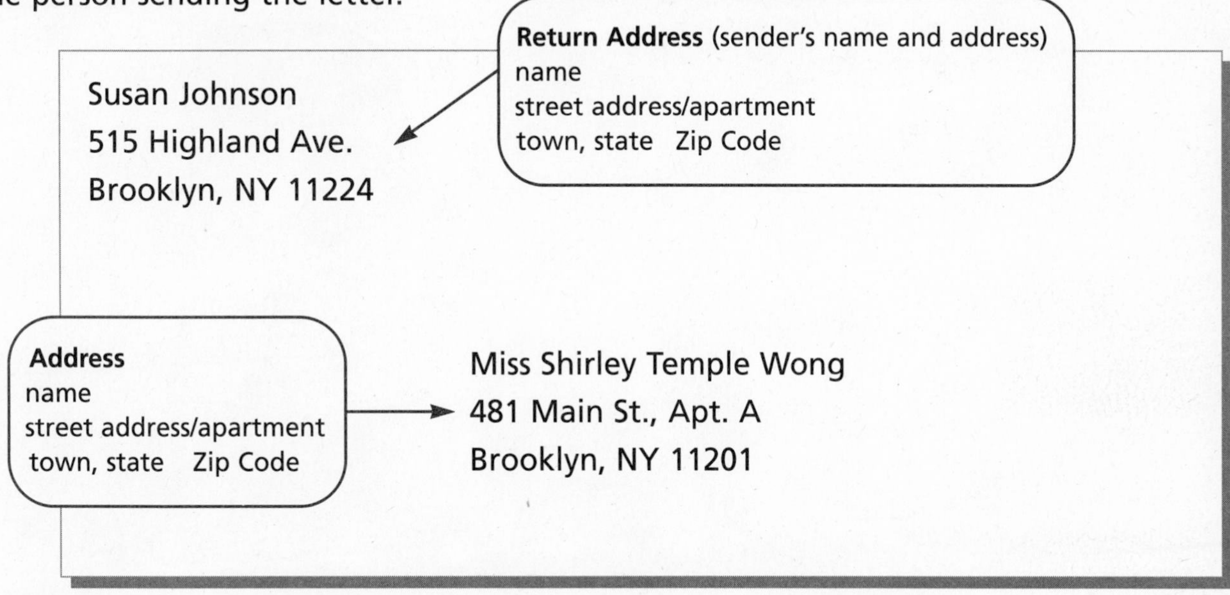

In the center of the address label, write the name and address of someone you write to. Write your return address in the upper left corner of the label. Cut out the label and use it on your letter.

Name

Winking and Blinking

On Shirley's first day at an American school, her teacher thought there was something wrong with her eyes. Solve the puzzle to find out why Shirley kept blinking at people.

Write the base word or suffix of each word. Then write each numbered letter on the line with the matching number at the bottom of the page.

1. suffix of *retirement* ___ ___ ___(12) ___
2. base word of *correction* ___ ___(6) ___(9) ___ ___ ___ ___
3. suffix of *courtship* ___(2) ___ ___ ___(17)
4. base word of *festivity* ___(8) ___ ___(14) ___ ___(3) ___ ___
5. suffix of *scarcity* ___(10) ___ ___
6. base word of *judgment* ___ ___ ___(13) ___(4) ___
7. suffix of *election* ___ ___ ___(5)
8. base word of *fellowship* ___(7) ___(11) ___ ___ ___ ___
9. suffix of *oddity* ___(16) ___ ___
10. base word of *achievement* ___(1) ___ ___(15) ___ ___ ___ ___

Shirley thought that blinking was

___(1)   ___(2) ___(3) ___(4) ___(5)   ___(6) ___(7)

___(8) ___(9) ___(10) ___(11) ___(12) ___(13) ___(14) ___(15) ___(16) ___(17).

Name ....

Diplomatically Speaking

honor	daring
exploit	foreign
embassy	diplomat
foreigner	escapade
reputation	ambassador

Match the words to their definitions. Write one letter of the word in each blank. Then use the numbered letters to solve the puzzle.

1. the headquarters of an official who represents his or her country ___ ___ ___ ___(10) ___ ___ ___(3)
2. what the public thinks of a person ___ ___ ___ ___(7) ___ ___ ___ ___ ___ ___(13)
3. a person from another country ___ ___(6) ___ ___ ___ ___ ___ ___ ___
4. a heroic act ___ ___ ___ ___ ___ ___(12) ___
5. a high-ranking official who represents his or her country ___ ___ ___ ___ ___(11) ___ ___ ___ ___ ___(2)
6. someone who is skilled at international relations ___(8) ___ ___ ___(5) ___ ___ ___ ___
7. respect ___(9) ___ ___ ___ ___
8. willing to take risks ___ ___ ___ ___ ___ ___(14)
9. from another country ___ ___ ___ ___(1) ___ ___ ___
10. an adventure ___ ___ ___(4) ___ ___ ___ ___ ___

Shirley was sad to leave her home in China. However, once she made some new friends in America, she realized that the following saying was true.

___(1) V ___(1) ___(2) ___(3)   ___(4) ___(5) ___(6) ___(7) ___(8)   ___(9) ___(10) ___(11)

___(10)   ___(11) ___(12) ___(5) V ___(1) ___(2)   ___(5) ___(12) ___(13) ___(12) ___(13) ___(14).

Name

Dog or Dragon

The Vowel Sounds in *shout* and *wall*

Some Spelling Words have the |ou| sound that you hear in ***shout.*** The |ou| sound is usually spelled with the pattern ***ou*** or ***ow***.

|ou| shout allow

The other Spelling Words have the |ô| sound that you hear in ***dawn.*** The |ô| sound is usually spelled with the pattern ***aw***, ***au***, or ***a*** before ***l***.

|ô| dawn fault wall

Spelling Words

1. **shout**
2. **wall**
3. **allow**
4. **counter**
5. **although**
6. **fault**
7. **frown**
8. **pause**
9. **dawn**
10. **straw**

My Study List
What other words do you need to study for spelling? Add them to My Study List for *In the Year of the Boar and Jackie Robinson* in the back of this book.

Shirley's story takes place during the Chinese Year of the Boar. Write each Spelling Word under the sign for the Chinese Year with the matching sound and spelling pattern.

|ou| **ou**

1. ______________________
2. ______________________

|ou| **ow**

3. ______________________
4. ______________________

|ô| ***a* before *l***

5. ______________________
6. ______________________

|ô| **aw**

7. ______________________
8. ______________________

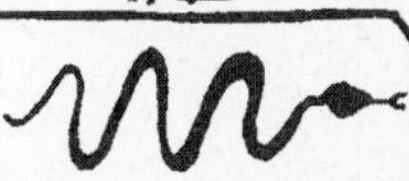

|ô| **au**

9. ______________________
10. ______________________

Name

Spelling Spree

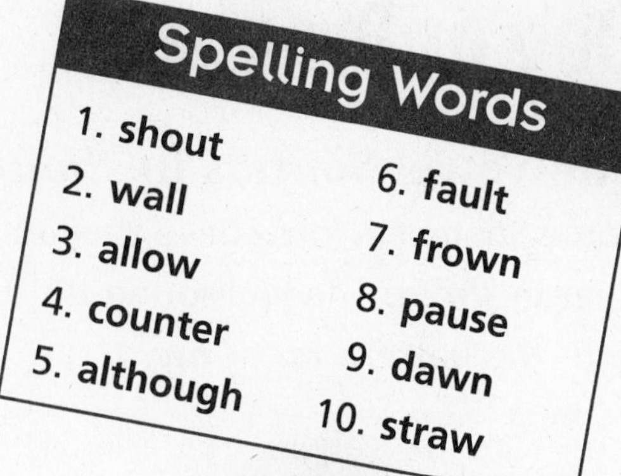

The Third Word Write the Spelling Word that belongs in each group of words.

1. floor, ceiling, ________
2. cupboard, shelf, ________
3. stop, start, ________
4. wheat, hay, ________
5. talk, whisper, ________
6. blame, mistake, ________

Proofreading Find and circle four misspelled Spelling Words in this letter. Then write each word correctly.

Dear Mai Mai,

Each day I awake at daun, and I pause to think of you. I wonder what you are doing today!

My new school is very different, altho I like it. My teacher is so nice. She will alow me extra time to do my work and does not froun if I make a mistake.

Your friend,
Shirley

7. ________
8. ________
9. ________
10. ________

School Days Think back to your first day in this school. Were you scared? Excited? Did you make new friends? Did you get lost? On a separate sheet of paper, write a short diary entry telling about your day. Use Spelling Words from the list.

Name

Lunch with Mr. P

Adjectives Mr. P wants to attract more customers to his store. Help him write an advertisement by adding adjectives.

What Kind

Shirley eats a **big, juicy** sandwich. It is **delicious.**

How Many

One student eats **many** meatballs.

Pick Mr. P's

Mr. P's tasty treats will make your mouth water! You can buy

__________ (what kind) frozen yogurt or __________ (what kind) pizza.

How would you like __________ (how many) __________ (what kind)

peanuts and a __________ (what kind) juice? Tired of candy? Mr. P has

__________ (what kind) fruit to refresh your mouth. Be sure to have

__________ (how many) pieces! And don't forget __________ (what kind)

popcorn. Just __________ (how many) bag will fill you right up. There are

__________ (how many) treats we haven't even mentioned.

Come to Mr. P's and try them all!

Name

In the Year of the __?__

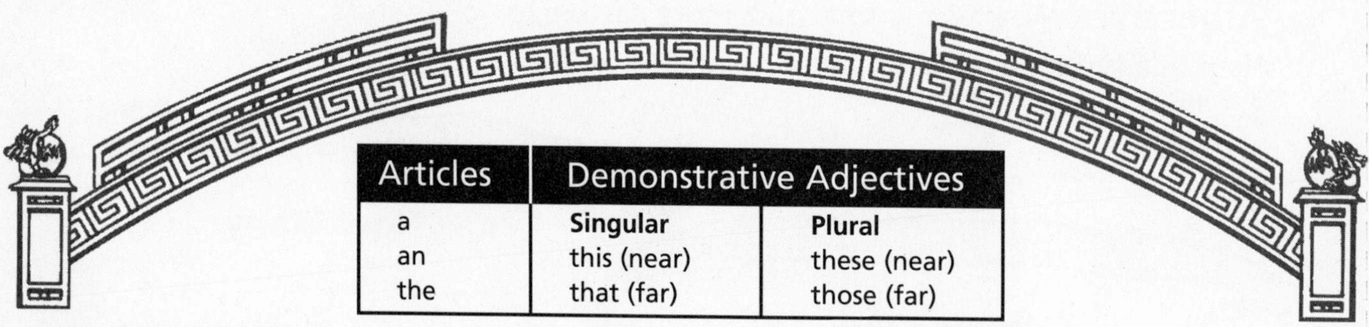

Articles	Demonstrative Adjectives	
a an the	**Singular** this (near) that (far)	**Plural** these (near) those (far)

Adjectives In the Chinese calendar, each year is named for one of twelve animals. Find the year you were born and write your own description of that year's animal. Then find the year of a friend's or a relative's birth and write a description of that animal. Underline articles, demonstrative adjectives, and descriptive adjectives.

Birth year ______________ Animal __________________________

Birth year ______________ Animal __________________________

Name

Painting with Words

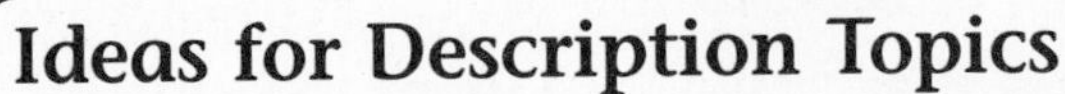

Ideas for Description Topics

- the school bus
- the bus driver
- the lady on the train
- my secret hangout
- lunchtime at school
- my homemade pizza
- the scene from my classroom window
- my favorite shoes
- my baseball bat
- my grandfather

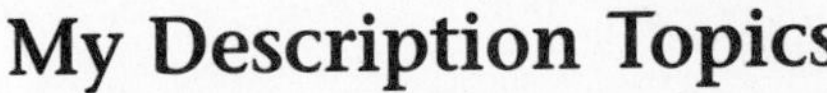

My Description Topics

List five people, places, things, or events that you know well enough to describe.

____

____

____

____

____

Think about each idea you wrote. Ask yourself these questions.

Have I seen this person, place, thing, or event recently?

Can I use at least three senses to describe it?

Would I enjoy writing about it?

Circle the topic you want to write about.

Name

Use Your Senses

Complete the cluster with descriptive details about how your topic looks, sounds, tastes, smells, or feels to the touch. Write exact words or descriptive phrases that you might want to use.

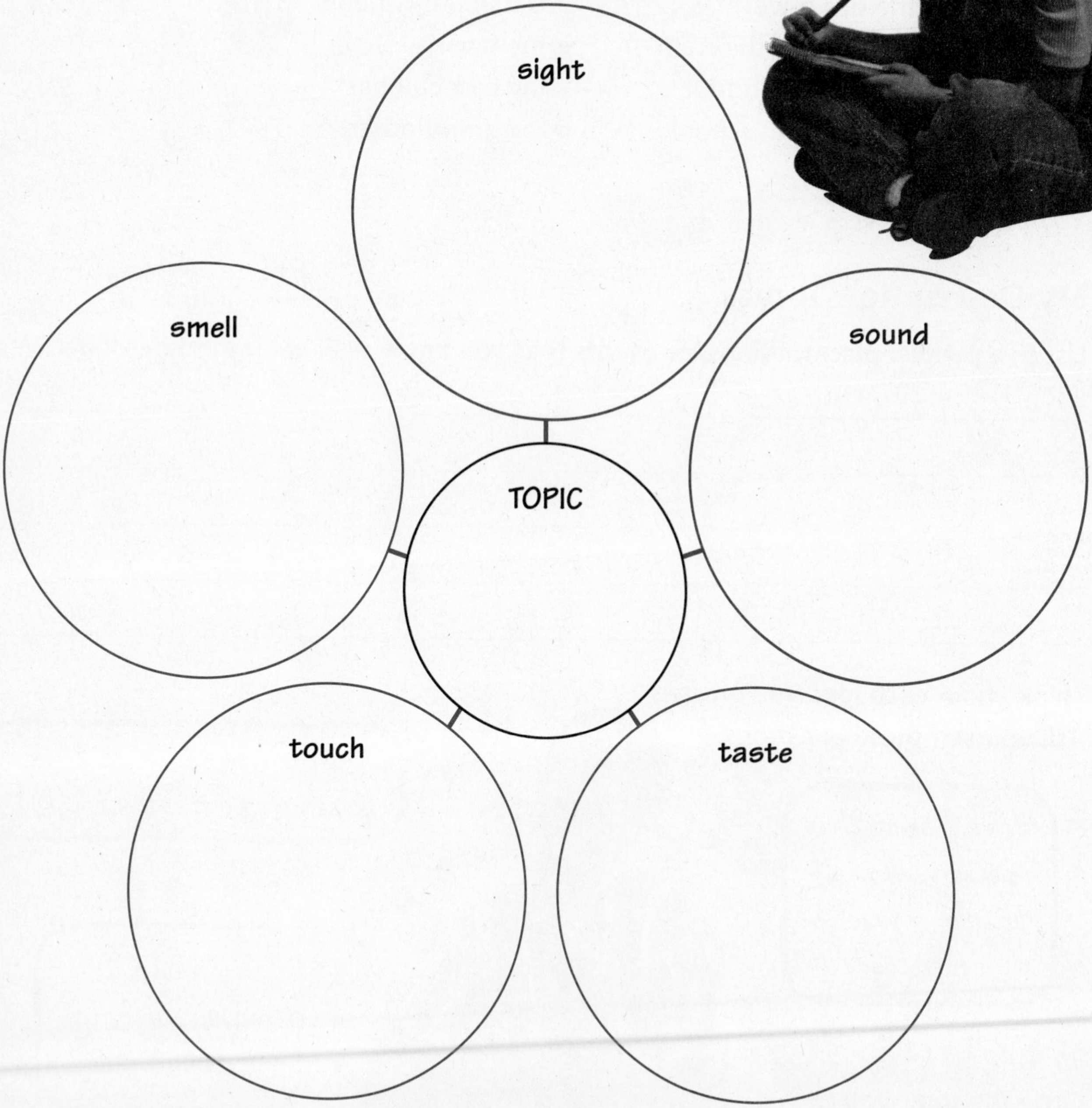

sight

smell

sound

TOPIC

touch

taste

Name

Taking a Fresh Look

Reread and revise your description, using the Revising Checklist. Then use the Questions for a Writing Conference to help you discuss your questions with a partner.

Revising Checklist

- ❑ Did I focus on describing my topic rather then telling about a personal experience?
- ❑ Did I use details that appeal to different senses?
- ❑ Did I use descriptive language, such as exact words, similes, and metaphors?
- ❑ Are the details organized in a way that is easy to follow?

Questions for a Writing Conference

- What is good about this description?
- What details are given? What other details would help fill out the picture?
- Are there any details that do not belong?
- Which general words could be replaced with exact words?
- What similes or metaphors are used? Are they helpful? Where could others be used?

Write notes to remember ideas and comments from your writing conference.

My Notes

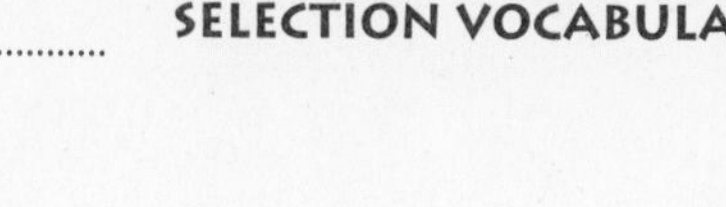

Name

Ready for Action

Read each sentence. After each sentence, write the word from the box that means the same as the underlined phrase.

gasped	grappled	swaggered	crouched	thundered

1. Alex lowered himself to the ground and waited. ____________
2. When Jake walked by, Alex jumped up and moved with a loud booming noise past him. ____________
3. Alex grabbed and struggled with the doorknob of the front door. ____________
4. Jake drew in breath sharply as he ran after Alex. ____________
5. Alex moved proudly into the house and announced, "I beat Jake!" ____________

Answer each question.

6. Have you ever gasped at something? Why?
____
7. Write about something that thundered when it moved. Why did it make a lot of noise?
____
8. Have you ever crouched in order to do something? Tell what it was.
____
9. Did you ever help someone who grappled with something? Tell how.
____
10. Have you ever swaggered because of something you did? Tell what it was.
____

Name

Spider Web

Read the quotes from *Like Jake and Me*, and then add the missing information.

"Do . . . you . . . need . . . me . . . to . . . help?"

Who says?____________________

To whom?____________________

Why?____________________

____

"Jake isn't the ballet type."

Who says?____________________

To whom?____________________

Why?____________________

____

"Maybe like Jake *and* you."

Who says?____________________

To whom?____________________

Why?____________________

____

"Wolf spider! Where?"

Who says?____________________

To whom?____________________

Why?____________________

____

"May I have this dance?"

Who says?____________________

To whom?____________________

Why?____________________

____

Name

Compare the Pair

Think of at least four ways that Virginia and the wolf spider are alike and four ways they are different. Then complete the Venn diagram to compare and contrast Virginia and the wolf spider.

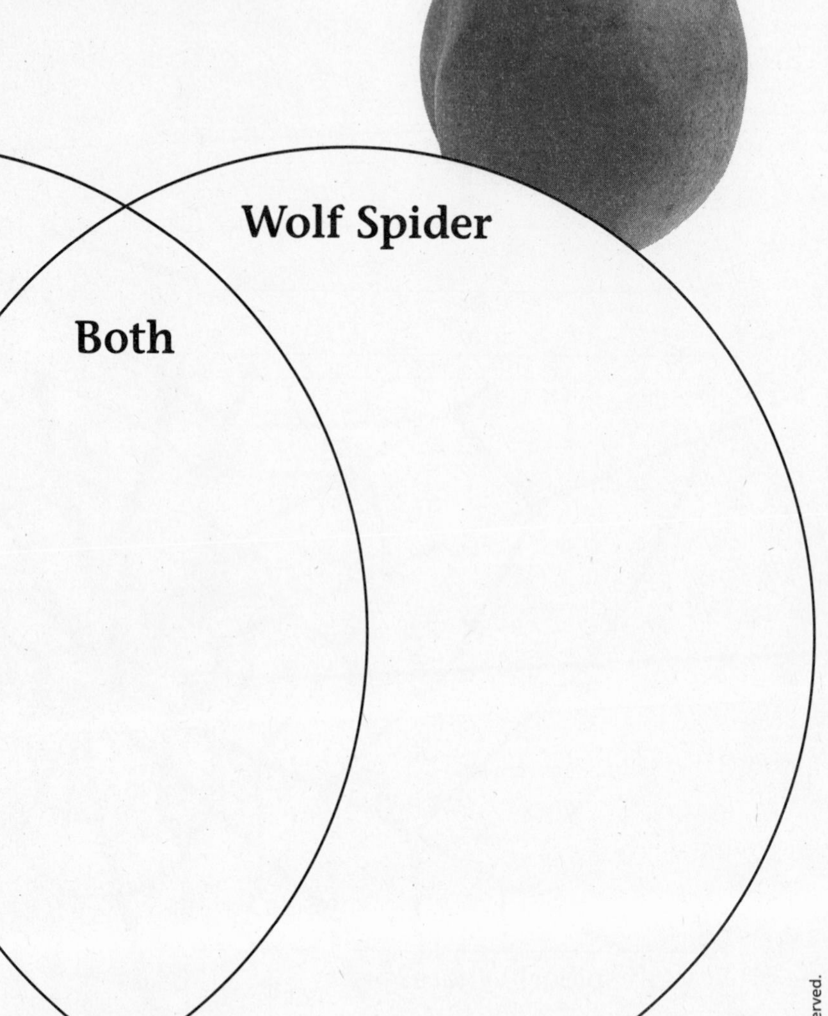

Virginia

Both

Wolf Spider

Now write a sentence comparing Virginia and the wolf spider.

Name

Poem Prompters

Having trouble writing a poem? Try one or more of these activities to spark ideas.

Frame a Poem

Create a frame for your topic that you can use for each line or to begin different sections.

Examples: If wishes came true . . .
Red is . . .
My mother says . . .
At night . . .

Write some frames for your own ideas.

Cool Words

Poetic language is all around you—just keep your eyes and ears open. Write down interesting words and phrases that you read or hear. Can you use any of them in a poem?

Be an Observer

Observe people. What are they feeling or thinking?

Observe things. What do they mean to you or remind you of?

Carry a notebook and write down your observations for a day. Can you find a poem in them?

Draw a Poem

Draw a picture of something important to you. Write your thoughts and feelings about it. Can you write a poem about it?

Name

Hide and Seek

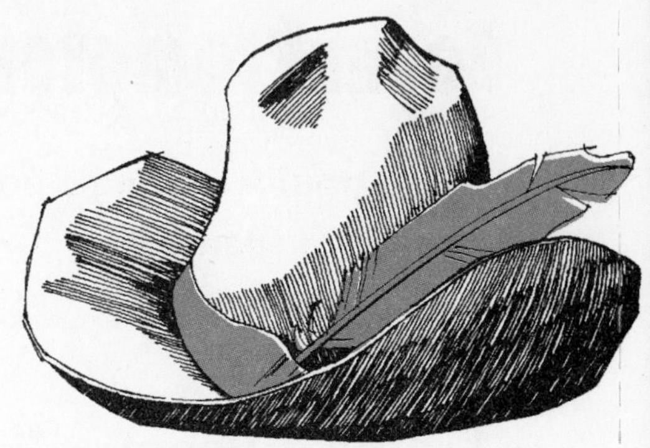

The wolf spider was as scared of Jake as he was of her. Solve the puzzle to find out where she hid. Use words from the box to fill in the blanks. Then unscramble the letters in the circles to spell the wolf spider's hiding place.

light	always	smart	trash	destroy	unhappy	mistake	after

1. an antonym for **heavy** ___ ___ ___ (___) ___
2. a synonym for **sad** ___ ___ ___ (___) ___ ___ ___
3. a synonym for **ruin** ___ (___) ___ ___ ___ ___ ___
4. an antonym for **before** ___ (___) ___ ___ ___
5. a synonym for **garbage** (___) ___ ___ ___ ___
6. an antonym for **stupid** ___ ___ ___ (___) ___
7. an antonym for **never** (___) ___ ___ ___ ___ ___
8. a synonym for **error** ___ ___ ___ ___ ___ ___ (___)

The wolf spider's hiding place:

___ ___ ___ ___ ___ ___ ___ ___

Name

Spider Synonyms

Each wolf spider is next to a definition. Each definition matches two synonyms. Cut out the synonyms and paste them next to the correct definition. Then write a sentence using one of the synonyms.

walked proudly

struggled

bent down low

spoke while out of breath

made loud sounds

grappled

panted

thundered

wrestled

gasped

crouched

strutted

squatted

boomed

swaggered

Name ....

Word Spiders

Final Schwa + *r* Sounds Each Spelling Word has more than one syllable and ends with the schwa sound + ***r***, shown as |ə**r**|. The schwa sound, shown as |ə|, is a weak vowel sound that is often found in an unstressed syllable. The final |ə**r**| sounds in words of more than one syllable are often spelled with the pattern ***er***, ***or***, or ***ar***.

|ər| spider color collar

Spelling Words

1. spider
2. silver
3. color
4. feather
5. bother
6. collar
7. cover
8. quarter
9. flavor
10. sugar

My Study List
What other words do you need to study for spelling? Add them to My Study List for *Like Jake and Me* in the back of this book.

Write the missing pattern to complete each Spelling Word around the spider. Then write each word under the correct spelling pattern.

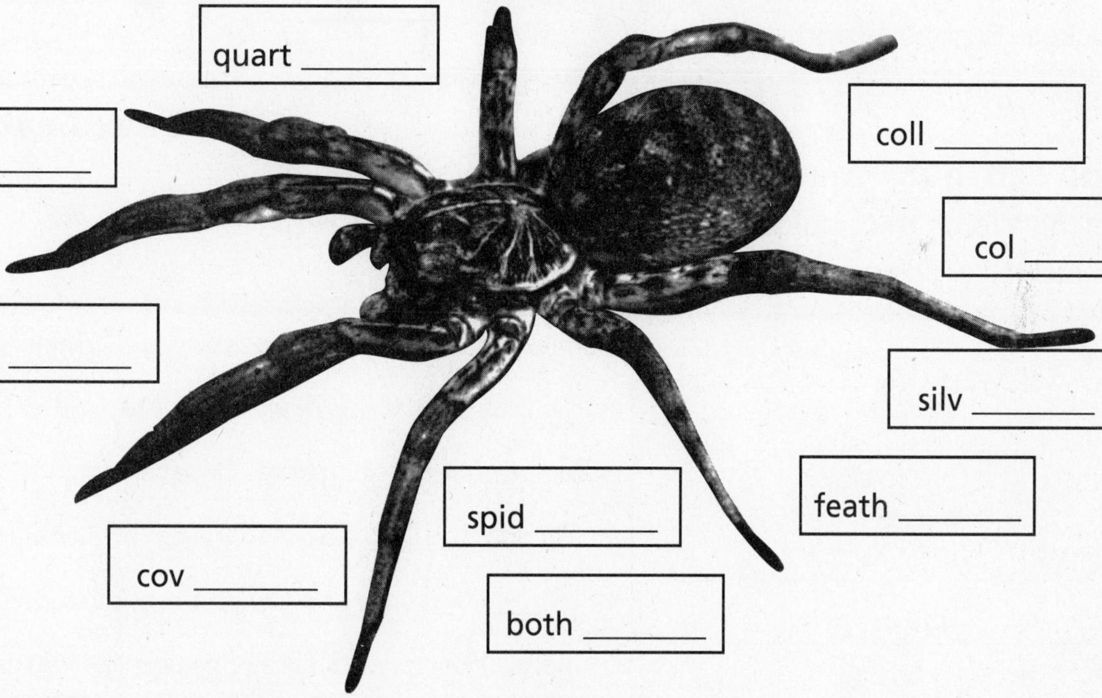

quart ______

flav ______

coll ______

col ______

sug ______

silv ______

feath ______

spid ______

cov ______

both ______

er		ar	or
1 ______	4 ______	7 ______	9 ______
2 ______	5 ______	8 ______	10 ______
3 ______	6 ______		

Name ....

Spelling Spree

Spelling Words

1. spider	6. collar
2. silver	7. cover
3. color	8. quarter
4. feather	9. flavor
5. bother	10. sugar

Proofreading Find and circle five misspelled Spelling Words in this ad. Then write each word correctly.

Surprise someone you love with one of these charming silver pins! Choose the cowboy hat with its tiny fether. Or order the spidar with its glittery eyes the coler of emeralds. Each is about the size of a quater and will look great on a shirt coller or pocket. Buy both and save!

1 ________________
2 ________________
3 ________________
4 ________________
5 ________________

Pear Leather Write Spelling Words to complete this recipe.

6 ________________
7 ________________
8 ________________
9 ________________
10 ________________

Pear Leather

Cut pears in chunks, but don't ____ to peel or core them. Put pears in a large ____ kettle. (Do not use aluminum.) Add one cup water or juice. Then ____ the kettle with a lid. Cook pears until they are soft. Strain and mash the pears. Sweeten them with one or more cups of ____; also add ginger or cinnamon for more ____. Put in a shallow pan and bake at 300° F for several hours until fairly dry and like leather.

Warning Words Alex wanted to help Jake chop and stack wood. What do you do to help around your house? Set the table? Take out the trash? On a separate sheet of paper, write a paragraph describing your chores. Use Spelling Words from the list.

Name ______________________

Knee Slappers

hairy	cheerful
hairier than #1	more cheerful than #1
hairiest of all	most cheerful of all

Comparing with Adjectives Here are some jokes Alex might try out on Jake. Complete each joke by writing the correct form of the adjective. Then write your own joke, using an adjective in a comparison.

1. Why is heat (fast) ______________ than cold?
2. Why is bowling the (quiet) ______________ sport of all?
3. Why is basketball the (disgusting) ______________ sport?
4. Which is (generous) ______________, a giraffe or a skunk?
5. What is the (easy) ______________ way to clean a tuba?
6. What are the (big) ______________ bugs in the world?
7. Which dinosaur is (scary) ______________ than a velociraptor?
8. Why are smiles (long) ______________ than frowns?
9. Who is the (nosy) ______________ superhero of all?
10. Who is the (well-traveled) ______________ superhero of all?

Answers:

1. You can catch cold.
2. You can hear a pin drop.
3. The players dribble all over the court.
4. A skunk: it gives everyone around it a scent.
5. With a tuba toothpaste
6. Gi-ants
7. A terror-dactyl
8. There's a mile between the beginning and the end.
9. Snooperman
10. Wander Woman

My Joke: ____

____

Name

Pear Patter

Comparing with Adjectives Virginia wants to sell jars of her pear preserves. She has tried to write a commercial for the local radio station, but she is not sure how she should use *good* and *bad* in comparisons. Help complete Virginia's commercial. Give her pear preserves a name, cross out each misuse of *good* or *bad*, and write the correct form over it. Add your own ending, using a comparison with *good* or *bad*.

Commercial for ______________________________
(name of product)

Want a sweet treat? Candy can be the baddest snack of all. In fact, few things are badder for you than candy. Instead, try ______________________. Made with the freshest, goodest pears, it is naturally delicious. Spread it on bread, or, for the goodest treat of all, eat it right out of the jar. But be careful. Every taste gets gooder and gooder, so you might eat the whole jar. Things could be badder, though. Just buy more!

Virginia: Try this ending.

____

____

____

____

Name

Batter Up

Use the words from the box to complete each part of the announcer's report. Then answer the question.

series	squad
backstop	foul

It's the Lions against the Lambs. The ________________ is tied at two games each. The score is 12 to 12 in the last inning. The Lions are up at bat. The batter swings . . . and it's a ________________ ball.

It's amazing! The Lambs' first baseman has thrown the ball all the way to the ________________ and now it's bouncing back onto the field!

Four runs! The Lions win with a roar! We have our new champions, the best ________________ in the country, the Lions!

What do you think it would be like to be in the play-offs?

____

____

____

____

Name

Baseball Ups and Downs

Answer each question.

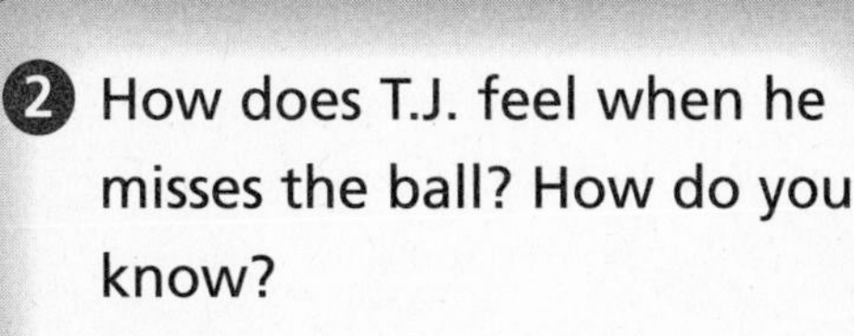

1. Why is winning the game important for the Elks?

2. How does T.J. feel when he misses the ball? How do you know?

4. What are T.J.'s and Moondance's problems?

3. Why do Marla, Mr. Williams, and Sister Carmelita help Moondance with his pitching?

Name

See It Both Ways: You Make the Calls!

Will the Elks make it to the play-offs? Complete each chart with three story events and two examples from your own experiences that support the predicted outcome.

WINNERS

EVENTS	EXPERIENCES	PREDICTED OUTCOME
1. 2. 3.	1. 2.	The Elks will make the play-offs.

LOSERS

EVENTS	EXPERIENCES	PREDICTED OUTCOME
1. 2. 3.	1. 2.	The Elks won't make the play-offs.

Name

Play Ball!

The sports editor wants to shorten this article to make room for photos. Rewrite the article, combining sentences to form new sentences with compound subjects or compound predicates. Use a separate sheet of paper if you need more space.

Lions Maul Tigers!

by Sheila Madigan

Yesterday the Lions and the Tigers fought to go to the play-offs.

The Lions were up first. They played brilliantly! The first batter got on base. The second batter got on base. The third batter got on base! The bases were loaded. Carlos Garcia was up next. Carlos Garcia hit a home run! The Lions cheered loudly. Their fans cheered loudly.

The Tigers were in trouble. Their pitcher loaded the bases two more times. He walked five batters. He struck out no one. That was only the first inning!

The Tigers were able to score two runs in the bottom of the first. The coach felt hopeful. The players felt hopeful. Then their luck ran out. They did not score again for the rest of the game.

The Lions played much better than the Tigers. They won the game easily. The final score was 21–2, Lions. The players are looking forward to the play-offs. Their coaches are looking forward to the play-offs.

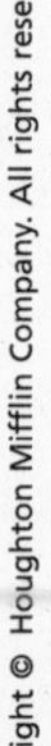

Name

Double Word Play

Solve each riddle by using a word from the box twice. Each use of the word will have a different meaning.

bleacher	pitcher	foul	bat	fan	fly	batter	ball

1. What would a baseball player who hits the ball make when he felt like having pancakes?
   He'd make a ______ ______

2. What would you call a rotten way to hit a ball out of bounds?
   It would be a ______ ______

3. What would you call a baseball player who throws water containers instead of baseballs?
   She'd be a ______ ______

4. What wooden object would a small, black, winged mammal use to hit a baseball?
   It would use a ______ ______

5. What would you call a small, black, flying insect that's hit straight up in the air?
   It would be a ______ ______

6. What would you call an electric appliance that cools a person who is loyal to one baseball team?
   You could call it a ______ ______

7. What would you call a person paid to turn the seats in the stadium white?
   You could call him a ______ ______

8. What would you call a fancy dance for small, white, round objects?
   It would be a ______ ______

Name

Team Picks

Each of the players has a word on his or her uniform. Write the correct player's number on the line next to the definition that matches that player's word.

1 backstop
2 foul
3 inning
4 umpire
5 pitched
6 play-offs
7 series
8 shortstop
9 squad

1. a ball hit outside the playing area _______
2. games played to determine a championship _______
3. a group of consecutive games _______
4. one of nine playing periods in a baseball game _______
5. fence behind home plate that stops the ball from leaving the field _______
6. position between second and third base _______
7. threw the ball toward the batter _______
8. a group of players on a team _______
9. referee who stands behind the catcher _______

On a separate sheet of paper, write a paragraph using the players' words.

Name ______________________________

Batting Practice

Final Schwa + *l* Sounds Each Spelling Word has two or more syllables and ends with the **schwa** sound + ***l***, shown as |**ə**l| or sometimes as only |l|. The final |əl| or |l| sounds are often spelled with the pattern ***le***, ***el***, or ***al***.

|əl| or |l| eagle level special

Spelling Words

1. eagle
2. example
3. special
4. double
5. single
6. signal
7. level
8. normal
9. towel
10. model

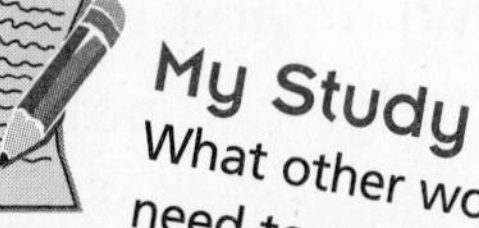

My Study List
What other words do you need to study for spelling? Add them to My Study List for *Me, Mop, and the Moondance Kid* in the back of this book.

Be a power hitter! Fill in the pattern that spells the schwa + *l* sounds in each Spelling Word in the ballpark.

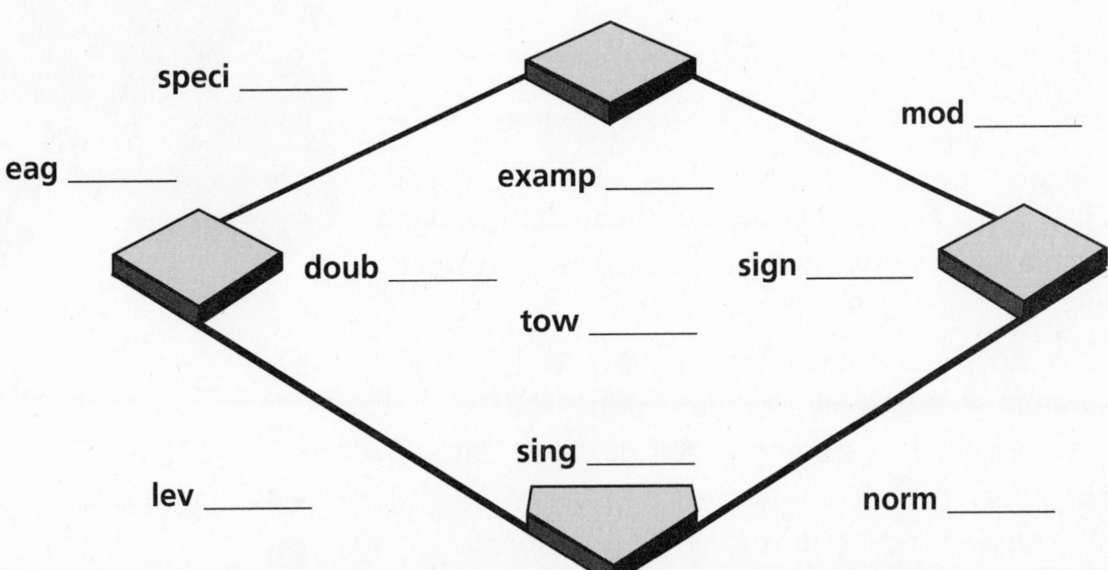

Now write each Spelling Word under the correct spelling pattern.

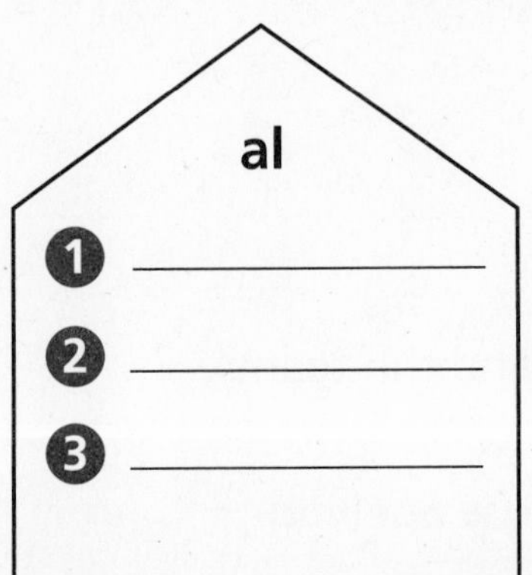

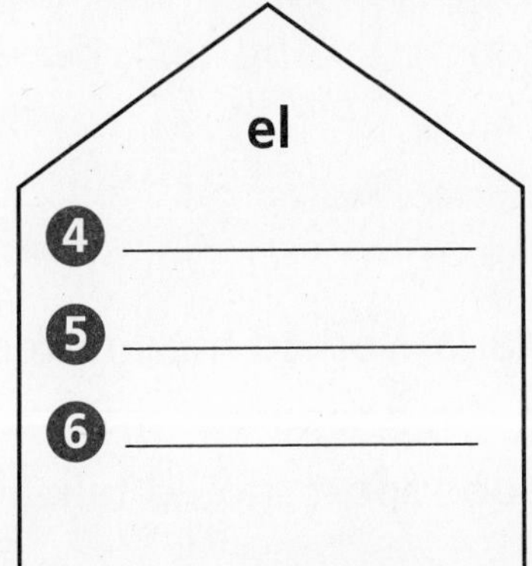

le
7 ______
8 ______
9 ______
10 ______

Name

Spelling Spree

Spelling Words

1. eagle
2. example
3. special
4. double
5. single
6. signal
7. level
8. normal
9. towel
10. model

Tongue Twisters **Write a Spelling Word to complete each tongue twister.**

1. Steve slammed a ____ that sent Sam sliding to second.
2. Nina's nightly nightmares were not ____.
3. Leon's leaning lodge was not on ____ land.
4. Each eager ____ flew east easily.
5. Sue slowed to a stop as soon as she saw the ____.
6. Tammy tried to use Todd's T-shirt as a ____.

1 ____________ 4 ____________

2 ____________ 5 ____________

3 ____________ 6 ____________

Proofreading **Find and circle four misspelled Spelling Words in this news story. Then write each word correctly.**

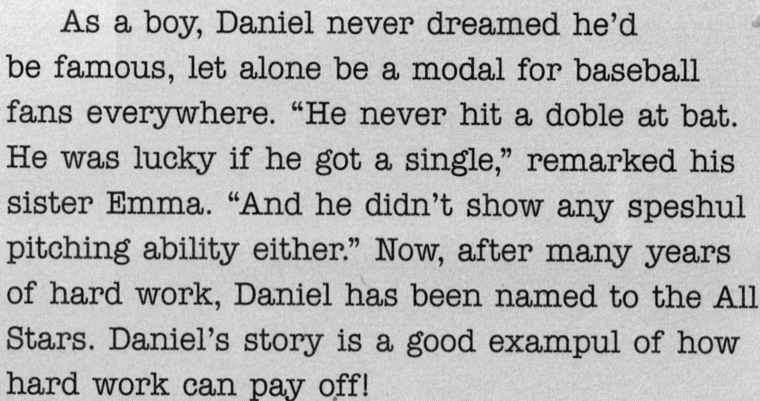

As a boy, Daniel never dreamed he'd be famous, let alone be a modal for baseball fans everywhere. "He never hit a doble at bat. He was lucky if he got a single," remarked his sister Emma. "And he didn't show any speshul pitching ability either." Now, after many years of hard work, Daniel has been named to the All Stars. Daniel's story is a good exampul of how hard work can pay off!

7 ____________

8 ____________

9 ____________

10 ____________

Award Winner Marla worked hard to teach T.J. and the team how to be good sports. On a separate sheet of paper, write a brief description of how a good sport should talk and act. Use Spelling Words from the list.

Name ....

Sports Extra!

action verb / direct object

The pitcher held the trophy.

Action Verbs and Direct Objects Complete the news story, using words from the box. If the word is an action verb, circle the letter under **Action Verb**. If it is a direct object, circle the letter under **Direct Object**. Finally, write the circled letters in the blanks at the bottom of the page to find the answer to the riddle.

heard control owned it earned bat bases scored won name

Eagles Crush Pumas

The Eagles _______________ the series easily today. The Pumas' first three batters loaded the _______________. Then Abe Ruiz grabbed the _______________, watched the ball, and swung. The fans _______________ a loud crack, and the ball soared over the fence. Every player _______________ a run. The crowd joyously screamed Abe's _______________.

In the next inning, the Eagles took _______________ and never lost _______________. Tina Davis pitched and didn't give up a single run. At bat the Eagles _______________ the ball, scoring and triumphing, 9–4. They _______________ their trophy!

	Action Verb	Direct Object
1	Y	M
2	S	O
3	E	U
4	R	N
5	B	I
6	L	R
7	I	E
8	C	A
9	T	P
10	H	K

Question: What is harder to catch the faster you run?

Answer: __ __ __ __ __ __ __ __ __ __

Name

Hot Headlines!

Action Verbs and Direct Objects **Use one action verb and one direct object to complete each of these headlines from the sports pages of a newspaper.**

Example: New Hockey Team Breaks the Ice

HOMETOWN HITTERS

Coach Buono

The Awesome Twosome

Undefeated Tadpoles

OLYMPIC STAR

Foul Ball

EXCITED FANS

Donovan's Defeat

Sudden Rainstorm

HORNETS

Name

Puzzled?

Use each word from the box once to complete the puzzle about the play.

casting	heroine	audition	recited	script	imitated

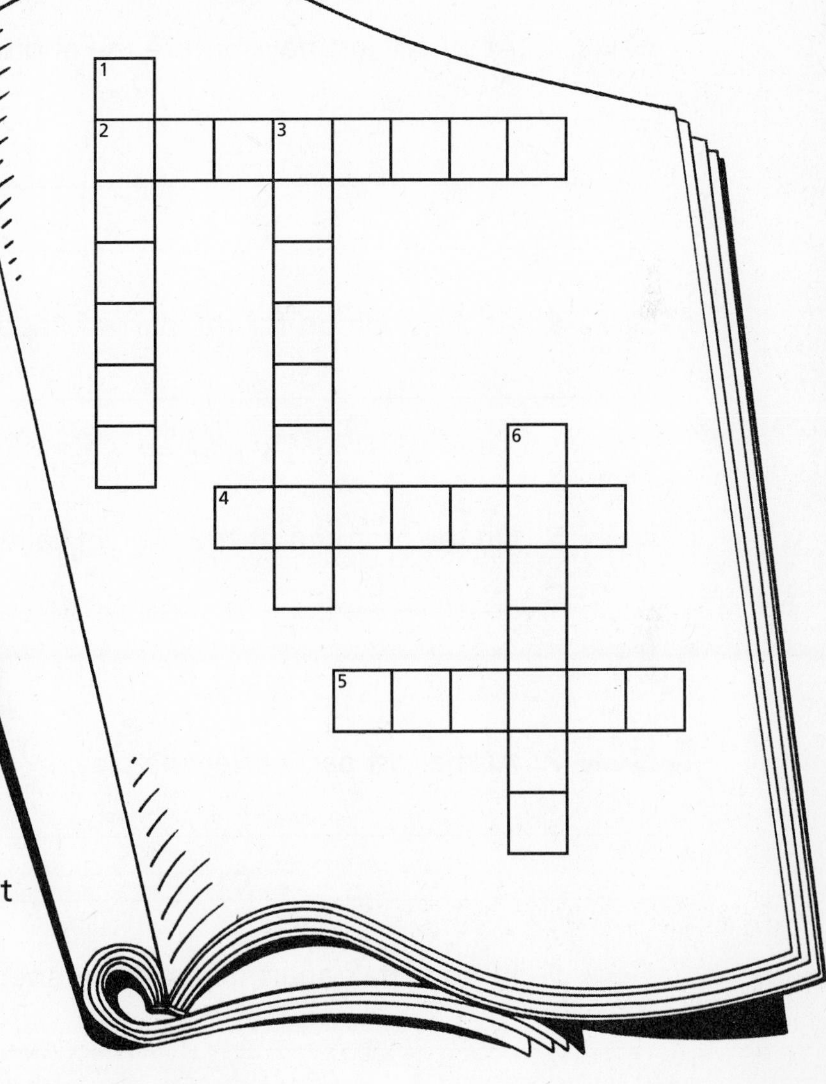

Down

1. the choosing of the actors for the parts in a play
3. acted like someone else
6. one of the main characters in a play

Across

2. try out for a play
4. repeated words from memory
5. what you read when trying out for a play

Write a sentence using two words from the puzzle.

Name

Scene by Scene

The writer forgot to complete the program for the play *Felita*. Think about what happened in each scene and complete the sentences.

Felita

Scene 1. At school just days before the audition,

Scene 2. At the audition for the part of Priscilla,

Scene 3. On the morning of the play, in Felita's kitchen,

Scene 4. At the cast party after the play,

Scene 5. In Abuelita's apartment after dinner, Felita

Scene 6. After school on Monday,

A00024 RESERVED Felita

A00025 RESERVED Felita

Name

Deal With It!

How does each character solve one of her problems? Complete the chart and answer the questions.

Character	Problem	Solution
Gigi	wants to be better than Felita at something	
Felita		

1. Is Gigi's way of dealing with her problem a good one? Why or why not? ________
____

2. How else could Gigi have handled her problem? ________
____

3. Do you think Felita solved her problem in the best way possible? Explain your answer. ________
____

4. Do you think Felita's and Gigi's problems could have been avoided? How?
____
____

Name

What's Wrong?

Felita's brothers took messages for her when she was out, but something was wrong with each one. For each message, tell what important information was left out.

MESSAGE 1

Saturday, 1:00
Felita,
A friend called.
Can you go to the park tomorrow at noon?

MESSAGE 2

Saturday
Felita,
Miss Lovett called.
She has some questions about the art project.
She will call back in two hours.

MESSAGE 3

Saturday, 2:30
Felita,
Consuela called.
She said something about the art project; important.
She won't be home until tomorrow night; will call back.

	What important information was left out?
Message 1	
Message 2	
Message 3	

Name

Stage Fright

Nervous actors forgot some of their lines in the Thanksgiving play. The number of syllables in each forgotten word or phrase matches the number of the scene it's from. Write the word or phrase next to the correct scene.

harvested their crops
the brave military captain
sat for supper at a long table

a Thanksgiving Day feast
turkey, corn, and cranberries
the most beautiful maiden in Plymouth

Thanksgiving Play

Act One

Scene 1: ______________________

Scene 2: ______________________

Scene 3: ______________________

Scene 4: ______________________

Scene 5: ______________________

Scene 6: ______________________

Scene 7: ______________________

Scene 8: ______________________

Scene 9: ______________________

Scene 10: ______________________

2248255
ADMIT
ONE
2248255
2248254
ADMIT
ONE

Name ________________________________

Make a Friendship Chain

Write each vocabulary word beneath its definition on one of the strips. Then cut the strips apart. On the back of each strip, write a sentence using the word you wrote on the front. Your sentences should create a paragraph.

audition	backstage
casting	heroine
imitated	narrator
props	recited
scenery	script

- the assignment of parts in a play ____________
- the person who tells the story ____________
- acted like someone else ____________
- to try out for a part in a play ____________
- objects other than scenery used on stage during a play ____________
- the text of a play ____________
- located behind the performing area of the stage ____________
- main female character of a play ____________
- painted pictures used on stage to represent real places ____________
- repeated, usually from memory ____________

Glue together the ends of the first strip. Your sentence should be on the outside of the link. Thread the second strip through the first one. Glue the ends of the second strip together. Continue until you have glued all the strips to make a chain.

Name

Crossword Pairs

Homophones The Spelling Words are pairs of homophones. **Homophones** are words that sound alike but have different spellings and meanings.

|sēn| seen viewed; looked at

|sēn| scene a short part of a play or movie

Complete each puzzle with a pair of Spelling Words. Write the homophone that fits each meaning.

Spelling Words

1. seen
2. scene
3. wear
4. where
5. bow
6. bough
7. great
8. grate
9. fair
10. fare

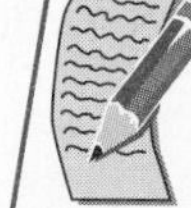

My Study List
What other words do you need to study for spelling? Add them to My Study List for *Felita* in the back of this book.

1
2
3
4
5
6
7
8
9
10

Across

2. part of a play or story
4. a large tree branch
6. to have on the body
8. according to the rules
10. terrific, remarkable

Down

1. viewed
3. to bend forward from the waist
5. at what place
7. money one must pay to travel
9. to rub against with a scraping sound

Name

Spelling Spree

Spelling Words

1. seen
2. scene
3. wear
4. where
5. bow
6. bough
7. great
8. grate
9. fair
10. fare

Proofreading Find and circle five misspelled Spelling Words in this play script. Then write each word correctly.

PAPI: Tito, whare is the can of oil? Your bike wheels grait on their axles, and the sound is driving me crazy.

TITO: Gee, Papi, I haven't sen it lately. Hey, Felita, can you find the oil can?

FELITA: Do you think it's fare, Tito, for me to have to look for the things you've lost? After all—oh, here it is!

PAPI: You're great at finding things, Felita! Take a bou!

1 ______________
2 ______________
3 ______________
4 ______________
5 ______________

Hink Pinks Write the Spelling Word that fits each clue and rhymes with the given word.

Example: a burning wheel **tire** fire

6 a part of a play in which the actors are high school students **teen** ______________

7 a cattle-shaped tree branch **cow** ______________

8 the money a rabbit gives to a bus driver **hare** ______________

9 a remarkable wooden box ______________ **crate**

10 clothing for a female horse **mare** ______________

Tryout Tales Imagine that you tried out for a lead role in the school play. On a separate sheet of paper, write the telephone conversation you had with your best friend that evening. Include details about how you felt as you read, who else tried out, and how well you think you did. Use Spelling Words from the list.

Name ____________________

Puerto Rico Calls!

Linking Verbs **Tío Jorge likes to talk to Felita about Puerto Rico. Create a travel brochure about the island. Pick the best word or words from the box to complete each sentence.**

- delicious
- swimmer
- island
- good
- smell
- spot
- delightful
- feel
- special
- taste
- small
- appears
- homesick
- beautiful

Puerto Rico ________ (linking verb) ________ (predicate adjective) on the map. However, it is a beautiful ________ (predicate noun) below Florida. The flowers ________ (linking verb) so ________ (predicate adjective) there. The bananas ________ (linking verb) really ________ (predicate adjective). The weather is ________ (predicate adjective). The island is a perfect ________ (predicate noun) for tourists. The ocean looks ________ (predicate adjective) from the beaches. You will enjoy its beauty even if you are not a ________ (predicate noun). Everyone's memories of Puerto Rico are very ________ (predicate adjective). Once you have visited Puerto Rico, you will always ________ (linking verb) ________ (predicate adjective) for our island!

Now write two sentences advertising Puerto Rico. Use a linking verb in one and an action verb in the other.

1. ____ (linking verb)

2. ____ (action verb)

Name

Special Delivery

Linking Verbs Help Felita finish a letter she might write to Gigi. Pick the word or words you need to complete each sentence. Then complete the postscript by writing one sentence using a linking verb and one using an action verb.

sorry	confident	looked	one	artist
fault	felt	fun	talented	angry
appeared	actress	happy	friends	

Dear Gigi,

I am ________ (predicate adjective) about our fight. It was my ________ (predicate noun). I ________ (linking verb) ________ (predicate adjective) about the play. I wanted the part of Priscilla. But you were the best ________ (predicate pronoun) for it. On stage you ________ (linking verb) calm and ________ (predicate adjective), not at all worried. You are a talented ________ (predicate noun). I am ________ (predicate adjective) too. I am a good ________ (predicate noun). My sets ________ (linking verb) almost real. Now that we have talked, I am ________ (predicate adjective) again. We will always be ________ (predicate noun)!

Love,

Felita

P.S. The play was so much ________ (predicate noun)!

1. ________ (linking verb)
2. ________ (action verb)

Name

Helping a Friend Get the Picture

Can you remember something that puzzled you when you saw it for the first time? Suppose you took Shirley someplace completely new to her. Imagine how things would look to her. Write a paragraph that tells about it.

Where will you and Shirley go?

___ We'll go to see the play that Felita's school is putting on.

___ We'll go to see T.J.'s team play ball.

___ We'll go to see ______________________________

____

Think about the actions or events that might seem strange to Shirley and list them in the chart.

What Shirley saw	What Shirley thought she saw

Pick one thing that puzzled Shirley. Write a paragraph telling what Shirley saw, what she thought she saw, and how you explained it. Share your paragraph with your class.

Checklist

Before you share your paragraph, use this list to check your work.

- ❑ I picked something that Shirley could easily be confused by.
- ❑ I was able to explain to her what she really saw.
- ❑ My paragraph tells clearly what happened.

Name

Catastrophe!

After you read each selection in Catastrophe!, complete the chart below and on the next page.

	The selection is an example of what kind of writing?	Describe the catastrophe featured in the selection.
Night of the Twisters		
Earthquakes		
The Story of the *Challenger* Disaster		

Name ....

Catastrophe!

After you read each selection in Catastrophe!, complete the chart.

	How do people in the selection react to catastrophe?	What did you learn about coping with catastrophes?
Night of the Twisters		
Earthquakes		
The Story of the *Challenger* Disaster		

If a disaster were to occur in your community, what would you do to help?

____

____

____

Name

Picking Up the Pieces

A tornado has hit! Help your sister pick up the pieces. Cut out and paste them on another sheet of paper to create five of your sister's toys. On each toy, write a word from the box that has about the same meaning as the rest of the words.

jolt	huddled	flickering	sobering	head-on	jammed

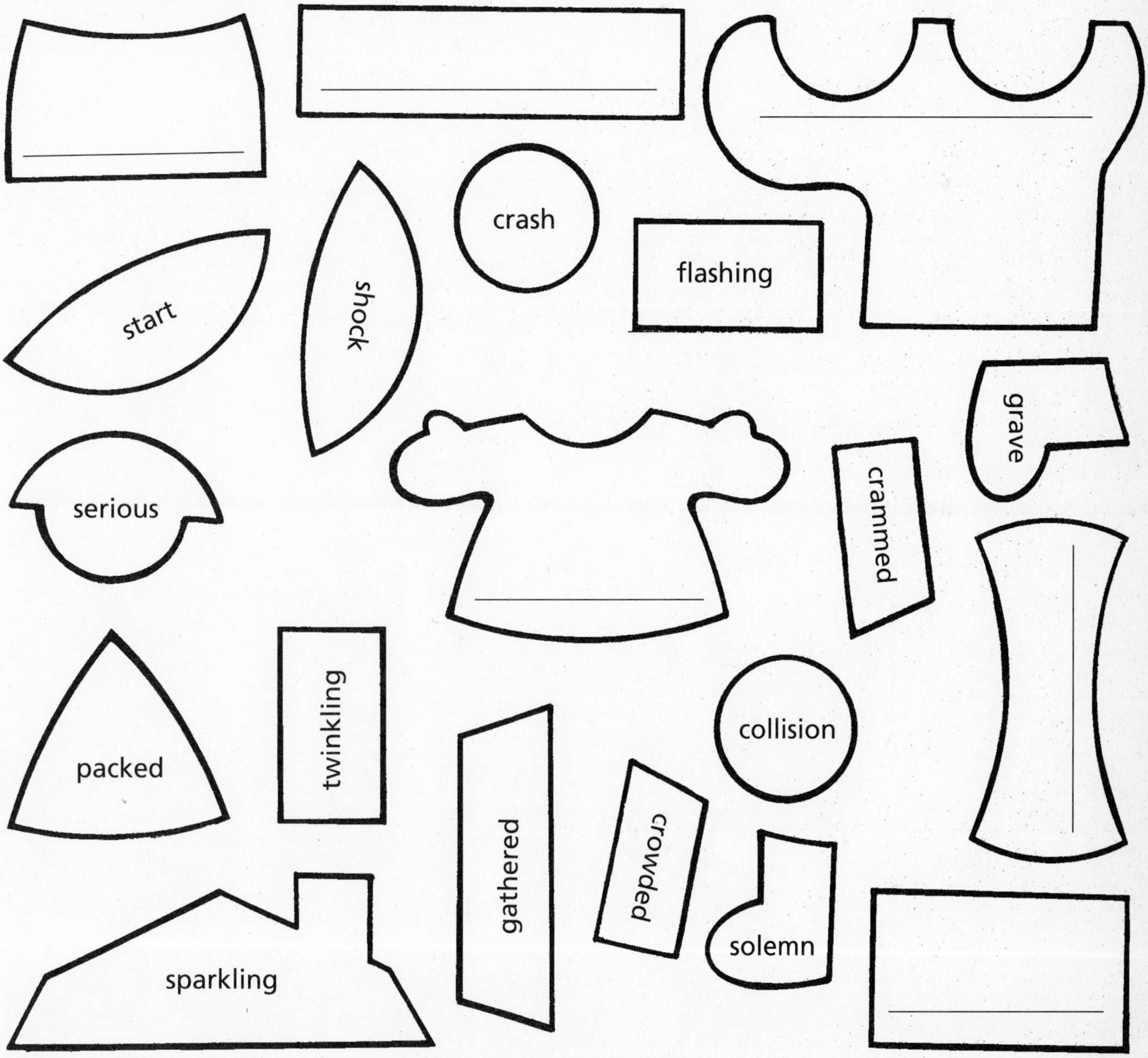

crash

flashing

start

shock

grave

serious

crammed

collision

packed

twinkling

gathered

crowded

solemn

sparkling

Name

A New Spin on the Story

These pictures show items or places in Dan's house. Next to each picture tell how the item or place played a part in what Dan, Arthur, or Ryan did during the tornado.

1. ______________________________

2. ______________________________

3. ______________________________

4. ______________________________

5. ______________________________

Name

Twister Terror!

Complete the sentences to illustrate some of the cause-effect relationships in *Night of the Twisters.* Then show which part of each sentence is the cause and which is the effect by completing the chart.

1. Dan calls his grandmother on the phone because ______
2. When the radio dies and the television flashes the emergency warning, Dan decides to ______
3. Arthur tries to run outside because ______
4. When Ryan gets tangled in the mobile, Dan can't ______

	Cause	Effect
1		
2		
3		
4		

Name

Get the Scoop

Choose a recent event that you think would make a great news article. Find out the facts. Conduct interviews, if possible. Record your information on this page. Then use the information to write your news article on a separate sheet of paper.

Event: ______

What happened? ______

______

When did the event happen? ______

______

Where did the event happen? ______

______

Why did the event happen? ______

______

Who was involved in the event? ______

______

Whom can I **interview** about the event? ______

______

What are other **details** about the event? ______

______

______

______

______

______

______

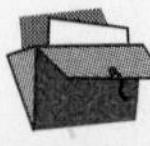

Name

Tornado Is to Twister as Fear Is to . . .

 is to 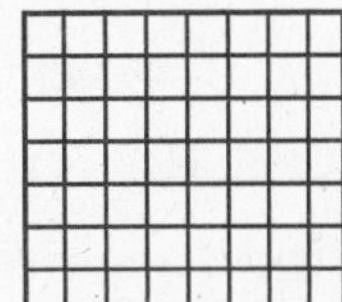 as  is to 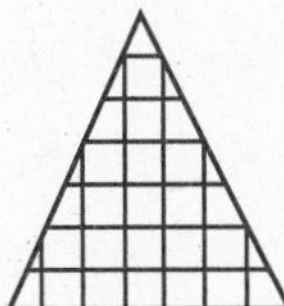

Look for similar relationships in analogies.

Write the best word to complete each analogy.

1. Tornado is to wind as flood is to ________.
   storm water lifeboat

2. Rain is to drop as snow is to ________.
   cold white flake

3. Hot is to sweat as cold is to ________.
   sweater chilly shiver

4. Harm is to damage as rush is to ________.
   danger hurry late

5. Chair is to sit as ladder is to ________.
   climb tall paint

6. Afraid is to fearless as cause is to ________.
   reason create prevent

7. Building is to basement as flower is to ________.
   root blossom stem

8. Shelter is to protect as shake is to ________.
   collapse tremble steady

9. Telephone is to talk as paper is to ________.
   mailbox write letter

10. Siren is to emergency as doorbell is to ________.
   ring door visitor

Name

Tornado Terms

Match each word from the box with its definition. Write only one letter of the word in each blank. Then use the numbered letters to decode four names for kinds of tornadoes.

startled
sobering
scrambled
jammed
jolt
siren
huddled
flickering
deafening
head-on

1. blinking unsteadily

   ___ ___(13) ___ ___ ___ ___ ___ ___ ___ ___

2. extremely loud ___ ___ ___ ___ ___ ___(8) ___ ___ ___
3. head-to-head collision ___(4) ___ ___ ___ – ___ ___
4. a sudden jerk or shake; a shock or surprise ___ ___ ___ ___(1)
5. making one feel serious ___ ___(5) ___ ___ ___ ___(9) ___ ___
6. surprised and somewhat frightened ___ ___ ___ ___(10) ___ ___ ___ ___
7. a device that makes a loud warning noise ___(7) ___ ___ ___(12) ___
8. packed tightly together; stuck ___ ___(11) ___ ___ ___ ___(3)
9. moved quickly, especially by crawling or climbing

   ___ ___(2) ___ ___ ___ ___ ___ ___ ___

10. crowded or pushed closely together ___ ___(6) ___ ___ ___ ___ ___

1 ___
W
9 ___
7 ___
1 ___
12 ___
10 ___

2 ___
y
2 ___
13 ___
5 ___
8 ___
12 ___

W
4 ___
9 ___
10 ___
13 ___
W
9 ___
8 ___
3 ___

W
11 ___
1 ___
12 ___
10 ___
7 ___
p
5 ___
6 ___
1 ___

Name

Cleanup Time

Compound Words Each Spelling Word is a compound word. A **compound word** is made up of two or more shorter words. Compound words can be written as one word, as a hyphenated word, or as separate words.

hall + **way** = hallway
built + **in** = built-in
first + **aid** = first aid

Spelling Words

1. hallway
2. upstairs
3. flashlight
4. everything
5. driveway
6. built-in
7. first aid
8. baby-sit
9. already
10. all right

My Study List
What other words do you need to study for spelling? Add them to My Study List for *Night of the Twisters* in the back of this book.

Help clean up the mess left by the tornado! Fill in the missing part of each compound word to form a Spelling Word. Then write the word under the correct heading.

drive________
hall________
________stairs
baby________
every________
________ right
built________
________light
________aid
al________

One Word

1. ________
2. ________
3. ________
4. ________
5. ________
6. ________

Hyphenated Word

7. ________
8. ________

Separate Words

9. ________
10. ________

Name

Spelling Spree

Spelling Words	
1. hallway	6. built-in
2. upstairs	7. first aid
3. flashlight	8. baby-sit
4. everything	9. already
5. driveway	10. all right

Safety Sense Write a Spelling Word to complete each game card from a board game about safety.

1. You list emergency phone numbers when you ________________ a neighbor's child.
Move ahead 1 space.

2. You wait in the cellar as a tornado passes, so you are not hurt. You are ________________.
Move ahead 3 spaces.

3. You bandage your friend's sprained ankle because you know ________________.
Take an extra turn.

4. You leave your bike in the ________________. Now your dad can't park the car.
Lose 1 turn.

Proofreading Find and circle six misspelled Spelling Words in this TV announcement. Then write each word correctly.

Spring's here alredy, so be prepared for tornado alerts! Buy fresh batteries for your falshlight and radio now. Also check your first aid supplies. Put evrything you'll need for an emergency in a handy spot like a hall-way closet or billt in cupboard. If you can keep spare supplies upstars too, so much the better. Know the safest spot in your home to wait out a twister. Be smart—be ready!

5. ________________
6. ________________
7. ________________
8. ________________
9. ________________
10. ________________

Acrostic Capture Dan's experience in a poem. Begin each line with a letter from the word *twister*. Tell what Dan felt, saw, and heard. The lines do not have to rhyme. Use Spelling Words from the list.

Name ______________________________

It Was Like This . . .

Singular	Plural
A tornado causes much damage.	Tornadoes cause much damage.
It approaches rapidly.	They approach rapidly.
Dan tries his best.	Dan and Arthur try their best.
I know about tornadoes.	You know about tornadoes.

Subject-Verb Agreement **Arthur wants to appear on TV. Help him finish his version of events for the producer. Write the correct form of the verb shown in parentheses. Use the present tense.**

Example: This memoir ____tells____ (tell) exactly what happened.

I ______________ (recall) every second of that day. Here I am at my friend Dan's house. Suddenly a siren ______________ (blare) shrilly. Dan and I ______________ (know) that sound well. It ______________ (mean) that a tornado is coming! Dan ______________ (dash) to the telephone. He ______________ (try) his grandmother's number, but the phone line ______________ (buzz) loudly. I ______________ (remain) calm, but Dan ______________ (become) more and more upset. Nervously he ______________ (watch) the TV screen. It ______________ (flash) the letters *CD*, *CD*. Then the lights and TV ______________ (go) out. He ______________ (scream). Calmly I ______________ (remind) him about his baby brother. We ______________ (hurry) upstairs to get Ryan. Dan ______________ (carry) the baby but does not know where to go. "You ______________ (remember)! The basement!" I ______________ (shout).

Name ....

Help!

Subject-Verb Agreement **After the tornado, people placed newspaper ads. Finish them by adding the correct present tense forms of *be* and *have*. Then write one ad, using *be* or *have* in the present tense.**

Classified Ads

Lost dog! Rex ______ (be) large and tan. His tail and one ear ______ (be) white. Please call if you ______ (be) the one who finds him.

If your water pipes ______ (be) still broken, call Polly the Plumber. She and her assistants ______ (be) the best you can ______ (have).

Be prepared for the next tornado! We ______ (have) flashlights for sale. Each light ______ (have) its own long-lasting batteries.

I ______ (have) three pet iguanas. They ______ (have) no home right now. If you can keep them until our house is rebuilt, please call.

I got lost in the storm. I ______ (be) a small orange-striped cat. My owners ______ (be) lonely for me, I'm sure. Please come for me!

Tornado damage? If your dining table ______ (have) a broken leg or if you ______ (have) any other damaged furniture, call us for repairs!

____
____
____
____
____
____
____

Name

Quake with These Words

Follow the directions in each box. Then answer the questions in complete sentences using the underlined words.

1. Draw a picture of two objects colliding. Then write a caption using the word *colliding*.

2. Show what happens to boats when the ocean heaves. Then write a caption using the word *heaves*.

3. What happens when there is friction between two objects?

4. Why do you think stresses weaken or change the shape of something?

5. Where do you think strains can occur?

Name

You're the Expert

You are Dr. Rocky Tremble. You plan to give a speech that answers commonly asked questions about earthquakes. Fill in the note cards.

1. What causes an earthquake?

2. What is the difference between the movement of a dip-slip fault and a strike-slip fault?

3. Where do most of the earthquakes in the United States occur? Why?

4. What should you do if an earthquake occurs when you are indoors?

5. What should you do if you are outside during an earthquake?

6. Why are seismographs important tools?

Name ________________

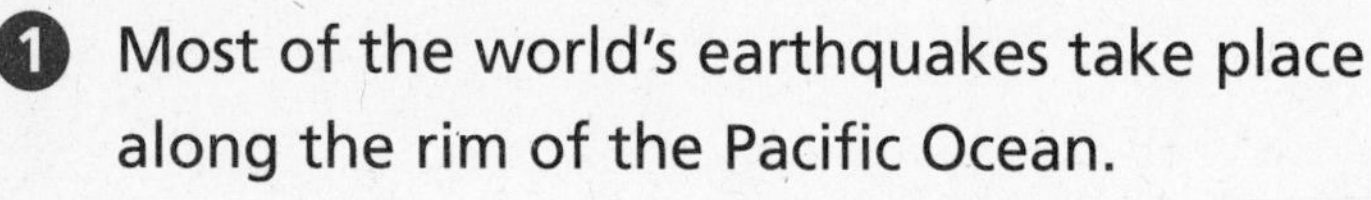

Generally Speaking

Read each of the statements. Circle each accurate generalization, and list a fact from the selection that supports it. Explain why the statements you left uncircled are overgeneralizations.

1. Most of the world's earthquakes take place along the rim of the Pacific Ocean.

2. Many earthquakes are destructive.

3. Earthquakes in densely populated areas are always dangerous.

Now make a generalization about which structure would be more likely to survive an earthquake. Use facts from the selection.

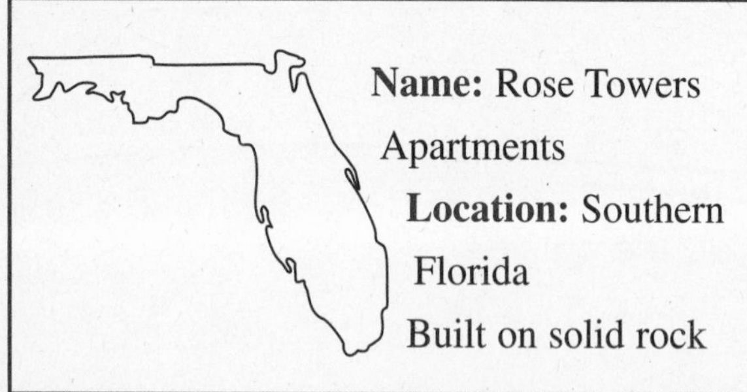

Name: Rose Towers Apartments
Location: Southern Florida
Built on solid rock

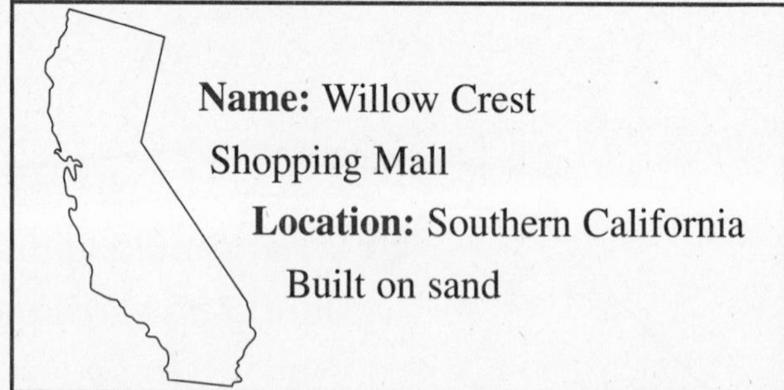

Name: Willow Crest Shopping Mall
Location: Southern California
Built on sand

Name

Use Your Own Words

Read the following article. Then paraphrase it on the lines below.

THE SAN FRANCISCO EARTHQUAKE OF 1989

It was 5:04 P.M. on the afternoon of October 17, 1989. At San Francisco's Candlestick Park, the third game of the World Series was about to begin. The two teams in the playoffs, the San Francisco Giants and the Oakland Athletics, had just finished batting practice. People were crowding into the stadium to watch their heroes play. Without warning, the ground and bleachers began to shake, a rumbling was heard, and chunks of concrete fell from the balconies.

Luckily, no one was injured at Candlestick Park, but that wasn't the case elsewhere in the San Francisco area. The quake had lasted a mere fifteen seconds but had caused a lot of damage. In West Oakland, the top half of a double-decker highway collapsed. Many buildings in the Marina District were destroyed, and a section of the Oakland Bay Bridge collapsed.

Despite the damage and the human lives that were lost, many parts of San Francisco looked untouched by the quake.

Name ....

Word Shake-Up

Write the word from the box that completes each sentence. If the word contains the word root *struct*, write the tinted letter on the house part labeled STRUCT. If the word contains the word root *rupt*, write the tinted letter on the house part labeled RUPT. Then unscramble the letters and complete the sentence at the bottom of the page.

bankrupt	instructions	structure	erupt
destruction	disrupted	construction	obstructing

1. A big earthquake can cause terrible _____.

   ___ ___ ___ ___ ___ ___ ___ ___ ___ ___ ___

2. During an emergency, follow _____.

   ___ ___ ___ ___ ___ ___ ___ ___ ___ ___ ___ ___

3. The damage to our home _____ our lives.

   ___ ___ ___ ___ ___ ___ ___ ___ ___

4. A fallen telephone pole was _____ traffic.

   ___ ___ ___ ___ ___ ___ ___ ___ ___ ___ ___

5. The _____ workers repaired the apartment building.

   ___ ___ ___ ___ ___ ___ ___ ___ ___ ___ ___ ___

6. When their shop was destroyed, they were left _____.

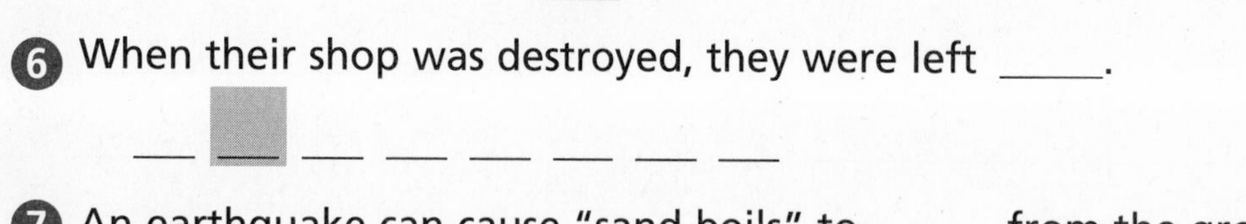

7. An earthquake can cause "sand boils" to _____ from the ground.

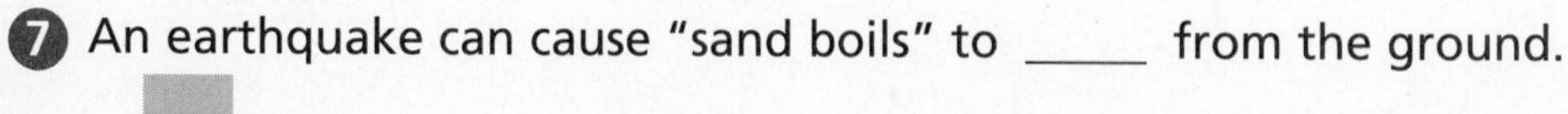

8. A building must have a strong _____ to withstand earthquakes.

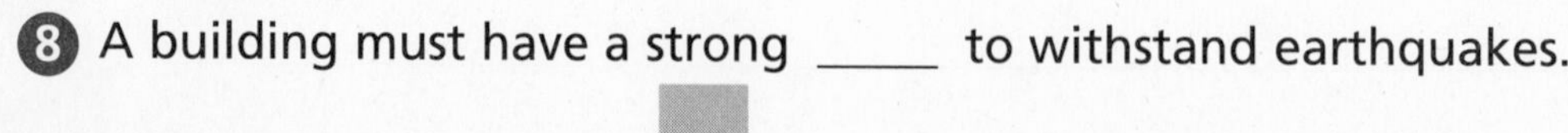

STRUCT
H
C
RUPT
L
C

Something that scientists use to measure earthquakes is the ____________ ____________.

Name

Rebuild the Building!

Repair the earthquake damage. Cut out the boxes at the foot of the page and paste them on the left side of the building. Match each vocabulary word with its definition. Then, on the back of this paper, write a short article about the earthquake. Use at least five vocabulary words.

	process of tearing down and ruining
	striking against each other
	vibrations
	changes in shape caused by pressure
	amount of force or strength
	forces that weaken or change the shape of something
	rises and falls
	rubbing together

tremors	destruction	friction	strains
colliding	intensity	heaves	stresses

Write a short article about the earthquake. Use at least five vocabulary words.

Name

Shake, Rattle, and Roll

Spelling Words

1. damage
2. surface
3. entire
4. solid
5. total
6. object
7. notice
8. suffer
9. modern
10. mirror

My Study List
What other words do you need to study for spelling? Add them to My Study List for *Earthquakes* in the back of this book.

The VCCV and VCV Patterns Each Spelling Word has two syllables. Some Spelling Words have the vowel-consonant-consonant-vowel (VCCV) pattern. To find the syllables in most **VCCV** words, divide the word between the consonants.

VC|CV
suf|fer

VC|CV
sur|face

The other Spelling Words have the vowel-consonant-vowel (VCV) pattern. VCV words are usually divided before the consonant if the first syllable has a long vowel sound and after the consonant if the first syllable has a short vowel sound. Divide each word before or after the consonant.

V|CV
to|tal

VC|V
dam|age

Write each Spelling Word under the correct pattern. Then draw a line dividing each word into syllables.

VCCV	VCV
1 ______	6 ______
2 ______	7 ______
3 ______	8 ______
4 ______	9 ______
5 ______	10 ______

Name

Spelling Spree

Spelling Words

1. damage
2. surface
3. entire
4. solid
5. total
6. object
7. notice
8. suffer
9. modern
10. mirror

Proofreading Find and circle six misspelled Spelling Words. Then write each word correctly.

Almost 2000 years ago a Chinese scientist invented an "earthquake alarm." Like modurn seismographs, it recorded movements of the earth's surfus. Eight dragon heads jutted out from the kettle-like objekt. Each head held a soled metal ball, and a toad sat below. When the ground shook, the ball dropped into the toad's open mouth with a clang the scientist was sure to nottis!! Thus, he knew that somewhere in China, people had suffered earthquake dammage.

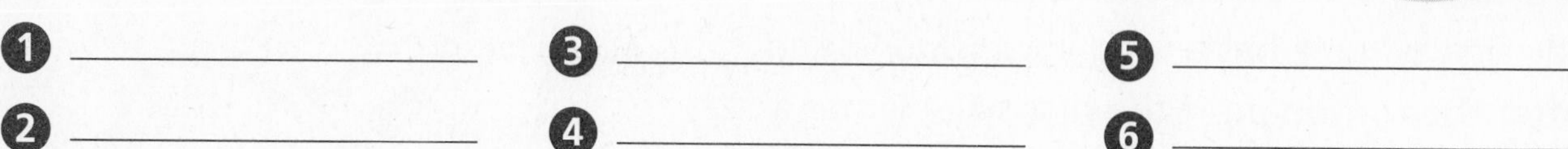

1 ____________ 3 ____________ 5 ____________

2 ____________ 4 ____________ 6 ____________

Headlines Replace the underlined words in each newspaper headline with a Spelling Word having a similar meaning. Remember to use a capital letter.

7. **Reflective Glass Shatters, Misses Sleeping Child**
8. Power Losses Affect Whole City
9. **Troy and Eltown Experience Quake Destruction**
10. **Added-up Cost of Quake Repair Reaches Millions**

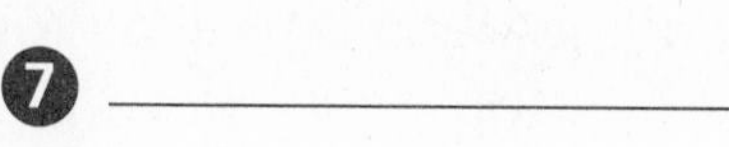

7 ____________

8 ____________

9 ____________

10 ____________

Disaster Relief Natural disasters can change people's lives forever. Can you help those people get back to normal? On a separate sheet of paper, list four practical ways to help. Use Spelling Words from the list.

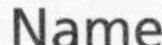

Name

New! Improved!

Past Tense Yesterday experts **predicted** a quake.	Present Tense Now the tremors **shake** us.	Future Tense Soon we **will repair** our house.

Verb Tenses **An inventor wants a patent on her new, improved earthquake-measuring machine. Help her fill out a patent application. Write the verb in the present, the past, or the future tense.**

National Patent Office Application for a Patent

Name of machine:	The Seismic Wonder
Purpose:	to measure the force of earthquake tremors

Explanation:

Five years ago I ________________ (notice) problems with earthquake-measuring scales. Immediately, I ________________ (start) work on my own machine. Now it is ready. Soon other machines ________________ (become) useless.

The Seismic Wonder is remarkable. In tests last year, it ________________ (perform) amazingly well. When it was tested in China, it ________________ (record) seismic shocks within a second. When it was tested in California, it ________________ (measure) slips in the San Andreas fault perfectly. The parts of the Seismic Wonder are simple. They ________________ (shift) through water to measure the smallest movement. As you watch, the needles ________________ (swing) to the correct number on the dial.

In the coming years, the Seismic Wonder ________________ (change) earthquake measurement forever. Everyone ________________ (use) this remarkable instrument.

Name ______________________

Tense Situation

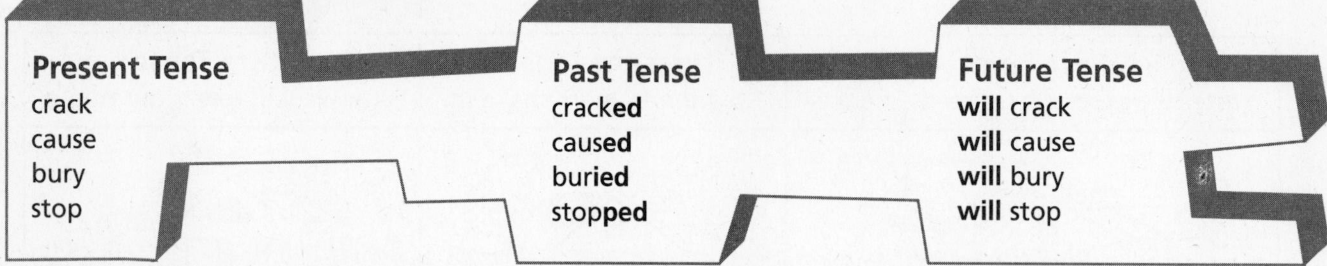

Present Tense	Past Tense	Future Tense
crack	crack**ed**	**will** crack
cause	caus**ed**	**will** cause
bury	bur**ied**	**will** bury
stop	stop**ped**	**will** stop

Verb Tenses **In the puzzle, read down or across to find the past tense forms of the verbs in the boxes. Circle the forms. Then write them on the lines.**

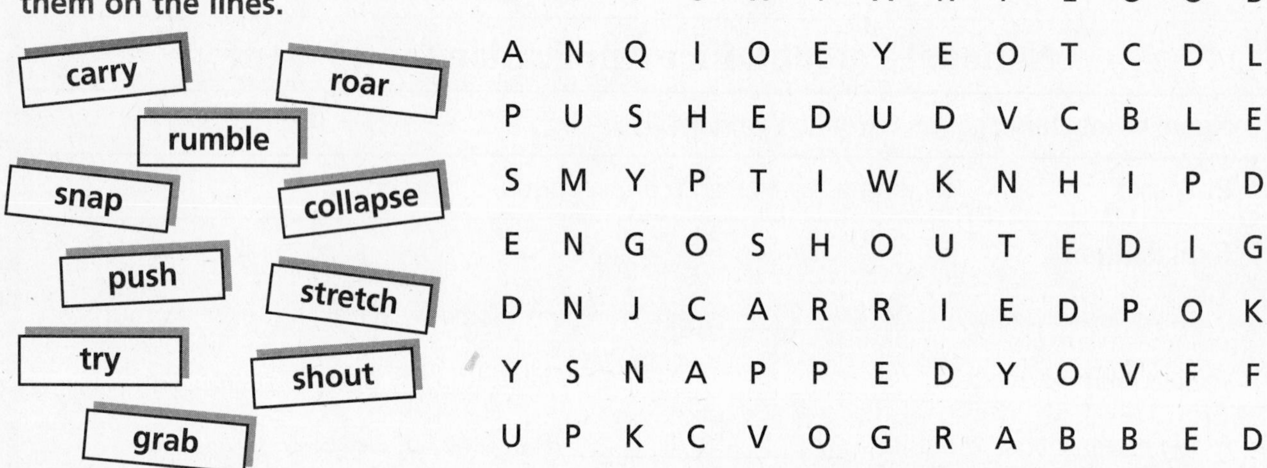

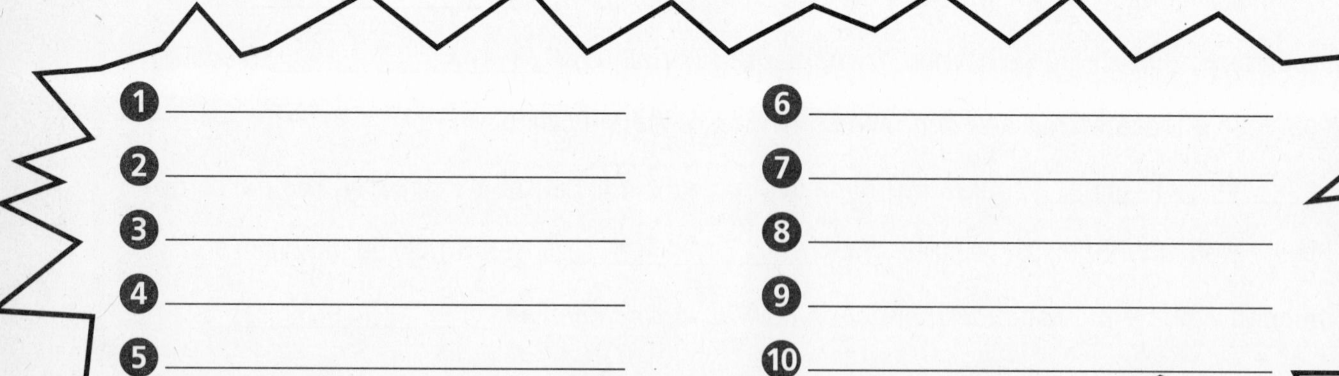

More! On another sheet of paper, write a short poem about an earthquake. Use at least five of the past tense forms.

PREWRITING Choose a Research Report Topic

Name

I Wonder Why . . .

Report Topics Are you curious about one of these topics? What other ones do they make you think of?

- avalanches
- poisonous insects
- Boston Tea Party
- cotton
- training for a marathon
- scuba diving
- Sojourner Truth
- weather forecasting
- The Great Wall of China
- Klondike Gold Rush
- Kamehameha the Great

My Report Topics Write five ideas that you might like to write about in a report.

1. ______
2. ______
3. ______
4. ______
5. ______

Ask yourself these questions about each idea you listed.

Now circle the topic that you will write about. You may want to check your library resources before you decide.

Name ______________________________

Be a Researcher

Write your report topic. Then fill in the first two columns of the chart to help you plan your research. In the column "What I Want to Know," write questions you would like to answer about your topic. Fill in the last column later when you have finished your report.

My Topic ______________________________

What I Know	What I Want to Know	What I Learned

Name

Taking Another Look

Reread and revise your report, using the Revising Checklist. Then use the Questions for a Writing Conference to help you discuss your report with a classmate.

Revising Checklist

- [ ] Have I stated my main ideas in topic sentences?
- [ ] Do all the facts in each paragraph support the main idea?
- [ ] Where should I add more information?
- [ ] Have I used my own words?
- [ ] Does my introduction prepare the reader for the report?
- [ ] Does my conclusion sum up the report?

Questions for a Writing Conference

- What do you like about this report?
- Does any part seem unclear? Why? Not enough facts? Unfamiliar words?
- Do any facts belong in other parts of the report?
- Do any parts seem out of order?
- Does any information seem not to belong?
- How could the introduction or conclusion be improved?

My Notes

Write notes to remember ideas discussed in your writing conference.

Name

A Tribute to *Challenger*

commemorate	grief
tragedy	mourned
sympathy	memorial

Use the vocabulary words to complete the plaque. Then answer the question.

This plaque is a ________________ to the seven astronauts killed January 28, 1986, when the space shuttle *Challenger* exploded shortly after takeoff. It was created to ________________ the seven brave heroes who lost their lives. As a nation, we ________________ the loss of *Challenger.* We expressed sadness and ________________ over the deaths of the *Challenger* crew. We send our ________________ to the families and friends of those seven brave astronauts who sacrificed their lives for science. The *Challenger* explosion is a ________________ we will never forget.

What kind of tribute would you make to honor the astronauts killed in the *Challenger* disaster?

____

____

____

____

____

Name

Countdown to Disaster

Explain the sequence of events surrounding the *Challenger* disaster by completing the sentences. Then answer the question.

Christa McAuliffe is chosen to be the first

McAuliffe travels to the Johnson Space Center, where she meets and trains with

The launch of the shuttle is delayed for three days because of

Seventy-four seconds after the *Challenger* is launched, it

Rescue efforts are attempted, but

People show their grief for the astronauts who died by

How did you feel when you read the description of the *Challenger* explosion?

Name

Think for Yourself

Draw conclusions by answering the questions in the charts.

Facts
How did Christa McAuliffe react to being chosen to ride in the space shuttle?

Personal Experiences
How would you feel if you were chosen?

Conclusion
What would it be like to be chosen to ride the space shuttle?

Facts
How did students react to the disaster?

Personal Experiences
How did you feel as you read about the shuttle explosion?

Conclusion
What would it have been like to be one of Christa McAuliffe's students?

Name

A Business Matter

Use this page to help you plan your business letter.

Inside address

Name of person who will receive letter (and his or her title): ______

Company name (if there is one): ______

Address: ______

______

Greeting

Person's name or a general greeting: ______

Body

Purpose of letter: ______

______

Details I need to include: ______

______

______

______

Closing

______

Name

Compound Challenge

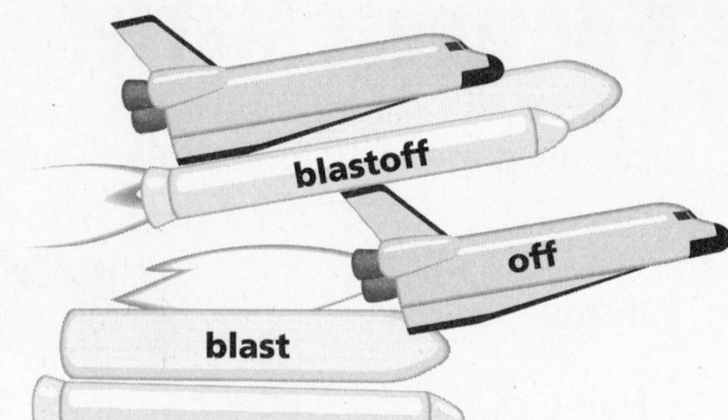

Each word in the box is a compound word made up of two smaller words. Search for the "word within a word" that matches each puzzle clue. Then complete the crossword puzzle.

skyrocket
stargazing
broadcast
earthbound
breathtaking
setback
airtight
runway
moonlight
safeguard

Across

3. wide
6. move swiftly
7. looking
8. road
9. the sun, for example
12. soil *or* our planet
14. to throw
16. opposite of forward
18. where birds fly
19. without leaks

Down

1. to protect
2. Earth has only one.
3. tied *or* headed
4. brightness
5. air inhaled and exhaled
10. craft that shoots into space
11. put
13. opposite of giving
15. not dangerous
17. contains oxygen

More! Write a crossword clue for one of the two words that make up the compound word *blastoff.*

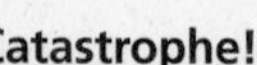

Name

In Honor of *Challenger*

Take a moment to remember the *Challenger* crew. Write each vocabulary word next to its definition. Then use at least five vocabulary words to write a paragraph or a poem honoring the *Challenger* astronauts.

1. deep sadness caused by disaster or loss __________
2. suddenly surprised or upset __________
3. something that is put up, kept, or done to help people remember a person or event __________
4. to honor the memory of someone or something __________
5. to feel or express sorrow for someone who has died __________
6. very sad event; terrible happening __________
7. bad luck __________
8. unwillingness to accept that something is true __________
9. expression of sorrow for the sadness of another person __________
10. something given or done to show respect or thanks __________

misfortune **commemorate** **tragedy** **grief** **tribute** **shocked** **memorial** **disbelief** **sympathy** **mourn**

Name

On to the Stars

Spelling Words

1. explode
2. instant
3. control
4. explore
5. address
6. struggle
7. express
8. empty
9. farther
10. sandwich

My Study List
What other words do you need to study for spelling? Add them to My Study List for *The Story of the Challenger Disaster* in the back of this book.

The VCCCV Pattern

Each two-syllable Spelling Word has the vowel-consonant-consonant-consonant-vowel (VCCCV) pattern. In each word, two different consonants spell one sound (as in *farther*) or form a cluster (as in *explode*). Divide each word into syllables before or after those two consonants. Look for familiar patterns, and spell the word by syllables.

VC | CCV:	**far | ther**
VCC | CV:	**sand | wich**
VC | CCV:	**ex | plode**

Find the Spelling Word that fits each clue, and write it under the correct heading. Then draw a line dividing each word into syllables.

Clues

1. two or more slices of bread with a food filling
2. containing nothing
3. at a greater distance
4. brief moment
5. to search for
6. to put into words
7. great effort
8. to speak to; to greet
9. to burst suddenly
10. power that checks and regulates an operation

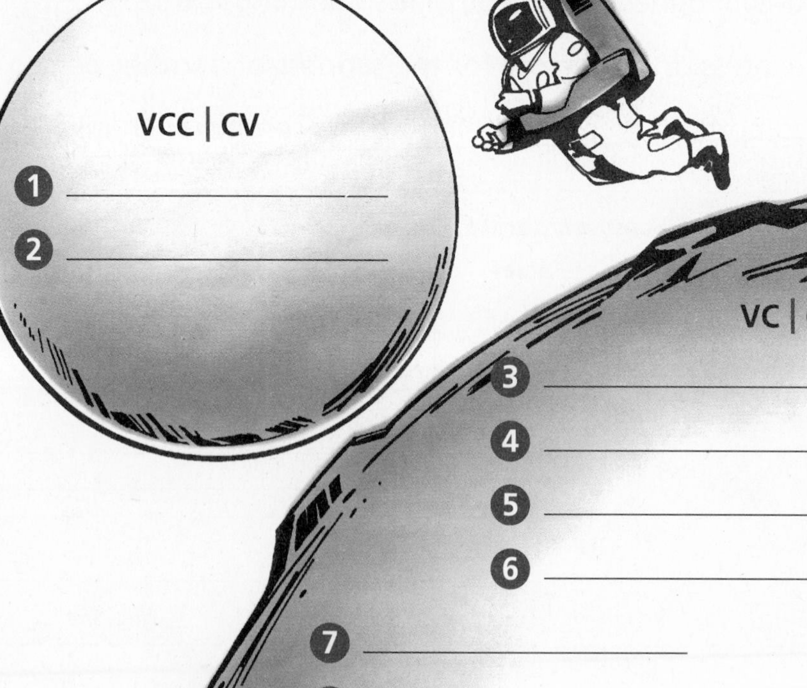

VCC | CV

1. ______________
2. ______________

VC | CCV

3. ______________
4. ______________
5. ______________
6. ______________
7. ______________
8. ______________
9. ______________
10. ______________

Name ....

Spelling Spree

Spelling Words	
1. explode	6. struggle
2. instant	7. express
3. control	8. empty
4. explore	9. farther
5. address	10. sandwich

Proofreading **Find and circle five misspelled Spelling Words on this monument. Then write each word correctly.**

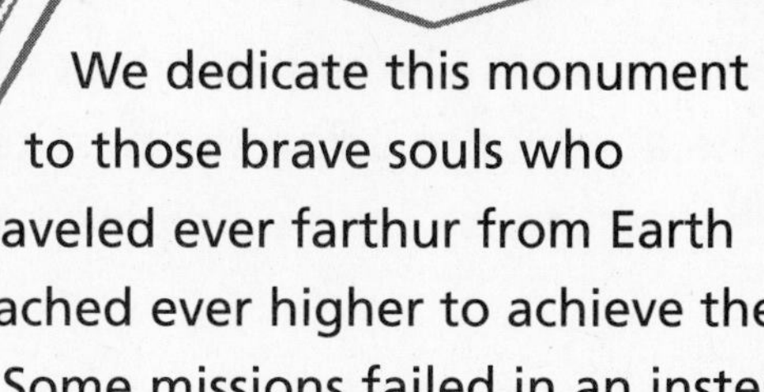

We dedicate this monument to those brave souls who traveled ever farthur from Earth and reached ever higher to achieve the impossible. Some missions failed in an instent; others succeeded only after years of strugle. Our space pioneers risked their lives to explor and settle the empty reaches of space. To all those who showed commitment and courage, we espres our heartfelt thanks. Touch the stars!

1. ____________________
2. ____________________
3. ____________________
4. ____________________
5. ____________________

Analogies **Write a Spelling Word to complete each analogy.**

Example: Close is to distant as nearer is to farther.

6. Occupied is to full as unoccupied is to ____________________.
7. Book covers are to book as bread slices are to ____________________.
8. Fence is to limit as leash is to ____________________.
9. Volcano is to erupt as bomb is to ____________________.
10. Greeting is to welcome as speech is to ____________________.

No Limit to Dreams Imagine it is the year 2150. What has the space program achieved since the *Challenger* disaster? On a separate sheet of paper, write a brief news story about the latest space mission. Explain the mission's purpose. Use Spelling Words from the list.

Name

Space Camp

	Verb	Past Tense	Past with Helping Verb
Regular	look	looked	(has, have, had) looked
Irregular	see	saw	(has, have, had) seen
	go	went	(has, have, had) gone

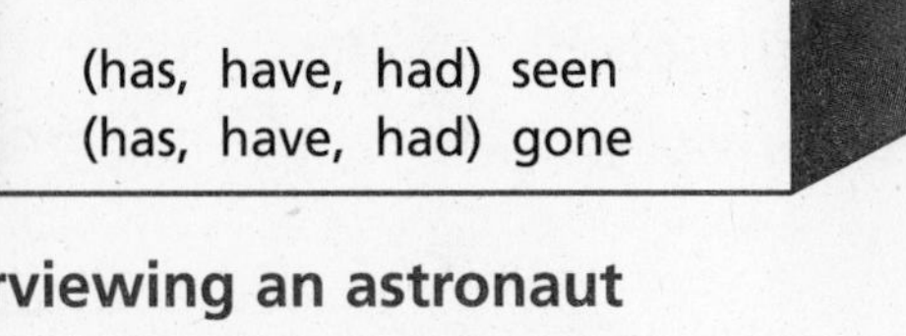

Irregular Verbs **You are a news reporter interviewing an astronaut in training. For each question, write a response using the past tense form of the highlighted verb or the past tense with a helping verb.**

Example:

Q. Did you **write** an application for this training camp?

A. I **wrote** an application and also went to an interview.

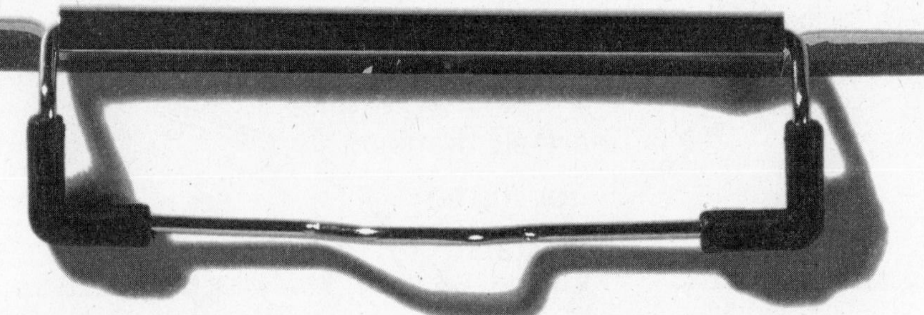

Q. Training camp began yesterday. When did you **come** to Houston?

A. ____________________

Q. Do the officers **make** you work hard?

A. They have ____________________

Q. Did you **go** on any training flights?

A. ____________________

Q. Do you **take** any tests during training camp?

A. Yes, I have ____________________

Q. When you were a kid, what did you **think** of space travel?

A. ____________________

Q. Will you **write** about your training experience?

A. Yes; in fact, I have ____________________

Name

Wish You Were Here!

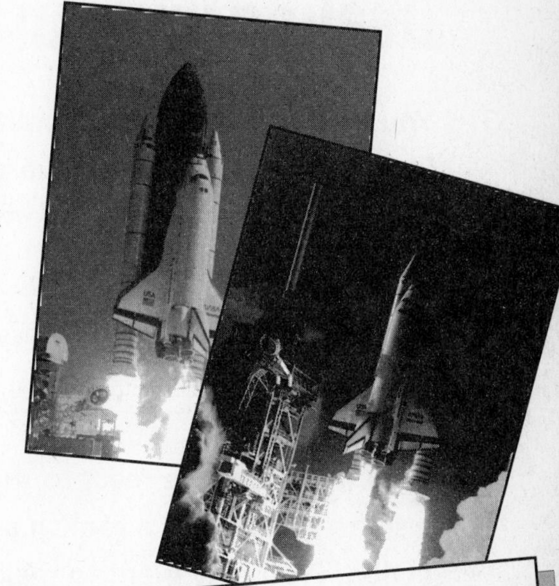

Irregular Verbs Your dream came true! You saw a shuttle launch in person. Write a post card describing the experience to a friend. Use five verbs from the box in the past tense form or the past with a helping verb.

bring	run	take	come	make
think	go	see	write	say

Place Stamp Here

To: ______________________

Name

Dealing with an Emergency

You know that people can get frightened and confused in an emergency. Planning and cool thinking are important for survival. Make a chart and a display that explain what can happen if people act correctly or incorrectly when disaster strikes.

First, pick a kind of emergency that you are familiar with.

The emergency: ______________________________

How might people react to the things that happen? Give examples of a smart action and a foolish action. Then give the likely results of each action. (You may want to make a chart like this on a separate sheet of paper.)

What Happens	How People React	The Results
	good:	
	bad:	
	good:	
	bad:	
	good:	
	bad:	

Turn your chart into a mobile. Write the "What Happens" events on tag-board cards and attach them to a coat hanger. On separate cards, write responses to the events and the results of the responses. Have one of your group present your work to the class.

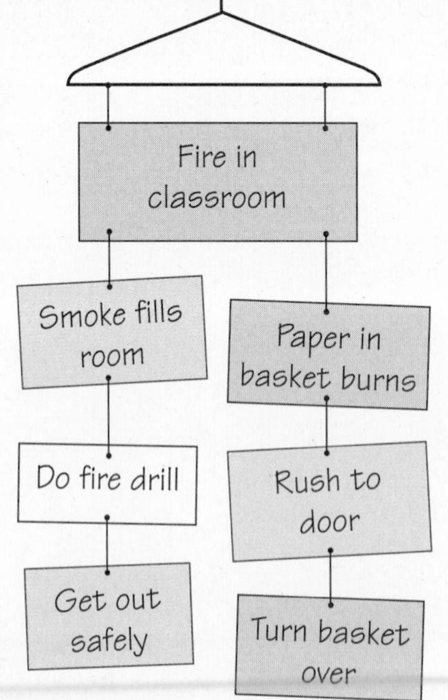

Revising Checklist

- ❑ We picked a common emergency and described what it might involve.
- ❑ We explained how people might try to cope with the emergency.
- ❑ We explained the likely results of their actions.

Cynthia
Name

From the Prairie to the Sea

Complete the chart below and on the next page with information from each selection. Then use that information to answer the questions.

	What problems or challenges did the characters face?	What did the characters do for fun or for pleasure?
Along the Santa Fe Trail	The problems the characters face is that there was a thunderstorm	The characters do for fun or for pleasure is that the childern play games and the people would gethered around the fire and the men would tell stories
Children of the Wild West	The problems the character face is that	The characters do for fun is play games and help their parents
Pecos Bill		

For the characters you have read about, do you think the hardships outweighed the benefits of living in the West in the 1800s? Explain your answer.

Name: cynthia Gutierrez

From the Prairie to the Sea

Complete the chart with information from each selection. Then use that information to answer the questions.

	How did the characters change throughout the story?	What were the attitudes of the characters toward the West?
Along the Santa Fe Trail	The characters change throughout the story is that they felt in the beginning is	The attitudes of the character is
Children of the Wild West	The charaters change throughout the story is that they	the attitudes of the charaters is they had courage and nevergive.
Pecos Bill		

Based on the characters you have read about, how important was the land and the surroundings in the West to the people who lived there? Explain your answer.

Cynthia Gutienrez
Name

Trail Words

Write each word from the box on the correct line.

caravan	vast	desolate	mesa	epidemic	wallows	emigrant

Traveling the Santa Fe Trail

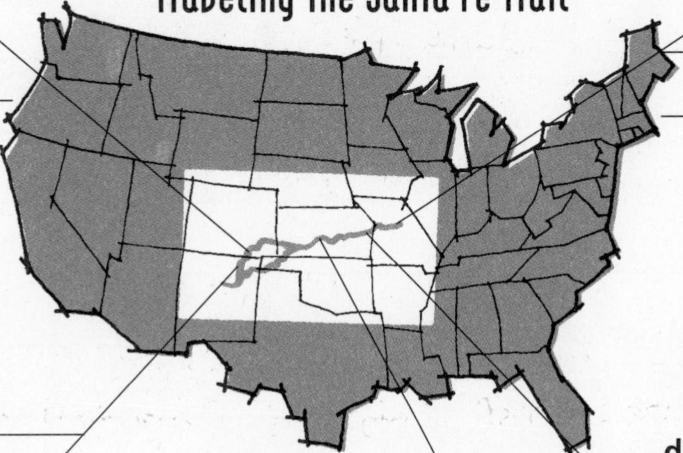

sights
vast

transportation
caravan

description
mesa

travelers
emigrant

dangers
epidemic

Now choose at least three words from the box. Use them to write a short paragraph describing a journey to the West in a covered wagon.

On my Journy there were new comers somepeople drank wallow water but I didn't. We were on top of a mesa and saw that we were almost there.

Name

Rating the Trail

Use information from *Along the Santa Fe Trail* to complete Marion's report of the trip.

CONESTOGAS, INC.
Customer Satisfaction Survey

Trail you took: santa fie

Leader of your caravan: A frenchman calle d pierre

Traveling companions: Mother and

Typical daytime schedule: do chores gather buffalo chips

Typical evening activities: play games like ball games leapfrog and dare base and told stories

Most exciting parts of trip: seening the sunset and watching the buffalos herd

Most frightening parts of trip: a thunderstorm came

Did you reach your destination? ☐ yes ☑ no

If not, why? because the mother lost her money, Jewelry and didint have enough money to pay the passage

Current residence: ____________

Overall rating of Conestogas, Inc.:

☐ excellent ☐ good ☐ fair ☐ poor

Name

Propaganda Out West

TAKE THE SANTA FE TRAIL TO CALIFORNIA

Take the Santa Fe Trail to California. It's safe and beautiful. On a recent journey, the weather was beautiful, and the travelers arrived in Santa Fe in record time.

Everyone is getting rich in California! You can too! Mr. Edward Walsh, a mining expert, says,

"The gold in California is so plentiful that you can find gold nuggets in no time!"

Find an example of each type of propaganda on the posters. Write the example after each propaganda technique.

1. Omission of facts: 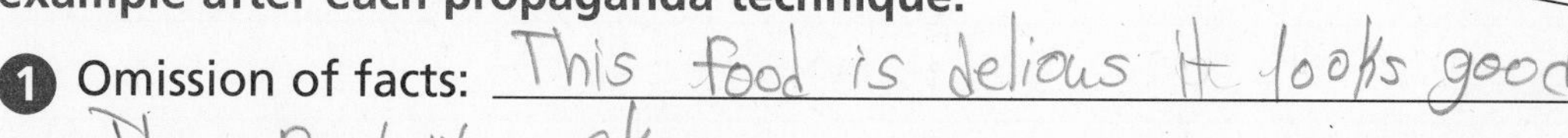 This food is delious It looks good This food its okay
2. Overgeneralization: 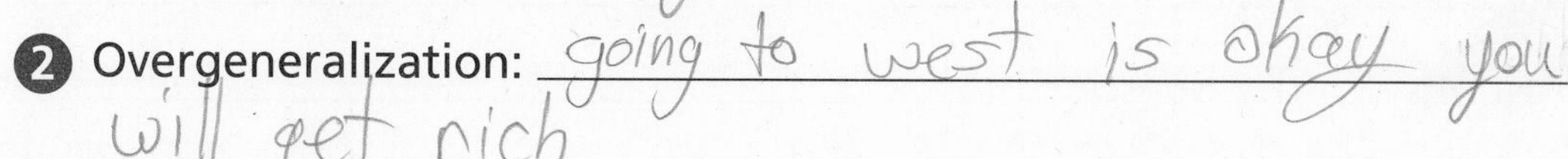 going to west is okay you will get rich
3. Bandwagon:
4. Testimonial: 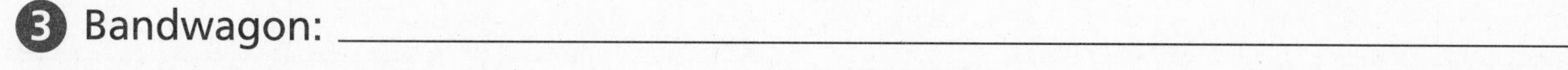 Brittney spears in the chermical of the pespi

Now write a propaganda statement of your own. Your goal is to make people stay in the East or the Midwest and not travel on the Santa Fe Trail. Write the statement and then tell which technique you used.

5.

Name ______________________

I'll Answer That

Circle an essay question that you would like to write about. Use the space below to plan and write your answer.

A. Explain the advantages and disadvantages of traveling in a wagon train. Use details from *Along the Santa Fe Trail* to support your answer.

B. Describe and discuss some of the things the narrator enjoyed about traveling on the Santa Fe Trail.

C. Compare and contrast the narrator and her brother, Will.

1. Are there any key words in the question? If so, what are they? ______________________

____

2. Plan your answer: ______________________

____

____

____

3. Write your response to the question: ______________________

____

____

____

____

____

____

____

____

____

Name ....

Spectacular Westward Transportation!

Some words in the covered wagon contain the word root *port*, which means "carry." Others contain the word root *spec*, which means "look." Write the words that match each clue. Then write each numbered letter in the space with the matching number to find a message.

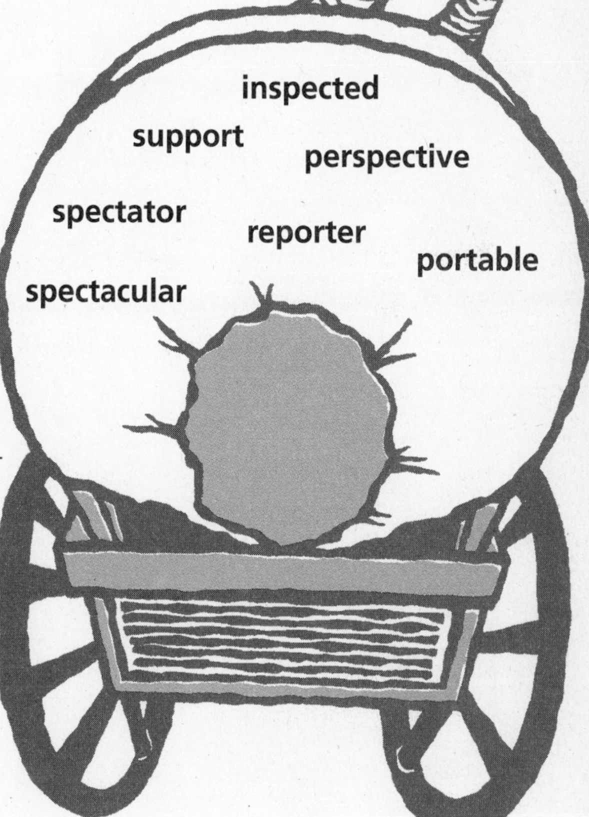

1. looked at closely for problems or mistakes

   __ __ __ __ __ __ __ __ __ (5, 11, 8)

2. describes something you can carry

   __ __ __ __ __ __ __ __ (6)

3. describes something fantastic to look at

   __ __ __ __ __ __ __ __ __ __ __ (10, 7)

4. someone paid to carry back information about an event

   __ __ __ __ __ __ __ __ (4)

5. a point of view or way of looking at something

   __ __ __ __ __ __ __ __ __ __ __ (15, 3, 9)

6. someone who looks on at an event

   __ __ __ __ __ __ __ __ __ (2, 14)

7. to carry the weight of something

   __ __ __ __ __ __ __ (1, 13, 12)

Those who traveled the Santa Fe Trail needed

a __ __ __ __ __ __ of __ __ __ __ __ __ __ __ __!

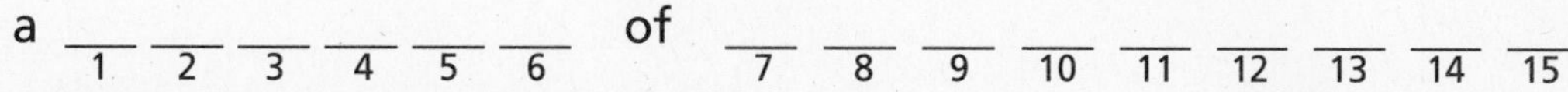

Name

Travel the Santa Fe Trail!

You are a traveler on the Santa Fe Trail. Pause at the landmarks listed below to write one-sentence journal entries about your experiences. Use the vocabulary words in the box.

epidemic	corral	en route
caravan	turbulent	wallows
emigrant	mesa	desolate
plaza		

Name

Wagon Words

Adding *-ed* or *-ing* Each Spelling Word is made up of a base word and an ending. A **base word** is a word to which a beginning or an ending can be added. When a base word ends with **e**, drop the **e** when adding ***-ed*** or ***-ing***.

decide + ed = decided   stare + ing = staring

When a one-syllable word ends with one vowel and a single consonant, the consonant usually is doubled when ***-ed*** or ***-ing*** is added. When ***-ed*** or ***-ing*** is added to a two-syllable word, the consonant usually is not doubled.

plan + ing = planning   depart + ed = departed

Change the base words on the buckets into Spelling Words. Decide whether or not each base word has a spelling change when an *-ed* or *-ing* is added. Then write the Spelling Word formed from each base word on the correct wagon.

Spelling Words

1. **planning**
2. **decided**
3. **departed**
4. **staring**
5. **offered**
6. **slipping**
7. **numbered**
8. **scattered**
9. **healing**
10. **knitted**

My Study List
What other words do you need to study for spelling? Add them to My Study List for *Along the Santa Fe Trail* in the back of this book.

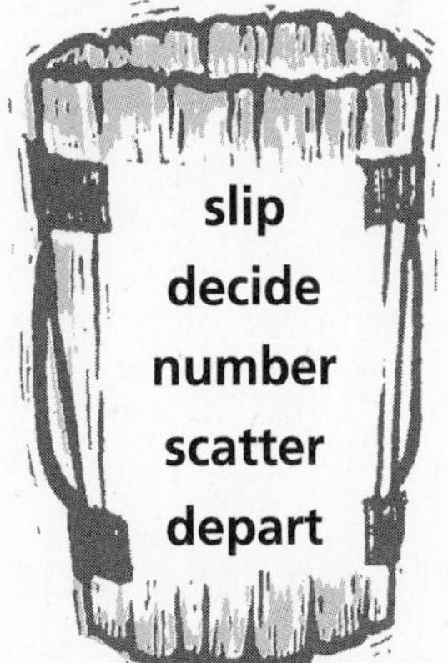

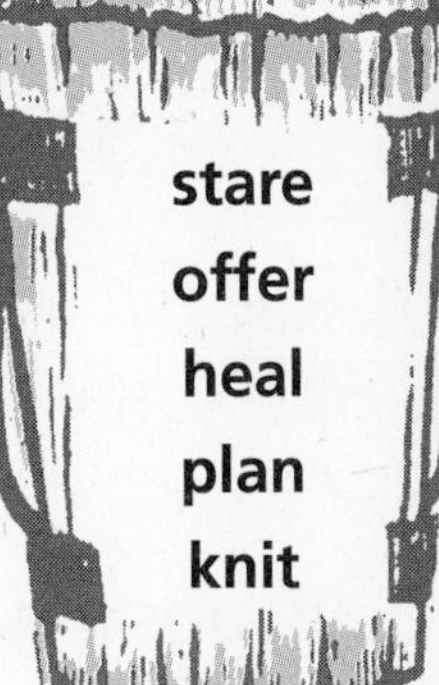

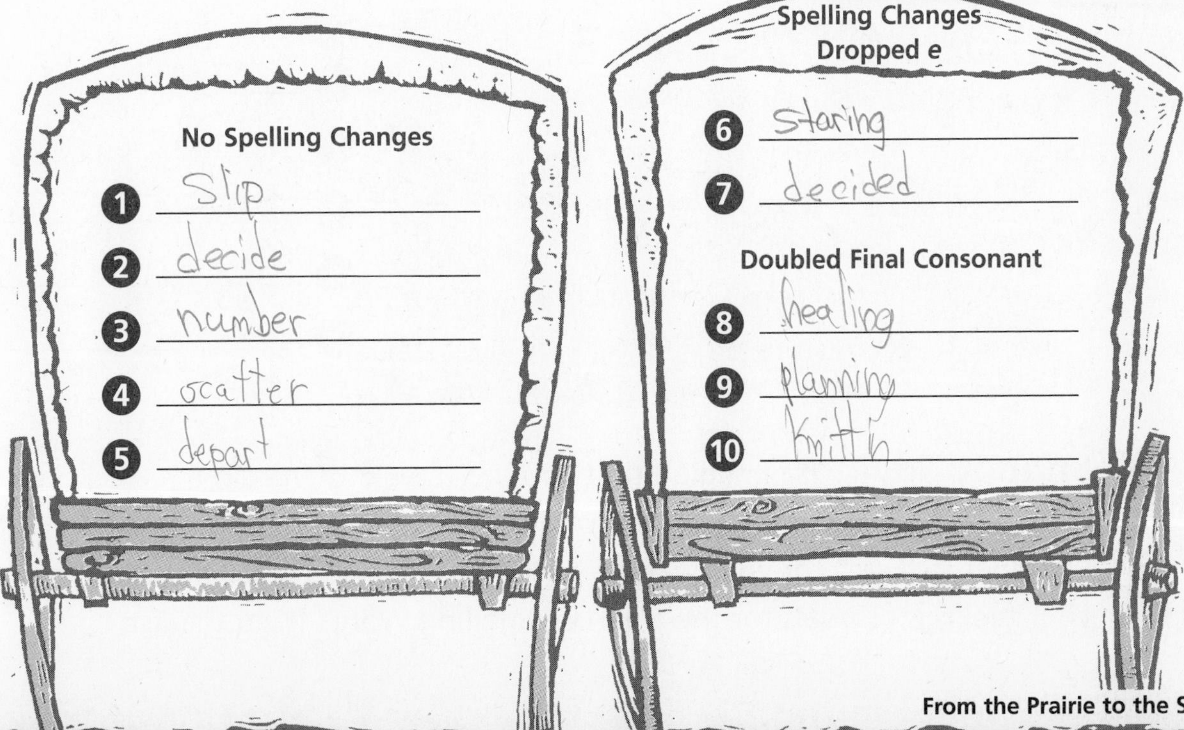

Name

Spelling Spree

Spelling Words

1. planning
2. decided
3. departed
4. staring
5. offered
6. slipping
7. numbered
8. scattered
9. healing
10. knitted

Trail Talk Write a Spelling Word to complete this conversation between two wagon train mules.

Hee: Mrs. W has knitted two hats and a sweater already!

Haw: Yes, but she's missing all the sights, such as the flowers scattered throughout the grass. They make me hungry.

Hee: Say, when do we stop for lunch? Soon, I hope.

Haw: I'm looking forward to planning out of this harness.

Hee: That herd of buffalo we just passed probably numbered over a thousand. And all of them kept staring at us.

Haw: They probably wondered why we're pulling this wagon but were too shy to ask! Heeee-hawwwwwwwwwwwwww!

Proofreading Find and circle five misspelled Spelling Words on this poster. Write each word correctly.

GOODS FOR SALE

To be ofered by Captain Dunn at a fair price, which will be desided the day of sale! He departid Kansas by wagon train in April and is planing to arrive here in five weeks. Goods will include buckles, needles, and other metal pieces (numbered at over 500) as well as cloth and medicine for heeling pains and fever.

1. offered
2. decided
3. departed
4. planning
5. healing

Snappy Sayings Imagine that you are traveling west in a covered wagon in 1852. On a separate sheet of paper, design three "bumper stickers" for your wagon. Each message should tell about your feelings or goals for the trip. Use Spelling Words from the list.

Name

The Way West

Punctuating Dialogue **Read this conversation. Notice how the dialogue is punctuated.**

"What would you take with you in a covered wagon?" Louis asked.

"I'd take all my favorite foods," Maria replied, "and plenty of water."

Sarah said, "You would need blankets to stay warm."

"I'd take a telephone," Chris added. "I could call for extra supplies."

"The emigrants did not have telephones!" Louis exclaimed.

Add the correct punctuation to Aja's story about a wagon train traveling west. Use proofreading marks to show her where to indent (¶), where to insert punctuation (‸), and which letters to capitalize (≡). Then, on a separate sheet of paper, copy the dialogue. Show the correct indents, punctuation, and capital letters.

Example: ¶ "how high the river is!" cried little Tad. ¶ "what shall we do?" asked Sarah.

we can't drive the wagons across said Father. we'll have to make a ferry. what does that mean asked Sarah. it means said Father that we'll pull our wagon back and forth across the river with long ropes. Once we unload our things, our wagon will be a ferry for others. will our wagon carry other wagons asked Tad. they'll be emptied, taken apart, and carried across in pieces said Father.

Name ______________________________

Western Word Search

Punctuating Dialogue **Find the words in the puzzle. They run across, down, and diagonally. Then use at least six of the words to write sentences that include direct quotations.**

A	O	T	P	R	A	I	R	I	E	L	D
D	W	R	B	U	F	T	A	M	J	R	R
J	C	A	L	I	F	O	R	N	I	A	B
O	A	V	G	J	W	U	F	A	L	M	U
U	L	E	O	O	V	E	L	F	I	U	F
R	E	L	X	U	N	T	S	E	F	L	F
W	S	X	S	R	O	S	N	T	A	E	A
A	D	V	E	N	T	U	R	E	M	S	L
G	O	N	N	E	W	M	E	X	I	C	O
T	R	N	E	Y	W	E	S	J	L	Y	T
P	R	A	I	R	O	J	X	L	Y	F	F

- California
- New Mexico
- prairie
- wagons
- buffalo
- mules
- family
- travel
- West
- adventure
- journey
- trail

1. ______________________________

2. ______________________________

3. ______________________________

4. ______________________________

5. ______________________________

6. ______________________________

Name

Did I Tell You About the Time I . . . ?

Do these suggestions give you any topic ideas?

a funny misunderstanding

a big decision

caught in a storm

a scary experience

when I met someone important

getting a pet

when I lost something

learning something new

my moment of triumph

My Personal Narrative Topics **Write five experiences you have had that would make interesting stories.**

1 __________

2 __________

3 __________

4 __________

5 __________

Ask yourself these questions about each idea you wrote.

Can I remember details about what happened?

Would this interest my audience?

Would I enjoy writing about this?

Should I focus on only one part of this experience?

Now circle the topic you want to write about.

Name

Remembering the Details

Make a photo album for your narrative. Write your topic at the top of the page. Then draw "photos" of the important events in the order that they happened. List as many details as you can about what you saw, heard, smelled, touched, tasted, and how you felt.

Name

Making It Better

Reread and revise your story, using the Revising Checklist. Then use the Questions for a Writing Conference to help you discuss your story with a classmate.

Revising Checklist

- ☐ Does the beginning lead into the story in an interesting way?
- ☐ Does this story describe the experience the way I remember it? Where should I add more details or make them more vivid?
- ☐ Where can I use dialogue to bring this experience to life?
- ☐ Did I tell how I felt?

Questions for a Writing Conference

- What is good about this story?
- Does the beginning open the story in an interesting way?
- Is the order of the events clear?
- Were any parts confusing?
- Where are more details or dialogue needed to make the experience clearer?

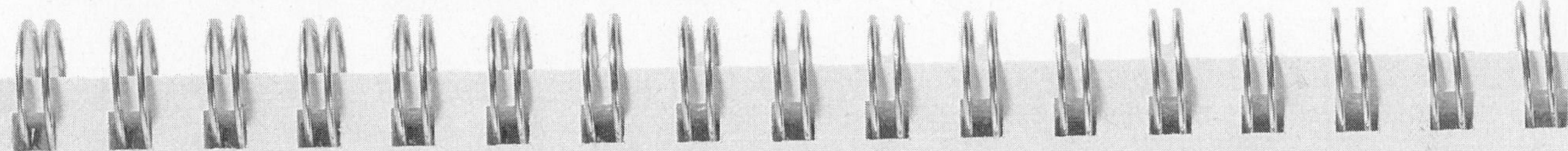

Write notes to help you remember ideas discussed in your writing conference.

My Notes

Name ______________________________

A Letter from the Wild West

Use the words in the box to complete the letter.

culture	civilization
customs	traditional
primitive	myths
sacred	

Dear Anne,

When I first left Chicago to move to Oregon, I thought I would never see ______________________ again, but now I am getting used to it. We have seen some Sioux. They seemed very ______________________ at first. Now, however, I see that their ______________________ isn't better or worse than ours, it's just different. They have their own ______________________ to explain the world around them. They believe that buffalo are ______________________ and should only be killed if necessary.

In spite of the differences, I have also seen some Sioux ______________________ that are similar to ours. Sioux children play some of the same games we do, and as they grow up, boys and girls learn ______________________ tasks that their parents have learned. Boys learn to hunt and ride, and girls help with cooking or caring for other children. The more I learn about the Sioux people, the more I think we are more alike than different.

Your friend,
Marie

How might a Sioux child have described the settlers who moved onto Sioux land during the days of the Wild West? Use three of the words from the box to write a description on a separate sheet of paper.

Name

Growing Up in the West

Complete the chart to show how relations between American Indians and pioneers changed as more settlers moved to the West. List three samples in each section. An example is provided for you.

First Encounters	Many Settlers Arrive in the West	Late 1800s—Many Settlers in the West
most American Indians friendly	at first, small skirmishes	many American Indians forced to live on reservations

List three things a Sioux boy did.

Which activity is most like something you do, and how?

Name

Understanding Judgments

Judgments are made based on knowledge and beliefs. Answer the questions about the judgment used in the choices below.

1 The young Sioux Ohiyesa shot a tiny arrow at a huge moose, even though he knew he would not be able to kill it.	
What judgment did he make?	Why?

2 The American Indians made many treaties with the European settlers. Most of these agreements were not honored by the newcomers.	
What judgment do you think the Indians made when making these treaties?	Why?

3 A Sioux chief referred to "a great equality" in men's and women's work.	
What judgment did the chief make about the value of work?	Why?

4 The European settlers often came into conflict with the Indians.	
What judgment did the settlers make?	Why?

5 You are an American Indian in 1850. A white settler appears at your camp.	
What do you think you would do?	Why?

Name

Step by Step

Use this chart to help plan your instructions. List each step, and give details that your audience would need to know to do each step.

MATERIALS

STEPS	DETAILS
STEP 1	
STEP 2	
STEP 3	
STEP 4	
STEP 5	

Name ....

People Prefer Prefixes

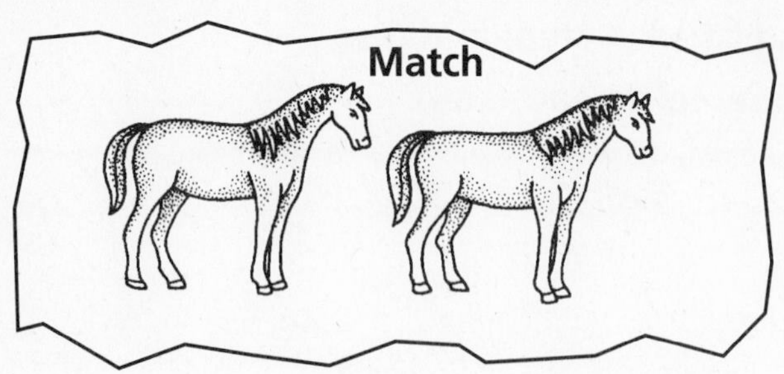

Prefixes make a difference. In the letter spaces, write the word from the blanket that best completes each sentence. Then write the letters that appear in a triangle, circle, or box into their matching shapes. Unscramble the letters in the shapes to spell the names of three Native American groups.

disprove
disbelieve
exhale
exception
misplaced
misread
excuse
discourteous
mischief
misuse
displease

1. His little sister is always getting into ___ ___ ___ ___ △ ___ △ ___ .
2. People soon learn to ___ ___ ___ ○ ___ ○ ___ ___ ___ ___ a liar.
3. I like all fruit with the ___ □ ___ ___ ___ ___ □ □ ___ of grapefruit.
4. We looked all over for the ___ ___ ___ △ ___ △ △ ___ ___ key.
5. It is ___ ___ ___ ___ ___ ○ ___ ___ ○ ___ ___ ___ to interrupt when someone is speaking.
6. Write your name clearly so that I won't ___ ___ ___ ___ ___ △ ___ it.
7. A fact is something you can't ___ ___ ___ ○ ___ ○ ___ ___ .
8. She had a good ___ ___ ___ □ □ ___ for being late.

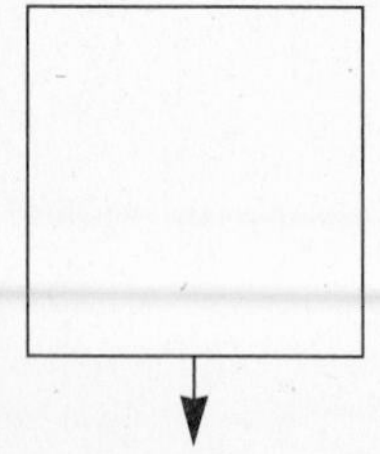

____

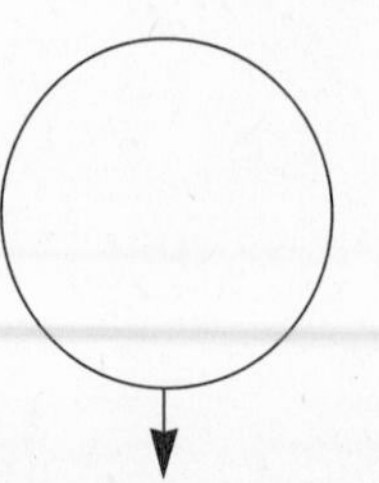

____

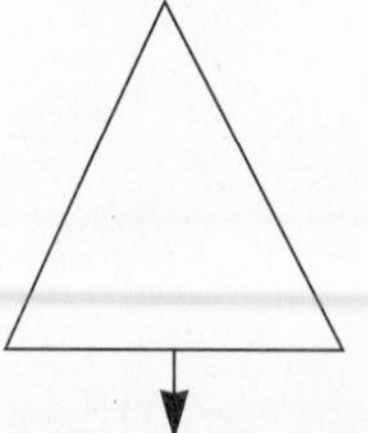

____

Name

Draw on Your Knowledge

Above each vocabulary word, draw the picture that appears beside the definition of that word.

1. 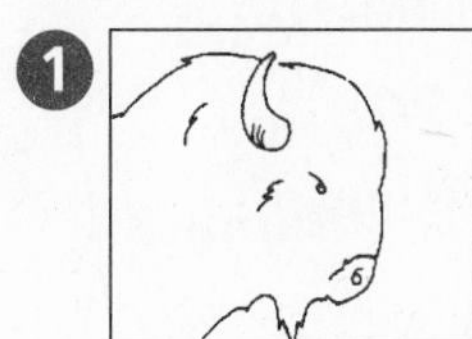 stories that explain the beliefs of a people

2. 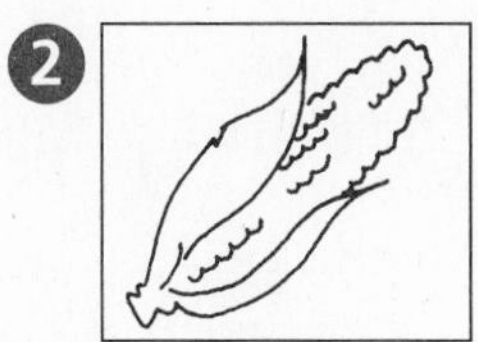 passed down from parents to children

3. 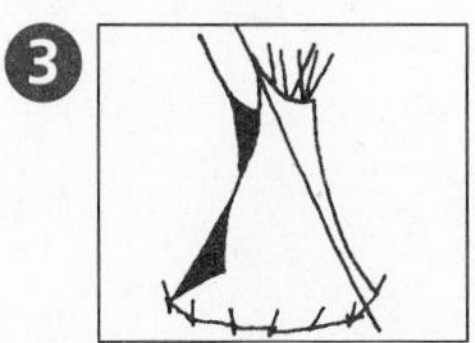 a people's beliefs, ways of living, products, and laws; education, refinement

4.  the everyday practices of a group of people

5. 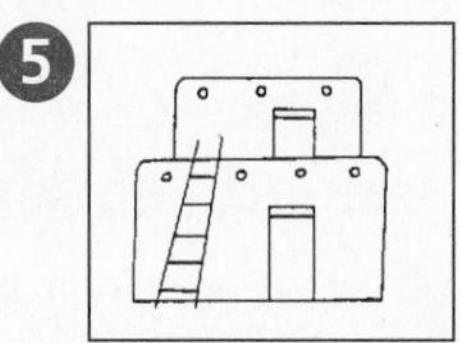 a kind of culture and society developed by a group of people

6. 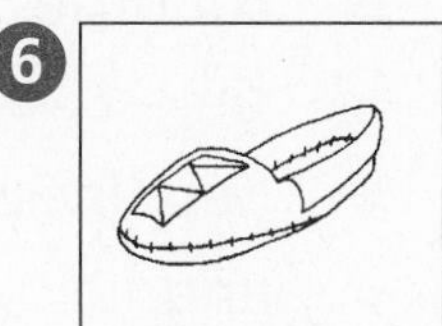 holy, deserving of great respect

7. 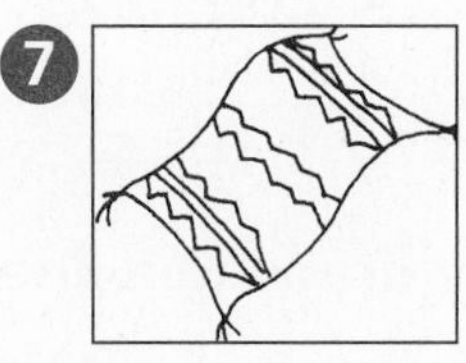 in an early stage of development

primitive

civilization

sacred

traditional

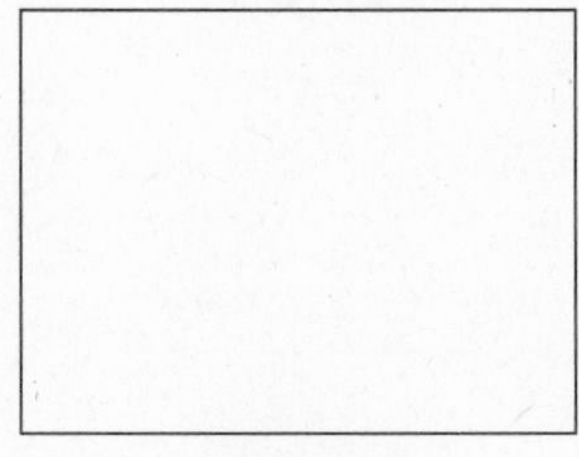

culture

customs

myths

On a separate sheet of paper, write three sentences that use two vocabulary words each.

Name

Tipi Match

Changing Final *y* to *i* Each Spelling Word is made up of an ending or a suffix added to a base word. Each base word ends with a consonant and *y*. If a word ends with a consonant and *y*, change the *y* to *i* when adding ***-es***, ***-ed***, ***-er***, ***-est***, or ***-ness***.

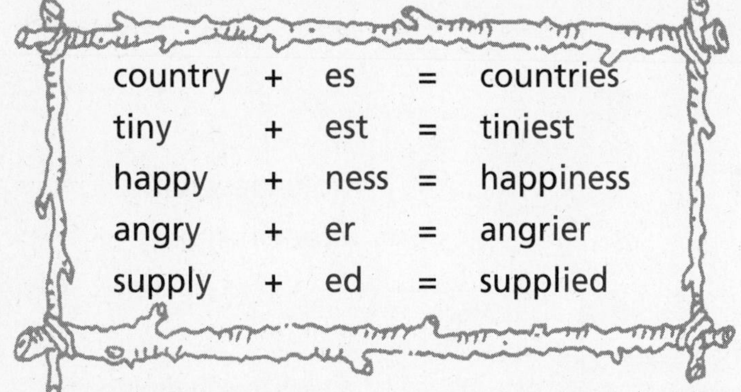

country	+	es	=	countries
tiny	+	est	=	tiniest
happy	+	ness	=	happiness
angry	+	er	=	angrier
supply	+	ed	=	supplied

Spelling Words

1. **countries**
2. **supplied**
3. **happiness**
4. **hurried**
5. **angrier**
6. **enemies**
7. **tiniest**
8. **nastiest**
9. **grassier**
10. **friendliness**

My Study List
What other words do you need to study for spelling? Add them to My Study List for *Children of the Wild West* in the back of this book.

Form Spelling Words by drawing a line from the base word to the correct ending. Then cross out the letter in the base word that is replaced by *i* when the ending is added. Write each Spelling Word that you have formed.

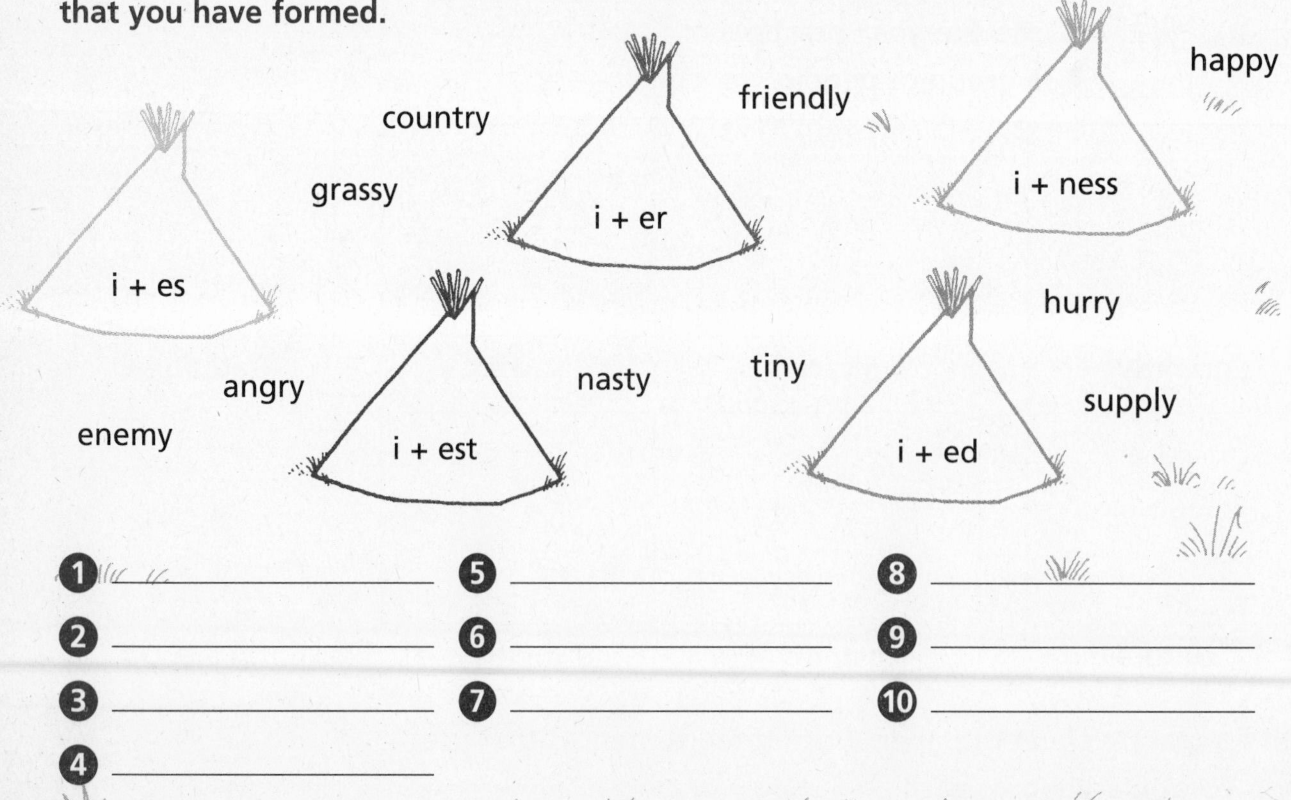

1. ______________________
2. ______________________
3. ______________________
4. ______________________
5. ______________________
6. ______________________
7. ______________________
8. ______________________
9. ______________________
10. ______________________

Name ______________________________

Spelling Spree

Spelling Words

1. countries
2. supplied
3. happiness
4. hurried
5. angrier
6. enemies
7. tiniest
8. nastiest
9. grassier
10. friendliness

Word Weave Use the clues to write the Spelling Words that complete this puzzle.

1 __ __ __ __ __ __ __ __ __ 1. joy

2 __ __ __ __ __ __ __ __ 2. opposite of kindest

3 __ __ __ __ __ __ __ 3. smallest

4 __ __ __ __ __ __ __ 4. rushed

5 __ __ __ __ __ __ __ 5. opposite of friends

Proofreading Find and circle five misspelled Spelling Words in this song verse. Then write each word correctly.

Once we wandered grasier prairies,
Life supplyed by buffalo.
Then came changes, agrier faces —
Say good-bye to all we know.
Days of plenty, evening frendliness,
Lights from campfires shone on happiness.
Different sights now, strange new countrees,
Puzzled by life's changing show,
Say good-bye to all we know,
Say farewell to all we know.

 ______________

7 ______________

 ______________

 ______________

A Day in the Life Imagine you are a Kiowa, Comanche, or Navajo child in the 1800s. On a separate sheet of paper, write a diary entry that tells what your day would be like. What chores did you do? How did you spend your spare time? Use Spelling Words from the list.

Name ....

Game Day

Subject and Object Pronouns

Finish your journal entry about yesterday's game day by writing the correct pronouns. Above each one write S for subject pronoun or O for object pronoun. Then write a final sentence, using a subject pronoun or an object pronoun.

Subject Pronouns	
I	we
you	you
she, he, it	they

Object Pronouns	
me	us
you	you
her, him, it	them

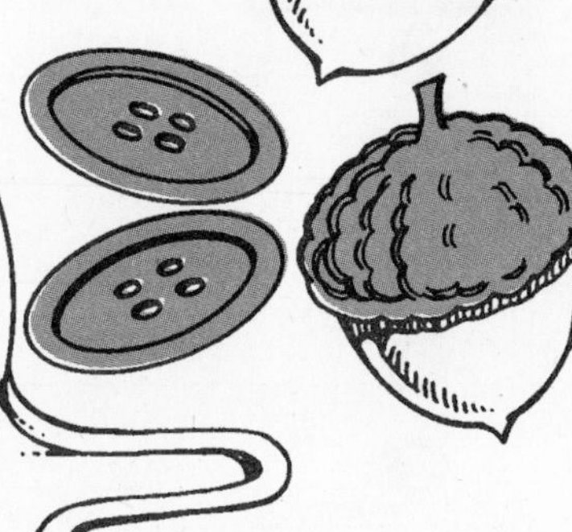

Example: ___S We___ had a wonderful time yesterday! (We, Us)

_______ (I, me) went with several friends to game day in the village. First, _______ (we, us) watched the breath-holding contest with Yancy and Nita. _______ (He, Him) offered the prize to _______ (she, her). Then _______ (they, them) won the three-legged race as we cheered _______ (they, them) on. Later a girl showed yo-yo tricks to my brother and _______ (I, me). Then _______ (she, her) gave a yo-yo to _______ (we, us). Next, Yancy and _______ (he, him) joined a game of blindman's bluff. At the end of the day, Yancy and _______ (I, me) rode horses. Horseback riding was the most fun for _______ (he, him).

____

____

Name

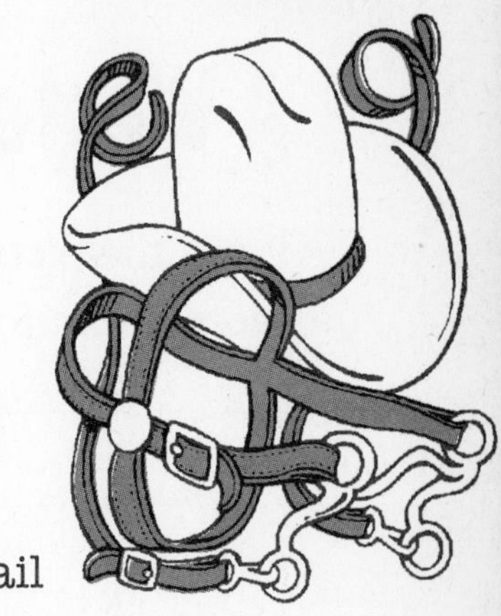

Heading West

Subject and Object Pronouns **Help Sam correct his letter. If a sentence contains an unnecessary double subject (a noun subject followed by a subject pronoun), use the delete sign ( ) to cross out one. Write subject or object pronouns above the underlined words.**

Example: This letter it is for my friend Kenji, and I want to mail
it **him**
this letter to Kenji soon.

Dear Kenji,

My mom she is planning a trip to the Great Plains. My family and I are looking forward to the trip. Because the Great Plains are vast and level, the Great Plains are great for riding horses. By the time a Native American boy was five or six, a boy might have a horse. Many Native Americans rode bareback. I want to ride like the Native Americans. My dad he said I might try riding bareback at my grandparents' house. My grandparents have two horses for my family and me. Riding bareback is hard, but I'm not scared to try riding bareback. María she says I'll probably fall off the horse. Sam'll show María that María is wrong! ______________________

____.

Sincerely,
Sam

Write a closing line for the letter. Use a subject pronoun and an object pronoun.

Name

A Western Scene

Label the picture, using the correct words from the box.

homestead	stagecoaches	cowpoke
hootenanny	coyotes	

Write a paragraph describing the picture.
Use all five vocabulary words.

Name

Put It Together

After reading *Pecos Bill*, complete the sentence on each puzzle piece. Then number the pieces 1 through 10, based on the order of the events in the story. Cut the pieces out and put them together, following the numbers. When you are finished, your puzzle will look like Pecos Bill's home state!

Bill rides a ____________ and makes it rain. ______

Bill wrestles a ____________ and turns it into a rope. ______

____________ invents the lasso. ______

Bill meets ____________ and wants to impress her. ______

Bill is raised by ____________. ______

Bill's group drives a herd of cattle to ____________. ______

Bill's parents accidentally leave him at the ____________. ______

Bill meets Chuckwagon Chuck and learns that he is ____________. ______

As they move the cattle, Bill's group suffers from the ____________. ______

The Bandana Bandits try to ____________ Bill and Chuck. ______

Name ....

How Great-Grandmother Dusted Texas

Read the tale. Use it to write simple directions for how to dust Texas. You can number the steps or use order words to show the sequence. Hint: There are seven steps.

Great-grandmother told me that when she was just a tiny cowgirl, she dusted the whole state of Texas.

One dry Texas spring, a powerful dust storm left knee-deep dust over all of Texas. Great-grandmother wanted to get rid of the dust, but how? She decided to hold a hootenanny.

Great-grandmother then built a huge dance floor. The singers and fiddlers began singing and playing, and the dancers began to turn and twirl. It was such fun that soon all of Texas joined in. All that singing and twirling set off a whirlwind. Great-grandmother caught the whirlwind in her sunbonnet and dragged it to the mouth of the Rio Grande River. She held the tip of the whirlwind down where the Rio Grande emptied into the Gulf of Mexico until every speck of dust in Texas landed there. The river and the gulf were so wet that the dust soaked up the water and settled down to form the muddy delta of the Rio Grande, which is still there today.

How to Dust Texas

____

____

____

____

____

____

____

____

Name ______________________

Cactus Caper

Read about Pecos Bill and the fast-talkin', low-down, cactus-rustlin' Texas Ted. Rewrite the paragraph into a scene for a play. Include stage directions in parentheses. Give your other characters appropriate cowboy names!

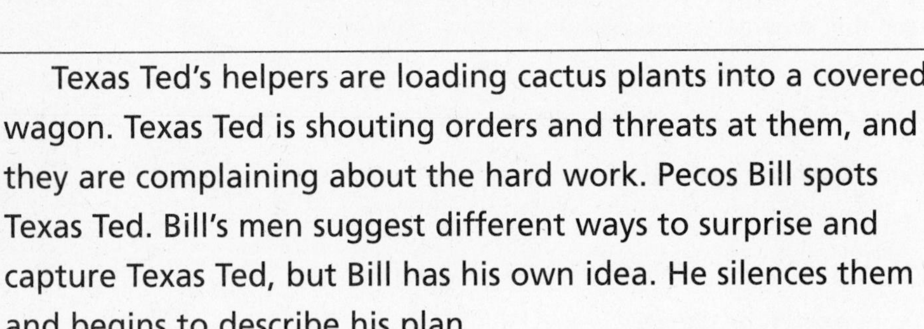

Texas Ted's helpers are loading cactus plants into a covered wagon. Texas Ted is shouting orders and threats at them, and they are complaining about the hard work. Pecos Bill spots Texas Ted. Bill's men suggest different ways to surprise and capture Texas Ted, but Bill has his own idea. He silences them and begins to describe his plan.

Copyright © Houghton Mifflin Company. All rights reserved.

Name

On Stage

Tale of a Contraction

The cow's mooing loudly.

Your school is going to stage *Pecos Bill*. You've taken notes at a meeting about props and special effects. Rewrite your notes without using a contraction or a possessive. Then organize your notes by writing **P** for possessive or **C** for contraction in each box.

Props Manager

Can-Do Special Effects Team

1. Bill's fishing pole is broken. ☐
2. We've found a drum for the thunder. ☐
3. Chuck's spurs jangle. ☐
4. You'll make it rain, right? ☐
5. We don't need to see the tornado; let's hear it! ☐
6. The bandits' bandanas are dirty. ☐
7. The cactus's suitcase is full. ☐
8. Sue's "Miss Kansas" sash is pretty. ☐
9. We can't use live coyotes; create sound effects. ☐

Name

Create a Cowboy Tale

In small groups, create a story using the numbered words. Begin by telling the group the definition of the word *homestead.* Then write the first sentence of a tall tale using *homestead*, and read it to the group. Then provide a synonym or a definition for *round up* and write a sentence using that phrase that continues the tale. Continue until all the numbered words have been defined and used in the story. Have a volunteer read the story to the class.

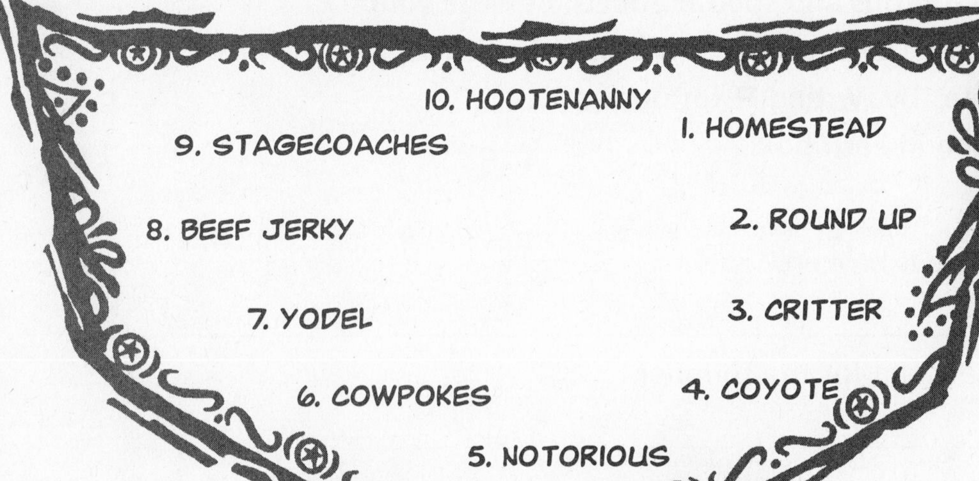

Name

Loopy Lasso Action

Adding -*ion* Each pair of Spelling Words is made up of a verb and a noun. The verb in each pair is the base word. The noun is formed by adding the suffix ***-ion*** to the verb. When a verb ends with **e**, drop the **e** before adding ***-ion***.

Verb:	act	create
Noun:	action	creation

Spelling Words

1. act
2. action
3. create
4. creation
5. direct
6. direction
7. possess
8. possession
9. narrate
10. narration

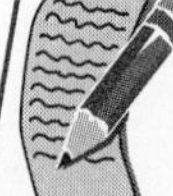

My Study List
What other words do you need to study for spelling? Add them to My Study List for *Pecos Bill* in the back of this book.

Write the verb form of a Spelling Word that fits each clue. Then add the suffix *-ion* and write the noun form of the Spelling Word.

CLUES

1–2 to perform; to behave
3–4 to instruct or order
5–6 to own; to have as a quality
7–8 to produce; to make
9–10 to tell; to read aloud

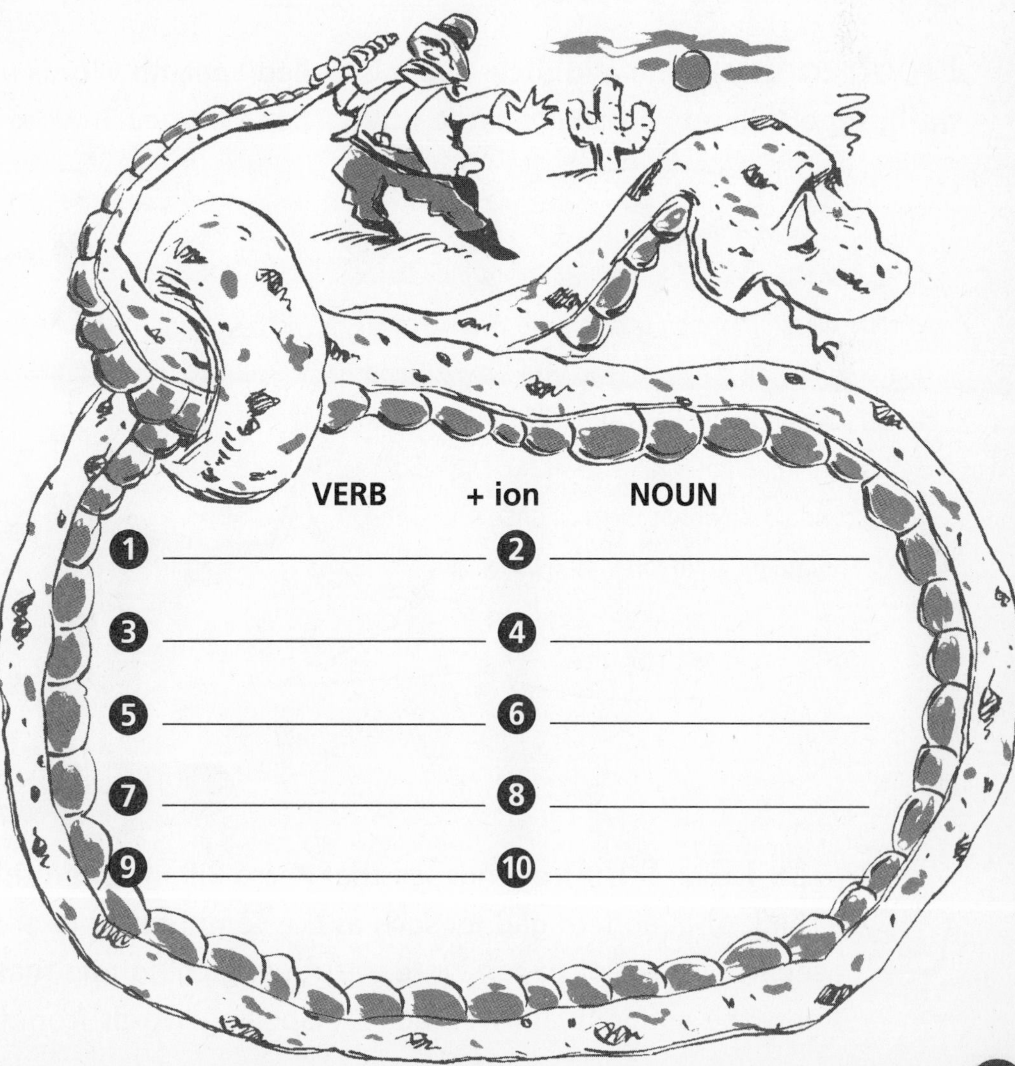

VERB	+ ion	NOUN
1 ______		2 ______
3 ______		4 ______
5 ______		6 ______
7 ______		8 ______
9 ______		10 ______

Name

Spelling Spree

Spelling Words

1. act
2. action
3. create
4. creation
5. direct
6. direction
7. possess
8. possession
9. narrate
10. narration

Tongue Twisters

Write a Spelling Word to complete Pecos Bill's favorite tongue twisters.

1. Does Atoka Al ________________ like an Arapaho or an Apache?
2. Nevada Ned never knew that ________________ was needed for the Natchez News.
3. Please pack each ________________ in your poncho, Panhandle Pete.
4. Why does Navajo Nell ________________ nearly every new announcement?
5. This contraption is a cute ________________ to catch coyotes!

Proofreading

Find and circle five misspelled Spelling Words in this traffic report about Pecos Bill's cattle drive. Then write each word correctly.

We're seeing plenty of acton on the trails today as longhorns move in the direcion of the stockyards. The cattle are clogging all major routes into town. Since cattle posess no understanding of traffic laws, they'll creat huge jams downtown for the next two hours. Should any cattle stroll onto your land, please stay calm but act quickly. Just derect the nearest cowpoke to the stray cow.

6. ________________

7. ________________
8. ________________
9. ________________

10. ________________

It's Like This Legends say that Pecos Bill invented the cattle drive. Think of a modern gadget such as the computer or laser scanner. On a separate sheet of paper, write a truth-stretching tale that explains how the gadget was invented. Use Spelling Words from the list.

Name ______________________________

Whose Cow?

Possessive Pronouns

The cattle drive is over, and the cows have been auctioned off. Help the auctioneer find each buyer's cow. Complete each sentence with a different possessive pronoun. Write your own sentences for the pictures.

Examples: Your cow has very short horns. The cow with very short horns is yours.

1. ______________ cow has very long horns.
2. ______________ cow is drinking water.
3. ______________ cow is eating hay.
4. ____
   ____
5. ____
   ____
6. The cow with long horns is ______________
7. The cow drinking water is ______________
8. ____
   ____
9. ____
   ____
10. ____
    ____

Name

Sing Along with Sluefoot Sue

Possessive Pronouns and Contractions with Pronouns

Help Sue finish her song. Write the correct contraction over each pair of underlined words and write the correct possessive pronoun in the blank.

Possessive Pronouns	Contractions
its	it's (it is, it has)
your	you're (you are)
his	he's (he is, he has)
their	they're (they are)
theirs	there's (there is)

I will sing you __________ (my, mine) song; it is about Pecos Bill.

Out here in __________ (our, ours) state we are amazed by him still.

He tamed a tornado with __________ (his, he's) rope made of snake
And gave cows to Kansas, where they are now eating steak.

(Refrain)

He has been raised by coyotes!

You have just got to know he is
The wiliest, smiliest, consarndest, gosh-darndest coyote kid in the West!

He invented the lasso, the roundup as well.

He has invented the yodel—taught the cowpokes __________
(they're, their) yell.

And if you had seen a cowpoke before Bill came through,

You would be right in believing he had improved on them, too.

(Refrain)

Name

Planning a TV Commercial

Imagine that Captain Aubry of *Along the Santa Fe Trail* could advertise his wagon train on television. Plan a TV commercial for him. Use the chart to help you plan.

Reread the beginning of *Along the Santa Fe Trail.* What hardships did pioneers face?	
What help could a leader such as Captain Aubry offer?	
What propaganda techniques could you use to persuade people to travel with Captain Aubry?	

Plan the pictures and script.

Pictures			
Script			

On another sheet of paper, make a final copy of your plan. Use it to present your plan to your group or class. Check the list to see that your work is complete.

Revising Checklist

- ❑ My work reflects the hardships described in *Along the Santa Fe Trail.*
- ❑ I've made good judgments about how Captain Aubry can help travelers.
- ❑ I can explain at least two propaganda techniques I have used.

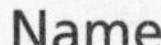

Name

Do You *Believe* This??

What "unbelievable" event happens in each selection? Fill out each column in the chart as you complete the selections in the theme.

	La Bamba	Willie Bea and the Time the Martians Landed
What is the genre of the selection?		
What surprising or unexpected event does the selection tell about?		
What causes this event to happen?		
How do people react to this event?		

What have you learned in this theme about how realistic and fantastic events can combine in what you read? ______________________________

____

____

Name

Do You *Believe* This??

What "unbelievable" event happens in each selection? Fill out each column in the chart as you complete the selections in the theme.

	McBroom Tells the Truth	Trapped in Tar
What is the genre of the selection?		
What surprising or unexpected event does the selection tell about?		
What causes this event to happen?		
How do people react to this event?		

Tell about a time in your own life when reality seemed hard to believe. ______

______

______

Name

A Golden Oldie

Use the vocabulary words to complete the sentences. Then answer the questions.

Hey, Dad, I just got this ______________________.

It's by a ______________________ called Willy and Wally. I think it's their first record, their ______________________, so it might be valuable.

Willy and Wally? I remember them! We used to ______________________ the words to their music! They had so much ______________________. They were in the ______________________ for years!

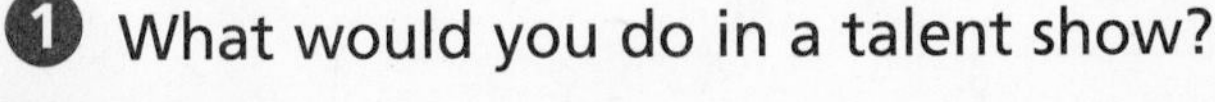

1. What would you do in a talent show? ______________________
2. How would you feel if you were making your debut as a performer? ______________________
3. What would you do to pantomime a song? ______________________
4. How would it feel to be in the limelight? ______________________

Name ________________________

Talent Scout's Report

Complete the talent scout's report about the main character and the events in "La Bamba."

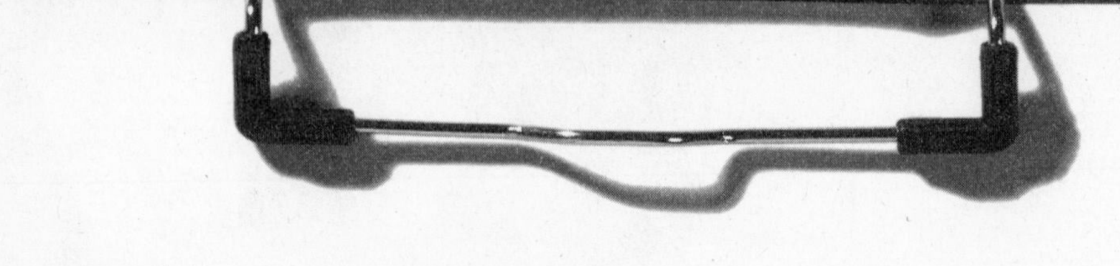

1. Performer's first name and talent: ________________________

2. Unusual events during the performance: ________________________

3. Audience reaction during the performance: ________________________

4. Performer's previous experience in front of an audience: ________________________

5. Performer's prospects for a future in show business: ________________________

Name

Sum It Up

Write a summary of "La Bamba" for a book jacket. Think about the story elements on the index card. Then write your summary using complete sentences.

Story Structure
Main character
Setting
Problem
Three events
Resolution

The story is about ______

Name

Who's on First?

These photographs were taken during a school talent show. Write a caption for each. Include at least one pronoun in each caption.

1

2

3

4

5

Name

The Spotlight's on You!

All the words in the spotlights begin with the prefix *con-* or one of its forms (*col-, com-*). Find the word that matches each clue and write it in the letter spaces. Then read the tinted letters down to find out what every performer wants.

The prefix *con-* (or *com-* or *col-*) means "together" or "with."

collection
contract
compound

compatible
compete
collapse
compare
companion

1. a written agreement ___ ___ ___ ___ ___ ___ ___ ___
2. able to live together in harmony ___ ___ ___ ___ ___ ___ ___ ___ ___ ___
3. to look for likenesses ___ ___ ___ ___ ___ ___ ___
4. a group of stamps, for instance ___ ___ ___ ___ ___ ___ ___ ___ ___ ___
5. someone to go places with ___ ___ ___ ___ ___ ___ ___ ___ ___
6. word made up of two or more other words ___ ___ ___ ___ ___ ___ ___ ___
7. what a waterlogged tent might do ___ ___ ___ ___ ___ ___ ___ ___
8. what athletes do ___ ___ ___ ___ ___ ___ ___

Write two sentences about "La Bamba," using a word from the spotlight in each.

____

____

Name ....

Preview a Performance

You are writing a preview of the school talent show for the school newspaper. Use the words on the curtains in your article about the scene shown.

limelight	forty-five record
pantomime	rehearsal
talent	slapstick
debut	melodramatic
duo	wings

____

____

____

____

____

____

____

____

Name

Song Sort

The Prefixes *in-* and *con-* Each Spelling Word is made up of the prefix *in-*, *im-*, *con-*, or *com-* and a base word or word root. A **prefix** is a word part added to the beginning of a base word or a word root. A prefix adds meaning to the word. A **word root** is a word part that has meaning, but unlike a base word, a word root usually cannot stand alone.

To spell a word with a prefix, think of the prefix and then the base word or the word root. Spell the word using its parts.

Spelling Words

1. impress
2. confuse
3. conduct
4. inhale
5. intent
6. command
7. immediate
8. compete
9. impolite
10. connect

My Study List
What other words do you need to study for spelling? Add them to My Study List for "La Bamba" in the back of this book.

Prefix	Meaning	Word	Meaning
in-, im-	in; toward;	inhale	to breathe in
	not; without	impolite	not polite
con-, com-	together; with	confuse	to mix up with
		compete	to strive together or with

Write each Spelling Word on the record with the matching prefix.

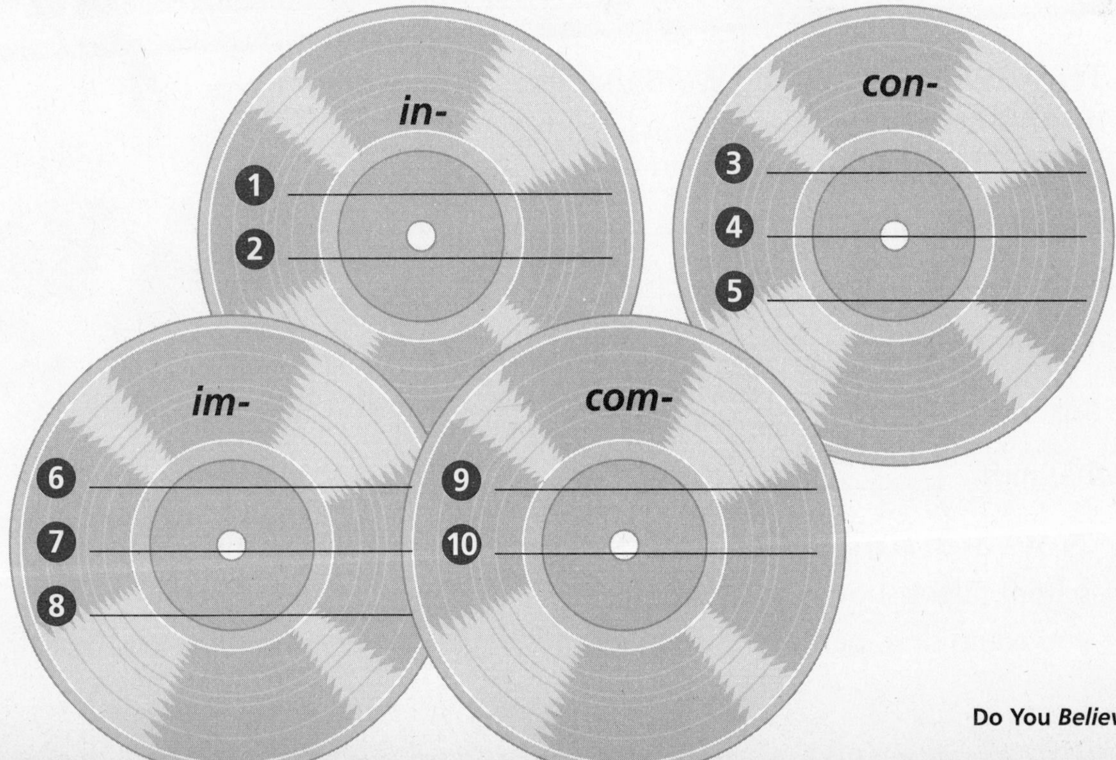

Name

Spelling Spree

Spelling Words

1. impress
2. confuse
3. conduct
4. inhale
5. intent
6. command
7. immediate
8. compete
9. impolite
10. connect

Proofreading Find and circle four misspelled Spelling Words in this school announcement. Then write each word correctly.

Do you sing or cunduct a band? Can you comand a dog to jump through a hoop? Would you like to conpete in a yodeling contest? If so, sign up today! Make imediate plans to be part of our Spring Talent Show. Have fun and impress your friends and family!!

1. ____________ 3. ____________
2. ____________ 4. ____________

Word Trios Write the Spelling Word that goes with each group.

5. rude, thoughtless, ____________
6. bewilder, muddle, ____________
7. affect, influence, ____________
8. determined, firm, ____________
9. join, link, ____________
10. breathe, sniff, ____________

Now Starring Imagine that you've been asked to perform in the school talent show. On a separate sheet of paper, write a short song that you could sing, perhaps to familiar music. Use Spelling Words from the list.

Name

Talent Tryout

Double Negatives **Read the poster. Use the proofreaders' delete mark ( ) to remove double negatives.**

Do not use double negatives in a sentence.

You haven't never been in a talent show like this! Imagine yourself on a dark stage. The audience isn't not making a sound. They are waiting for your brilliant performance. Suddenly, the lights shine. The crowd gasps. Nobody hasn't seen a costume like yours before. You couldn't never have a better time. So sign up to be in the show. Don't hide your talents—share them with the world. For more information, come to room 315 after school on Friday. You haven't got nothing to lose. You might even win!

Write a paragraph about your act. Your paragraph should have at least five sentences and use three negative words.

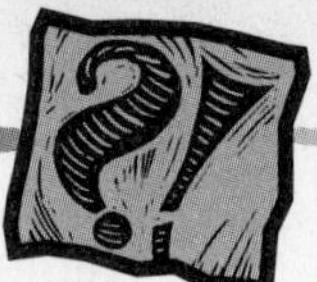

Name

Record Breakers

Double Negatives Manuel could use a rule book on caring for records. Use the negative word next to each picture to write the rule that goes with each picture.

Example: Do not touch the grooves. not

never 1 ______________________________

not 2 ______________________________

not 3 ______________________________

never 4 ______________________________

nothing 5 ______________________________

never 6 ______________________________

More! On a separate sheet of paper, write four rules about caring for a cassette tape or CD. Use a negative word in each rule.

Name

Martian Mania!

alien
Martians
Venus
universe
outlandish

Read each definition in the jack-o'-lantern. Then write the matching vocabulary word in each shape.

1. second planet from the sun
2. bizarre; strange

3. a being from outer space

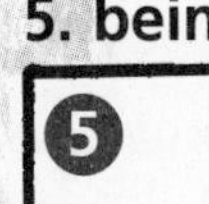

4. Earth, the galaxies, and space
5. beings from Mars

Use each vocabulary word in a sentence.

6. ______________________
7. ______________________
8. ______________________
9. ______________________
10. ______________________

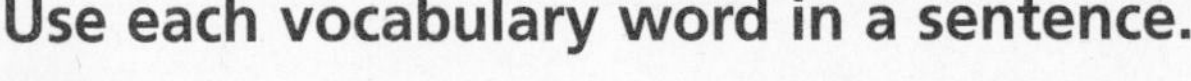

Name

What Really Happened?

Read each statement about *Willie Bea and the Time the Martians Landed.* Check **T** if it's true or **F** if it's false. Then answer the question.

		T	F
1	Willie Bea and Toughy Clay have heard on TV that aliens have landed.	___	___
2	Willie Bea has been invited to a costume party at the Kelly farm.	___	___
3	Toughy Clay has never been on the Kelly road before.	___	___
4	Willie Bea believes that beings from Venus have landed.	___	___
5	The children mistake a shooting star for an alien spaceship.	___	___
6	They both hear a loud rumbling they can't identify.	___	___
7	Toughy Clay explains that the shapes they see are really farm machines.	___	___
8	Willie Bea tries to escape and falls off her stilts.	___	___
9	Willie Bea mistakes a person's voice for an alien's.	___	___
10	The "aliens" turn out to be automobiles.	___	___

What really happened to the children in the story?

____

____

____

____

____

____

Name _______________

What Did *You* Notice?

Write your answers to the questions. The hints are there to help you.

1. What did the Kelly house look like? (**Hint**: Reread the third paragraph on page 561.) _______________

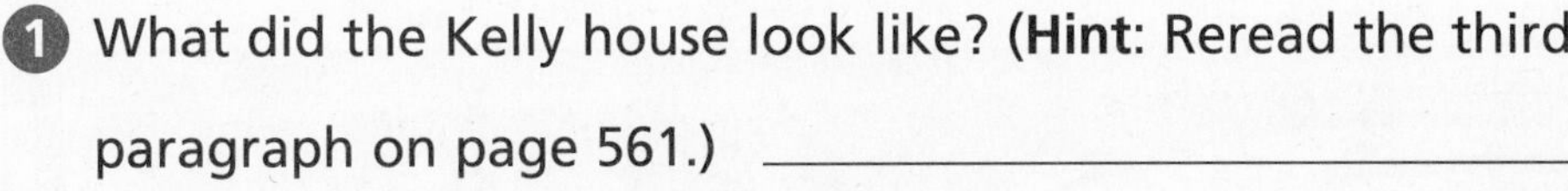

2. Which details let you know that Willie Bea is dreamy and imaginative? (**Hint**: Reread the eighth paragraph on page 562.) _______________

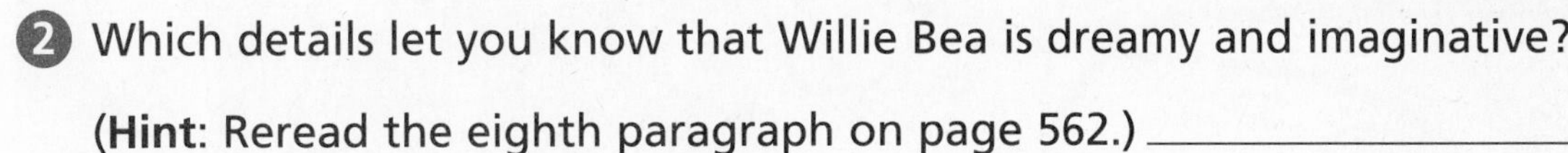

3. Which detail lets you know Toughy is nervous when Willie Bea asks him where he saw the monster? (**Hint**: Reread the last paragraph on page 562.)

____

4. What did Willie Bea see that made her "transfixed by the monsters"? (**Hint**: Reread the fourth paragraph on page 567.) _______________

____

Now use the details from the selection to draw a picture of one of the monsters Willie Bea thought she saw.

Name

Along the Winding Road

Each picture shows the same scene from a different point of view. Write three sentences under each one, describing what you see. Use adjectives and adverbs to describe the pictures clearly.

1 ______________________________

2 ______________________________

3 ______________________________

4 ______________________________

5 ______________________________

6 ______________________________

Name

Impossible Puzzle?

Write the word that matches each clue. (Use the code after each clue to help you.) Then write the numbered letters to solve the puzzle.

visible invisible

The prefix *in-* means "not."

exterior interior

The prefix *in-* means "within or into."

CODE Forms of the Prefix *in-*			
N	L	R	M
in-	*il-*	*ir-*	*im-*

1. not able to get a disease **CODE M**

   ___ ___ ___ ___ ___ ___
   (14, 12 under blanks 1, 2)

2. not perfect **CODE M**

   ___ ___ ___ ___ ___ ___ ___ ___ ___
   (5 under blank 4; 10 under blank 8)

3. not able to read **CODE L**

   ___ ___ ___ ___ ___ ___ ___ ___ ___ ___ ___
   (8 under blank 1; 3, 2, 7 under blanks 8, 9, 10)

4. to take air into the lungs **CODE N**

   ___ ___ ___ ___ ___ ___
   (1 under blank 3; 16 under blank 6)

5. not dependable **CODE R**

   ___ ___ ___ ___ ___ ___ ___ ___ ___ ___ ___ ___ ___
   (17 under blank 5; 11, 15, 6 under blanks 7, 8, 9; 13 under blank 11)

6. not handy **CODE N**

   ___ ___ ___ ___ ___ ___ ___ ___ ___ ___ ___ ___
   (4 under blank 6; 9 under blank 8)

irresponsible, environment, illiterate, immune, enclose, illegible, enforce, imperfect, inconvenient, envelope, encircle, illustrate, inhale

What Willie Bea really saw:

___ ___ ___ ___ ___ ___ ___ ___ ___ g   ___ ___ ___ ___ ___ ___ ___ ___
1 2 3 4 5 6 7 8 9   10 11 12 13 14 15 16 17

On another sheet of paper, write two sentences about the story. In each sentence, use a word with a form of the prefix *in-*.

Name

A Strange and Starry Night

Write each vocabulary word next to its definition. Then if you see the number 1, circle the first letter of the vocabulary word. If you see the number 2, circle the second letter, and so forth.

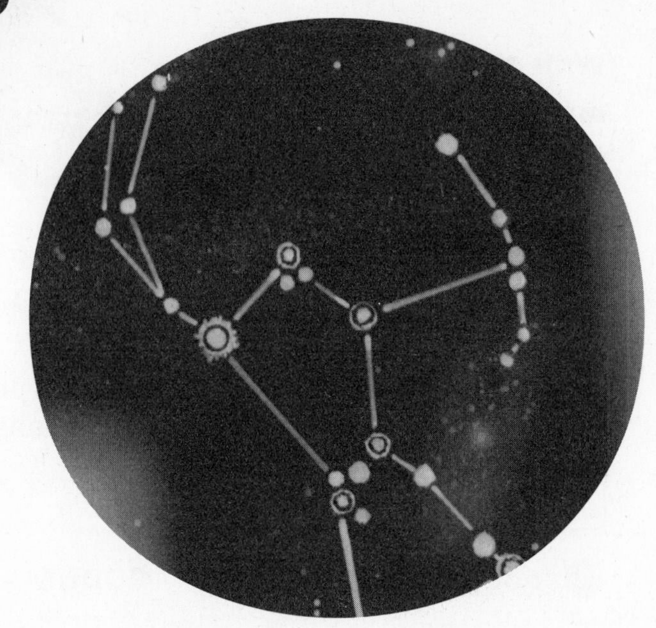

alien	Martians
bizarre	monstrous
celestial	outlandish
cosmos	universe
fantastic	Venus

(2, 8) beings from the planet Mars ____________________

(2) a being from another planet ____________________

(5) the second planet from the sun ____________________

(1, 3) unfamiliar and very strange ____________________

(2) everything that exists ____________________

(3, 4) unbelievable; existing only in imagination ____________________

(7) very strange or odd ____________________

(2) exceptionally large; scary-looking ____________________

(3, 7) having to do with the sky ____________________

(1) the orderly system of everything that exists ____________________

Unscramble the letters you circled to complete the sentence.

If Willie Bea had looked at the stars, she might have seen Orion and other

___ ___ ___ ___ ___ ___ ___ ___ ___ ___ ___ ___ ___ ___.

Name

Word Combine

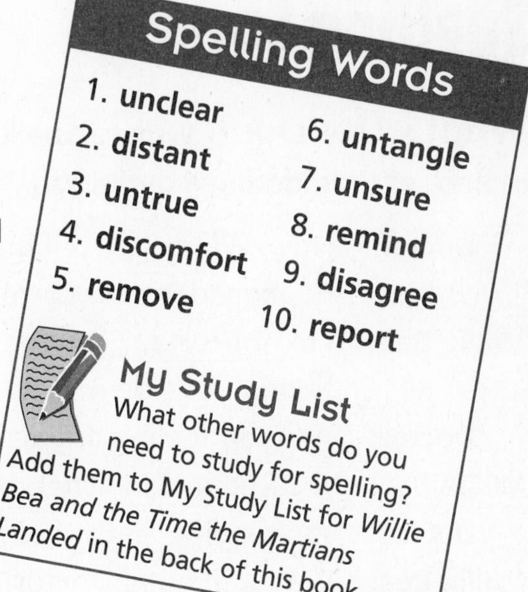

The Prefixes *un-*, *dis-*, and *re-* Each Spelling Word has the prefix ***un-***, ***dis-***, or ***re-***. To spell a word with a prefix, think of the prefix and then the base word or the word root. Spell the word using its parts.

Prefix	Meaning
un-	not; opposite
dis-	apart; opposite
re-	again; back

Word	Meaning
unclear	not clear
distant	standing apart; far off
remove	to take back or away

Make Spelling Words by adding the correct prefix to each base word or word root. Then write the Spelling Words.

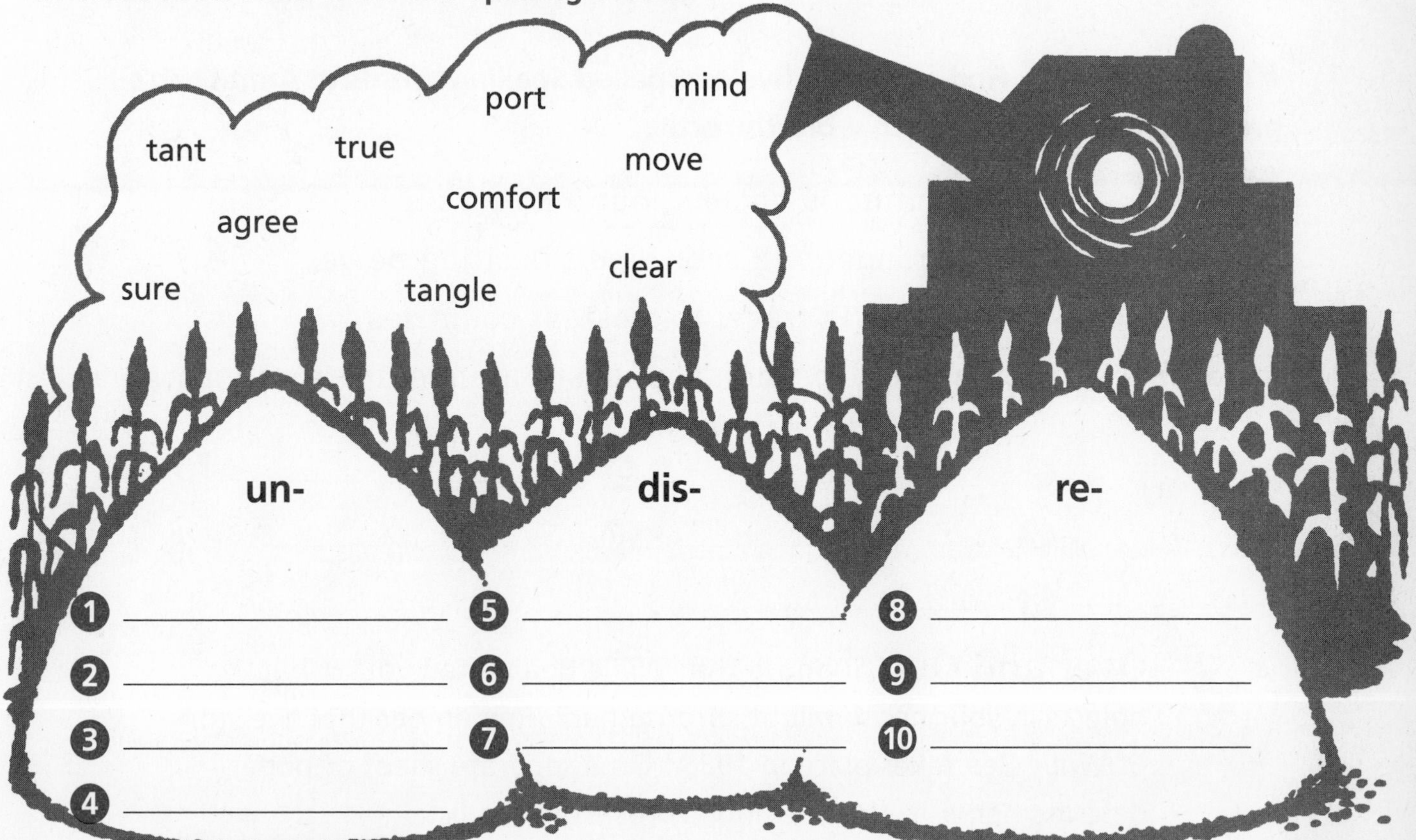

tant, true, port, mind, move, comfort, agree, clear, sure, tangle

un-

1. ______
2. ______
3. ______
4. ______

dis-

5. ______
6. ______
7. ______

re-

8. ______
9. ______
10. ______

Name

Spelling Spree

Spelling Words

1. unclear
2. distant
3. untrue
4. discomfort
5. remove
6. untangle
7. unsure
8. remind
9. disagree
10. report

What's Up, Doc? **Write a Spelling Word to replace each underlined definition.**

Doctor: Now, Willie Bea, tell me what happened in that cornfield.

Willie Bea: I'm not certain, Doctor. I remember falling. And then some farmers helped me take off my stilts.

Doctor: Are you feeling any pain?

Willie Bea: Just some mild aches, but I'm sure it's nothing serious.

Doctor: I think differently. You may have broken a bone.

Willie Bea: Wait a minute, Doctor! That light on your forehead does help me to remember about something! I saw Martians last night!

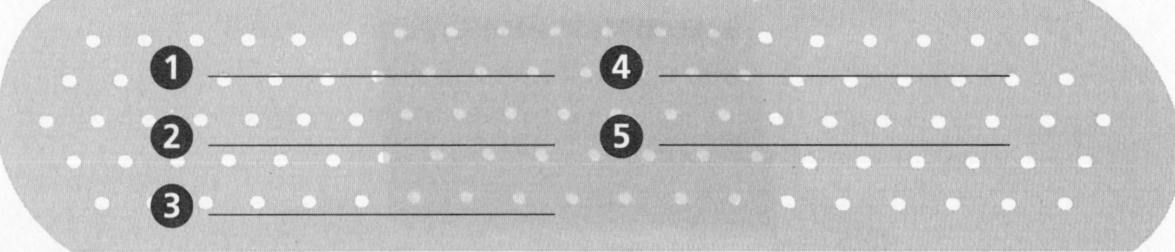

1 ______________ 4 ______________

2 ______________ 5 ______________

3 ______________

Proofreading **Find and circle five misspelled Spelling Words in Aunt Leah's predictions. Then write each word correctly.**

* Your future is uncleer, but follow your heart. *

* A stranger will soon riport exciting news.*

* You will travel to disstant countries.*

* Never tell unntrue tales, for then you must untangel more and more lies. *

6 ______________ 9 ______________

7 ______________ 10 ______________

8 ______________

Over and Out

Suppose that Willie Bea visited you. What objects in your house might surprise her? (Remember that the story of Willie Bea takes place in 1938.) On a separate sheet of paper, describe her visit. Use Spelling Words from the list.

Name

Never Did a Night Last Longer . . .

Adverbs **Toughy has already drawn pictures in his journal about the scary night. Help him complete his story. Write adverbs that tell *how, when,* or *where*. Then draw a final picture for the journal, and write a sentence using an adverb.**

When
first
later
second
often
then
next
today
yesterday

Where
there
outside
forward
somewhere
elsewhere

How
fast
nervously
happily
quickly
gently
suddenly
eerily

The sun sets ______ (when) in the fall. Willie Bea and I ______ (how) put on our costumes. We walked ______ (how) on our stilts. The moon shone ______ (how) over the fields, and the corn swayed ______ (how) in the night breeze. ______ (where) is the farmer who tried to stop us. The Kellys were having a party ______ (when). ______ (where) two combines were harvesting the corn. ______ (when) we saw a strange light! Willie Bea tried ______ (how) to get away.

______
______
______
______

Name

The Kelly Party

My light shines brightly.
I hold it tight.

My light shines **more** brightly.
I hold it tight**er** than before.

My light shines **most** brightly.
I hold it tight**est** of all.

Comparing with Adverbs

Write a summary of the party at the Kelly farm. Write five sentences using adverbs, comparing the actions of the people shown in the picture. Use adverbs from the box if you wish.

- soon
- sooner
- soonest
- fiercely
- more fiercely
- most fiercely
- fast
- faster
- fastest
- hungrily
- more hungrily
- most hungrily
- often
- more often
- most often
- noisily
- more noisily
- most noisily

Name

Put It in Writing

Write the correct vocabulary word on the line above each caption. Then write four sentences of your own, each using a different vocabulary word.

foreclose	bargain
deed	profit
legal	loophole

______
This officially allows Tim to own Tom's tree house.

______
Larry sells a bushel of corn but has to pay Mary for the seeds. This is the money he has left over.

______
Hester agrees to wash the dishes, and Chester agrees to dry them. This is what they've made.

______
If Peter doesn't pay her by next week, Polly will do this by taking back the bicycle he is buying from her.

______
This part of the agreement says that Will can't own Jill's pogo stick if he can't ride it in a week.

______
Little Clarinda says that if things aren't done according to the law, they're not this.

 ______________________________

____

 ______________________________

____

 ______________________________

____

 ______________________________

____

Name ______________________________

Who's Who and What's What?

Write the correct answers from the choices in the box.

Josh McBroom
Hector Jones
Melissa McBroom
the McBroom children

1. Who has the worst farmland in Iowa? ______________________
2. Who figures out how to find three moths in the daytime? ______________________
3. Who has pumpkin races on the farm? ______________________
4. Who spits out watermelon seeds on the McBrooms' farm? ______________________
5. Who tries to entertain Hector Jones as he rides with the McBrooms to their new farm? ______________________

Write the answer to each question.

6. What is the first trick that Hector Jones plays on the McBrooms? ______________________
7. What does McBroom have in his purse besides a ten-dollar bill? ______________________
8. What event turns the pond into good farming land? ______________________
9. What is the last trick that Hector Jones plays on the McBrooms? ______________________
10. What does Josh McBroom finally do to get rid of Hector Jones? ______________________

Name ______________________

Make It Real—or Fantasy!

Read the sentence starters. If the sentence is labeled F, add the ending that makes the sentence a fantasy. If it is labeled R, add the ending that makes the sentence realistic. Then write a fantasy sentence and a realistic sentence of your own.

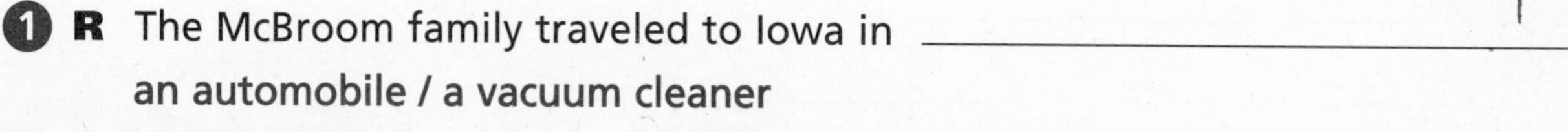

1. **R** The McBroom family traveled to Iowa in ______________________.
   an automobile / a vacuum cleaner
2. **R** They counted noses and found that ______________________.
   Larry was being counted twice / Larry had too many noses
3. **F** Heck Jones sold them a farm that turned out to be ______________________.
   a one-acre pond / a giant iceberg
4. **F** The water in the pond ______________________.
   evaporated in a sudden dry spell / was deep and muddy
5. **R** When McBroom planted seeds, ______________________.
   he planted them three inches apart / they grew instantly
6. **F** Heck Jones insisted that Josh McBroom owed him ______________________.
   three white moths / a unicorn
7. **R** The McBroom children learned to ride ______________________.
   corn stalks / bicycles
8. **F** Heck Jones went flying home ______________________.
   in an airplane / on a banana squash
9. **F** ______________________

   ____
10. **R** ______________________

    ____

    ____

Name

The Beanstalk and Jack

Read each sentence. Decide if the underlined word or group of words can be moved to another part of the sentence. If yes, rewrite the sentence, moving the word or words. If no, explain why not.

1. Jack planted the magical seed in the ground.

2. A beanstalk began to grow within seconds!

3. Jack watched the beanstalk shoot up above the rooftops.

4. Jack climbed the beanstalk rapidly.

5. Jack saw a sleeping giant when he reached the top.

Name

Automatic Fun!

Fill in the crossword puzzle. If the clue contains the word part *self*, use a word with the word root *auto*. If the clue contains a form of the word *write* or *record*, use a word with the word root *graph*.

polygraph
autocrat
autopilot
calligraphy
automatic
graphite
geography
paragraph
autograph
seismograph

Across

1. operating by itself
4. mechanism to let a vehicle steer itself
6. recorder of someone's truths or lies
8. a ruler who keeps all the power to himself or herself
9. fancy writing
10. the part of a pencil that writes

Down

2. your name when you write it yourself
3. recorder of earthquake signs
5. a way of organizing writing
7. study of the earth; writing about the earth

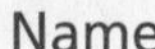

Name

Pick a Pair of Pumpkins

In the box, you will find five pairs of synonyms and one word that stands alone. Write the pairs of synonyms on the pumpkins by the pairs of children. Write the remaining word on little Clarinda's pumpkin. On a separate sheet of paper, write a sentence for each word on the pumpkins.

deed
escape clause
evict
legal
profit
lawful
contract
loophole
bargain
gain
foreclose

WILL JILL

CHESTER HESTER

PETER POLLY

TIM TOM

CLARINDA

MARY LARRY

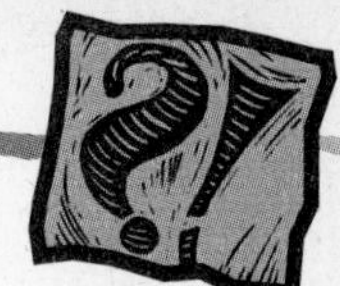

Name 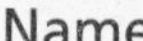

Suffix Patch

Words with Suffixes Each Spelling Word contains the suffix ***-ly***, ***-ful***, ***-ness***, ***-less***, or ***-ment***. A **suffix** is a word part added to the end of a base word. A suffix adds meaning to the word. The spelling of a base word is usually not changed when the suffix begins with a consonant.

Suffix	Meaning	Word
-ly	in a certain way	exactly
-ful	full of	wonderful
-ness	the condition or quality of	kindness
-less	without	countless
-ment	the condition of	excitement

Spelling Words

1. wonderful
2. countless
3. excitement
4. exactly
5. kindness
6. sleepless
7. mouthful
8. brightness
9. finally
10. government

My Study List
What other words do you need to study for spelling? Add them to My Study List for *McBroom Tells the Truth* in the back of this book.

Write each Spelling Word on the watermelon with the matching suffix.

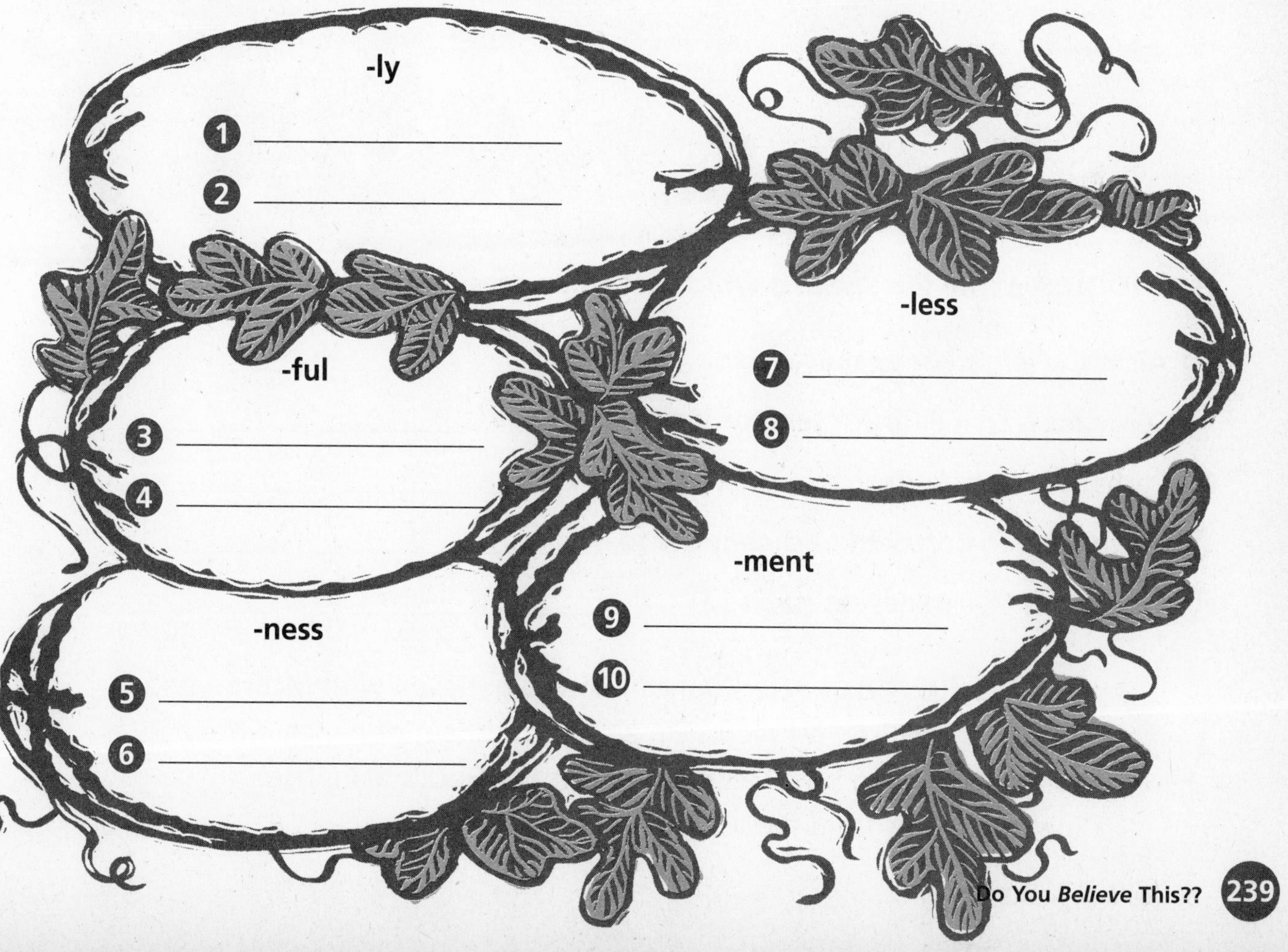

-ly

1. ____________
2. ____________

-ful

3. ____________
4. ____________

-ness

5. ____________
6. ____________

-less

7. ____________
8. ____________

-ment

9. ____________
10. ____________

Name

Spelling Spree

Spelling Words	
1. wonderful	6. sleepless
2. countless	7. mouthful
3. excitement	8. brightness
4. exactly	9. finally
5. kindness	10. government

Proofreading Circle five misspelled Spelling Words in the letter. Then write each word correctly.

Dear Mr. McBroom,

When I first tasted a mouthfull of your home-grown watermelon, I could hardly control my excitement! Its flavor was wunderful!! I knew I must have more. Now, after several sleepliss nights, I have finaly found you. I would like to buy the rest of your melons. Please do me the kindnes of answering as soon as possible.

Very truly yours,

Gwendolyn Goldgrabber

1. ____________
2. ____________
3. ____________
4. ____________
5. ____________

Analogies Write the Spelling Word that completes each analogy.

6. Air is to weightless as stars are to ____________.
7. Sergeant is to military as senator is to ____________.
8. Perhaps is to definitely as approximately is to ____________.
9. Yawning is to boredom as cheering is to ____________.
10. Clouds are to darkness as sun is to ____________.

Heck's Revenge Heck Jones plans to get even with McBroom by planting poison ivy seeds. On a separate sheet of paper, write a paragraph telling how McBroom might foil Heck's plan. Use Spelling Words from the list.

Name

Find the Farm

Prepositions and Prepositional Phrases

When Josh McBroom sent a map to his friend, he forgot to include prepositions in his directions. Add the correct prepositions.

about	by
above	down
after	over
around	past
at	to
before	under
beside	

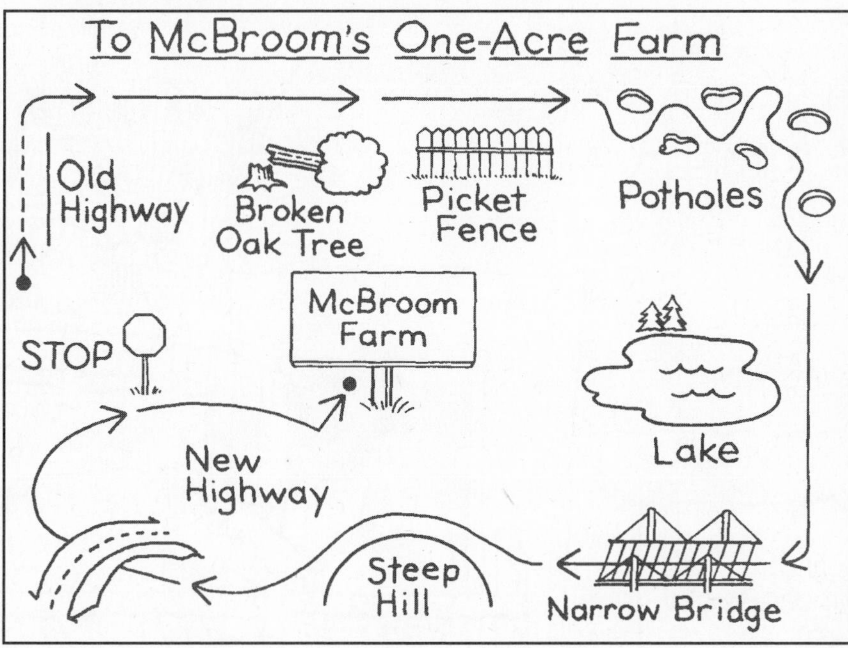

When you get ________________ the old highway, make a right turn. Soon you will drive ________________ a broken oak tree. Next, you will go ________________ a picket fence. Drive very carefully ________________ the potholes. As you drive ________________ the lake, you will have a lovely view. Then, cross ________________ a narrow bridge. Watch out as you drive ________________ a steep hill. Next, pass ________________ the new highway. Turn right immediately ________________ the stop sign. Finally, you will be ________________ the McBroom farm.

More! On a separate sheet of paper, write directions to tell how to get from the front of your school to your classroom. Include a prepositional phrase in each sentence. Then draw a map.

Name

On and Around the Farm

along	into
around	near
beside	outside
by	over
down	past
during	up
in	without

Prepositions and Prepositional Phrases

Write home about your visit to McBroom's farm. Write five sentences describing life on the farm. Use a prepositional phrase in each sentence.

Name

Let's Tell a Story!

Story Ideas

Do any of these ideas make you think of a story?

A new friend
On a spaceship
The missing page
A locked box
Adventures of a pencil
A rivalry between friends
The score is tied
The moose and the mosquito
A mystery bus trip
A talking tree

My Story Topics **Write five story ideas that you would like to write about.**

Ask yourself these questions about each idea.

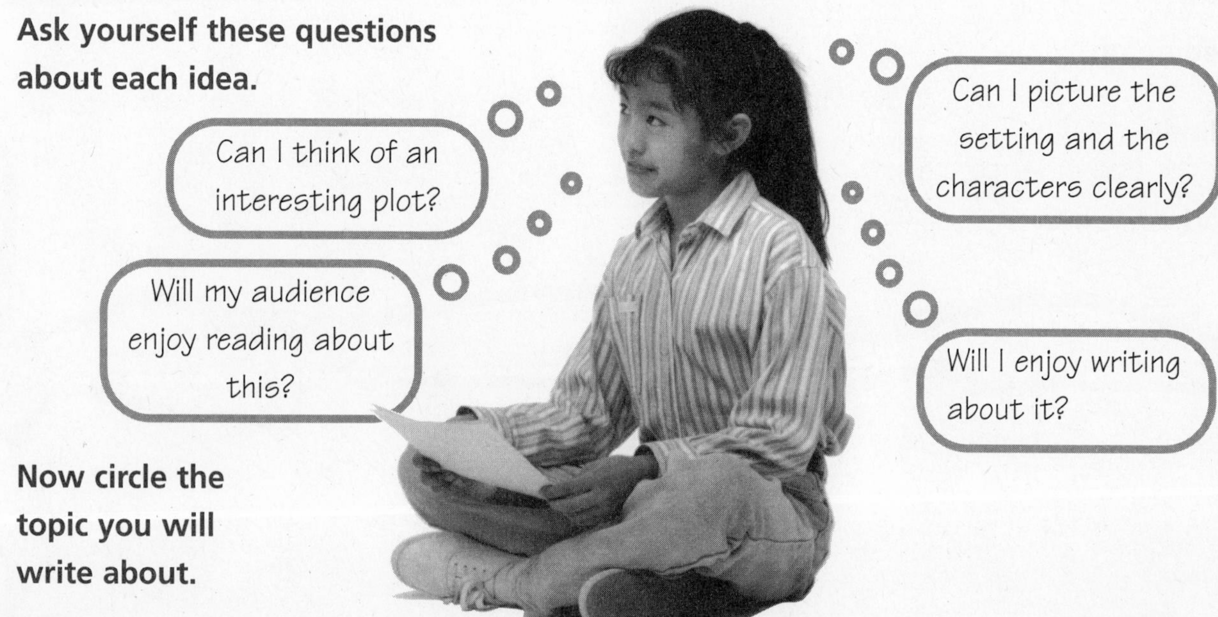

Now circle the topic you will write about.

Name

Who? Where? What?

Fill in the story map. Tell who your main characters are. Tell the setting, or where and when the story takes place. What problem do the characters deal with? What happens in the beginning, middle, and end? How do the characters solve the problem?

Characters

Setting

Place:

Time:

Plot

Problem:

Beginning

Middle

End

Solution

Name

Take Another Look

Reread your story to yourself and revise it, using the Revising Checklist. Then discuss your story with a classmate. Use the Questions for a Writing Conference to guide the discussion.

Revising Checklist

Ask yourself these questions about your story.

- ❑ Did I introduce the main characters, setting, and problem in the beginning?
- ❑ Does each event relate to the problem?
- ❑ Did I use details and dialogue to show what the characters are like?
- ❑ Did I use details to make the setting and action interesting and clear?
- ❑ Does the ending resolve the problem in a way that makes sense?

Questions for a Writing Conference

Use these questions to help you discuss your story.

- What do you like about this story?
- Are there parts that are unclear or do not seem to fit in? How could they be improved?
- Does the story *show* what the characters are like?
- Is the setting clear? Are more details needed?
- Where could dialogue be used to tell the action? to show what a character is like?
- Does the ending fit the characters and the story?

Write notes to help you remember ideas discussed in your writing conference.

My Notes

Name

Dig Up the Past

You are a scientist! The photos show your finds after a hard day of digging at the excavation. Use the words from the box to complete your log. Tell about your discoveries and what you did during the day.

impression	skeletons
fossil	excavated
preserved	extinct

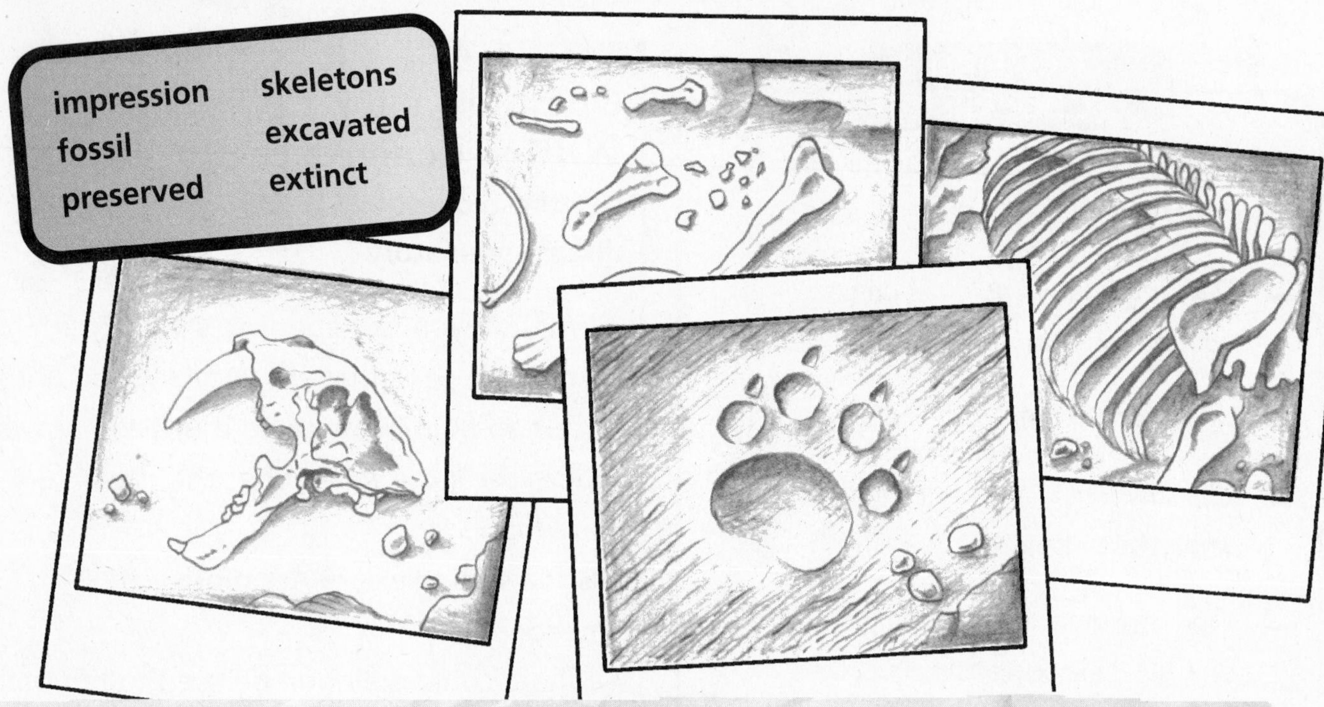

Scientist's Log

Date: ____________________

Place: ____________________

Job: ____

What a day! After a hard morning spent chipping away at rock, I found ______________

____

____

____

____

____

____

Name

Sticky Pictures

Write a description of what is happening to the animal. Explain how the animal will become a fossil.

Write a description of what the men are doing. Explain what they do with the fossils.

Name

Excavations Past and Present

What was the topic of *Trapped in Tar: Fossils from the Ice Age?*

What main idea is expressed in each photograph? Write the main ideas in the chart. Then list three details from the selection or the photos that support the main ideas.

Main idea:	Main idea:
Supporting details:	Supporting details:

On a separate piece of paper and using the information in the chart, write a brief summary of the selection.

Name

Excavation Explanation

Suppose you discovered some fossils in your neighborhood. Write an explanation telling how they would be excavated. Use the planner to help you organize your information. Then write your explanation.

FACT/DETAIL

FACT/DETAIL

FACT/DETAIL

FACT/DETAIL

FACT/DETAIL

Name

A Search for Meaning

Your friend doesn't know the meaning of some words in an article he's reading. Use context clues to help him figure them out and then write the meaning of each underlined word.

1. "A tree does not become petrified overnight. Centuries must pass before wood turns to rock." 1 ____________
2. "Today we know that pine, oak, willow, and monkey puzzle all existed more than one hundred million years ago." 2 ____________
3. "The remains of some creatures were preserved in layers of mud that eventually hardened to form sedimentary rock." 3 ____________
4. "Prehistoric corals did not live together in large groups but were solitary animals." 4 ____________
5. "Dinosaurs may have developed from archosaurs, early reptiles." 5 ____________
6. "Perfectly preserved mammoths were excavated from frozen mud. Even their hair and skin were intact." 6 ____________
7. "Meat of the fossil mammoths looked good to eat, but its taste was actually repugnant." 7 ____________
8. "By studying fossils, paleontologists provide a clearer picture of extinct life forms, making the prehistoric past less obscure." 8 ____________

Name ....

Ice Age Excavation

decay	impression
excavated	preserved
immersed	ancient
fossil	embedded
skeletons	extinct

Five Ice Age mammals are buried in the tar pit. Write the vocabulary words in the grid in the order in which their definitions appear. Write one letter in each box and don't skip any boxes! Write the letters from the grid on the blanks, matching the number below each blank with the number in each grid box.

a. extremely old
b. to break down; to rot
c. firmly placed in a surrounding substance
d. dug out of something
e. no longer existing
f. the hardened remains or imprint of a plant or animal from long ago
g. completely covered in liquid
h. a mark made by pressing
i. kept unharmed or undamaged
j. the frameworks of bones that support and protect the bodies of many animals

1	2	3	4	5	6	7	8
9	10	11	12	13	14	15	16
17	18	19	20	21	22	23	24
25	26	27	28	29	30	31	32
33	34	35	36	37	38	39	40
41	42	43	44	45	46	47	48
49	50	51	52	53	54	55	56
57	58	59	60	61	62	63	64
65	66	67	68	69	70	71	72
73	74	75	76	77	78		

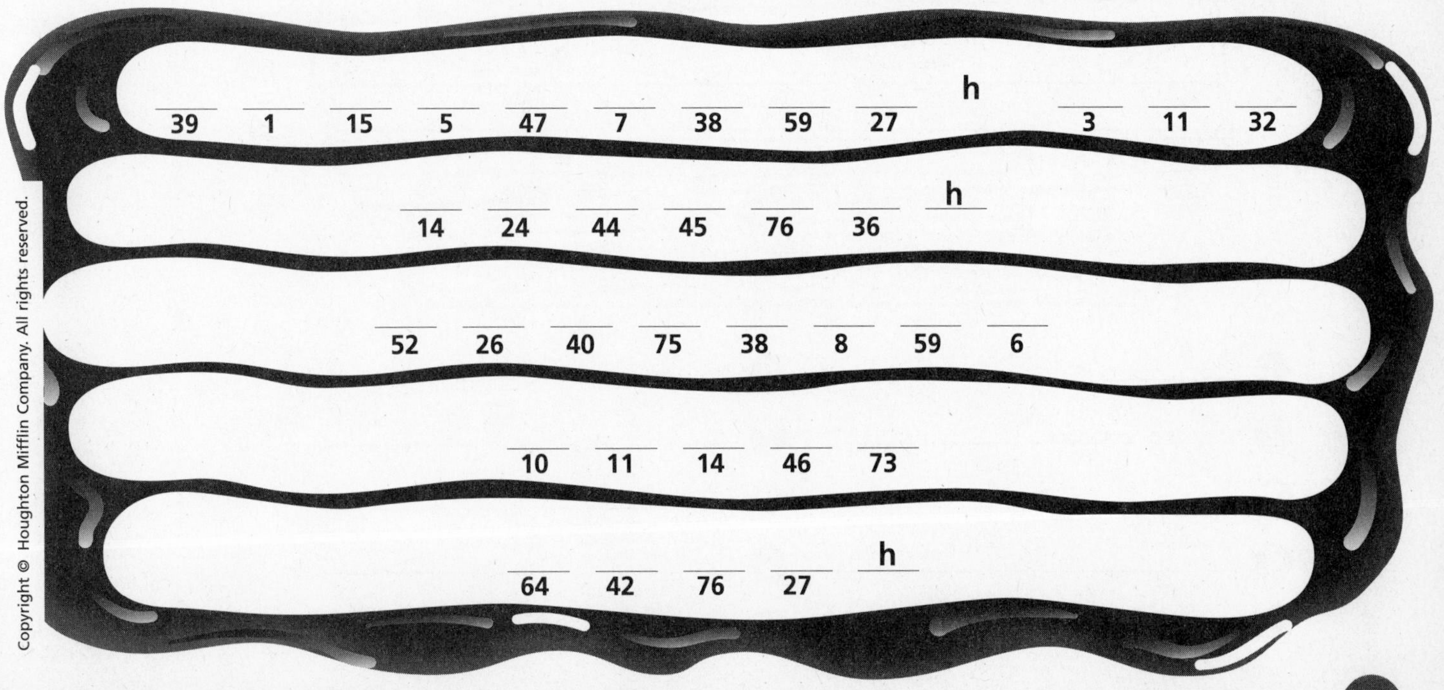

Name ______________________________

Prehistoric Puzzle

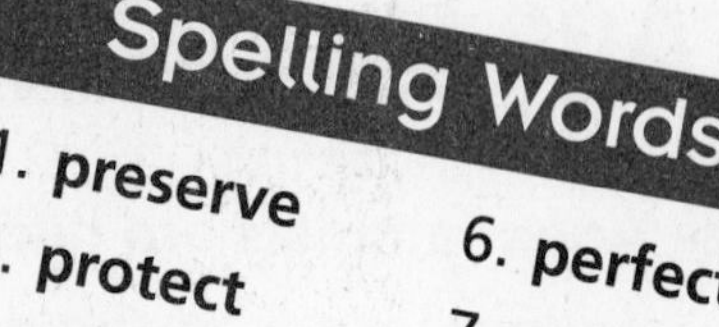

Spelling Words

1. preserve
2. protect
3. project
4. present
5. prevent
6. perfect
7. propose
8. permit
9. prefix
10. pronoun

My Study List

What other words do you need to study for spelling? Add them to My Study List for *Trapped in Tar: Fossils from the Ice Age* in the back of this book.

The Prefixes *pre-*, *per-*, and *pro-* Each Spelling Word has the prefix ***pre-***, ***per-***, or ***pro-***. To spell a word with a prefix, think of the prefix and then the base word or the word root.

Prefix	Meaning	Word
pre-	earlier; before	preserve
per-	through	perfect
pro-	forward; in front of	protect

Make Spelling Words by drawing a line from each prefix on a bone fragment to the matching word part. Then write the words.

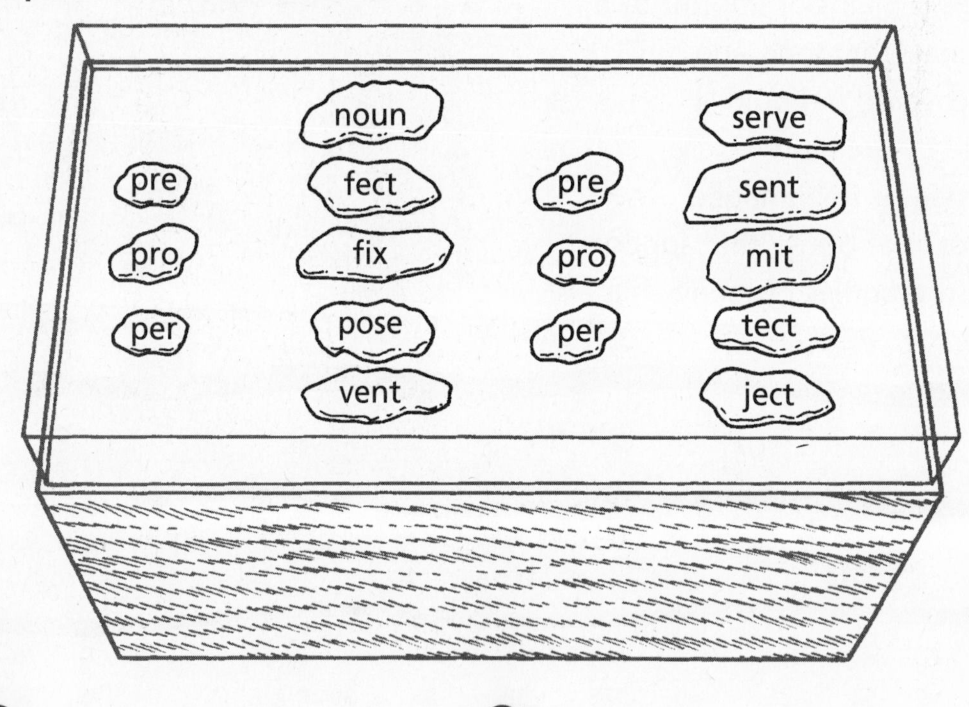

1. ______________________
2. ______________________
3. ______________________
4. ______________________
5. ______________________
6. ______________________
7. ______________________
8. ______________________
9. ______________________
10. ______________________

Name

Spelling Spree

Spelling Words

1. preserve
2. protect
3. project
4. present
5. prevent
6. perfect
7. propose
8. permit
9. prefix
10. pronoun

Proofreading **Find and circle five misspelled Spelling Words in this test for new tour guides. Then write each word correctly.**

- What does the museum feature at present?
- Why are animal skeletons often found in purfect condition?
- How does tar pretect and perserve animal remains?
- Why must scientists privent people from taking fossils from a dig site?
- How did scientists propos to save bone deposits that were uncovered when the new museum was being built?

1 ______________

2 ______________

3 ______________

4 ______________

5 ______________

Tar Puzzle **Find and circle the Spelling Word that is named in each clue. The word may appear across, down, or diagonally. Then write the words.**

6. *I, she,* or *it,* for example
7. a word part coming before a base word
8. at this time; now
9. allow
10. a large task or plan

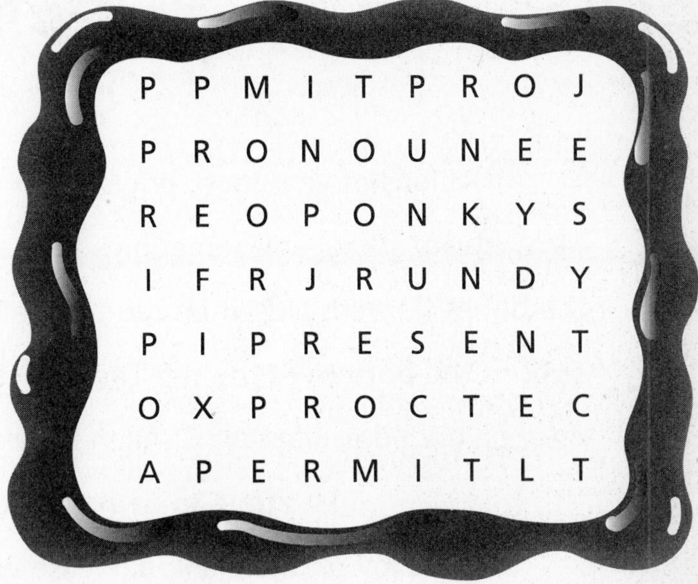

6 ______________ 8 ______________ 10 ______________

7 ______________ 9 ______________

Help Wanted A local museum must hire a paleontologist to direct fossil excavations and set up museum exhibits. On a separate sheet of paper, write a want ad. Include a description of the skills needed and the requirements of the job. Use Spelling Words from the list.

Name ....

This Place Is the Pits!

Object Pronouns in Prepositional Phrases You are in charge of training new tour guides for the La Brea tar pits. Your assistant has written a script but is unsure which object pronouns to use. Complete the script by filling in the correct object pronouns.

Millions of years ago, pools of tar seeped to the surface of the earth. The tar was very sticky, and sometimes animals got stuck in ______________. At first, the bones floated, but when the tar soaked through ______________, they sank to the bottom of the pit. They lay hidden for thousands of years. These tar pits once belonged to Captain G. Allen Hancock, so now this park is named after ______________. It's time to begin our tour.

This is my partner, Felicia. Please walk behind her and ______________. We are both wearing red badges, so it should be easy to keep track of ______________. We both know the area well, so come to ______________ or ______________ with questions. We want to be helpful to ______________. Remember, if you see any live sabertooth cats, please don't give food to ______________. We, however, haven't had lunch, so you can give it to ______________!

Name

A Post Card from Rancho La Brea

Using *I* and *me* **Julio wrote a friend after visiting the La Brea tar pits. He used *I* or *me* ten times, but he didn't always use them correctly. Use the delete sign (~~) to cross out his errors. Write the correct pronoun above the line.**

My brother and I
Example: ~~Me and my brother~~ will mail the post card.

Dear Juan,

Yesterday my family and me visited a place called the La Brea tar pits. Me and Dad were the first ones to jump out of the car and take a look. It was fun. Dad and I learned a lot about fossils. Of course, my little brother kept bothering Mom and me. A tour guide stood beside another boy and I. The other boy and I had the best view of things. When we got to the tar pits, we were careful. My brother and me always stood behind Dad. Well, I hope your summer isn't too boring. Maybe next year you and me can take a trip together. Look for Dad, Mom, and I next week.

See you soon,

Julio

On a separate sheet of paper, rewrite the post card.

Name

Making a Do-You-Believe Comic Strip

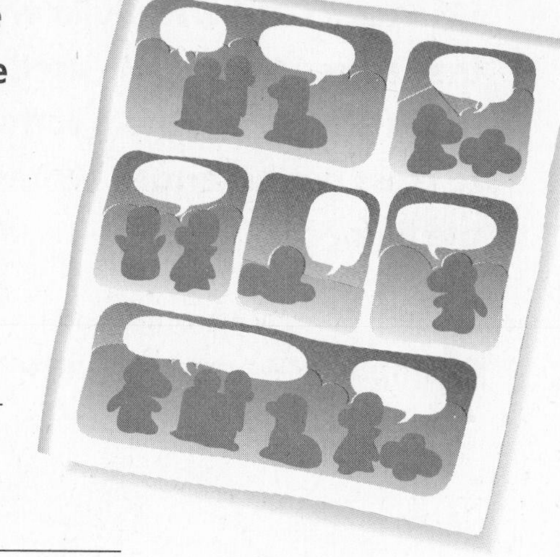

In small groups, discuss stories you know that mix up the real with the make-believe. Think, for example, of science fiction stories and tall tales. Use one of those stories, or make up one of your own, and turn it into a comic strip. This page will help you plan your strip. First, list some possible ideas for the comic strip.

1. ______
2. ______
3. ______

Pick the idea you like best. Make sure you have material for a Do-You-Believe strip.

- What is real in the story: ______
- What is unreal in the story: ______

Plan each frame, or box, in the comic strip. Try to make a story with interesting details.

- The first frame: ______
- The middle frames (as many as you need): ______

______

- The final frame: ______

Discuss your story with your partners. When you are satisfied that you have a good Do-You-Believe story, draw your comic strip. Your strip can have just pictures or pictures with words.

Checklist

- ❑ The comic strip has both real and make-believe ideas or events.
- ❑ It has details that make it an interesting story.
- ❑ It has a plot with a definite conclusion.

MORE SPELLING PRACTICE

MORE SPELLING PRACTICE

Contents

Name

Dive into These Words!

Words Often Misspelled Look for familiar spelling patterns to help you remember how to spell the Spelling Words on this page. Think carefully about the parts that you find hard to spell in each word.

Spelling Words

1. a lot
2. because
3. school
4. its
5. it's
6. tonight
7. might
8. right
9. write
10. again

My Study List
What other words do you need to study for spelling? Add them to My Study List for *Journey to Adventure!: Reading-Writing Workshop* in the back of this book.

Write the missing letters and a missing apostrophe in the Spelling Words below.

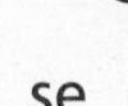

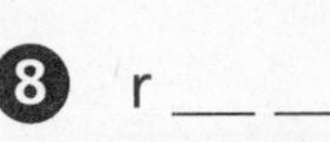

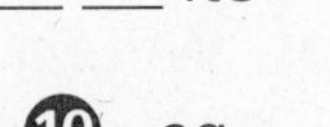

1. __ lot
2. bec __ __ se
3. s __ __ ool
4. it __
5. it __ __
6. ton __ __ __ t
7. m __ __ __ t
8. r __ __ __ t
9. __ __ ite
10. ag __ __ n

Write the Spelling Words to answer these questions.

11. Which word is a contraction of ***it is***?
12. Which word has the /ô/ sound you hear in ***pause***?
13. Which word has the /k/ sound spelled ***ch***?
14. Which word begins with a silent consonant?
15. Which word shows ownership?
16. Which word is made up of two words and means "many"?
17. Which word has an unusual spelling for the short ***e*** sound?

18–20. Which three words have the long ***i*** sound spelled ***igh***?

11 ______
12 ______
13 ______
14 ______
15 ______
16 ______
17 ______
18 ______
19 ______
20 ______

Name ....

Spelling Spree

Spelling Words

1. a lot
2. because
3. school
4. its
5. it's
6. tonight
7. might
8. right
9. write
10. again

Proofreading Find and circle five misspelled Spelling Words in this essay. Then write each word correctly.

My greatest fear is speaking in front of a group of people. I know that alot of my friends think this is silly, but it's a big problem for me. I dread the times when I have to speak at scool. One time I had to rite one sentence on a flip chart and then read it aloud to the class. I shook so badly that I actually knocked the flip chart on it's back!

With luck nothing like this will happen agin. I signed up for a public speaking class that starts next week. Who knows? Someday I might be thrilled to be asked to speak to thousands!

1. ____________
2. ____________
3. ____________
4. ____________
5. ____________

E-Mail Excitement Write a Spelling Word to replace each underlined clue in this e-mail message.

Hi, Jake!

I got some great news this evening. I was asked to join some of my friends on a rafting trip next week. We may even raft through some white water! I've heard it is so exciting! My parents said I could go for the reason that my dad is going along too. I must have done something correct lately to be so lucky!

6. ____________
7. ____________
8. ____________
9. ____________
10. ____________

Packing for Adventure What adventurous journey would YOU like to make? On a separate sheet of paper, list several items to pack for your trip. Explain what each item will be used for. Use Spelling Words from the list.

Name

Spelling Review

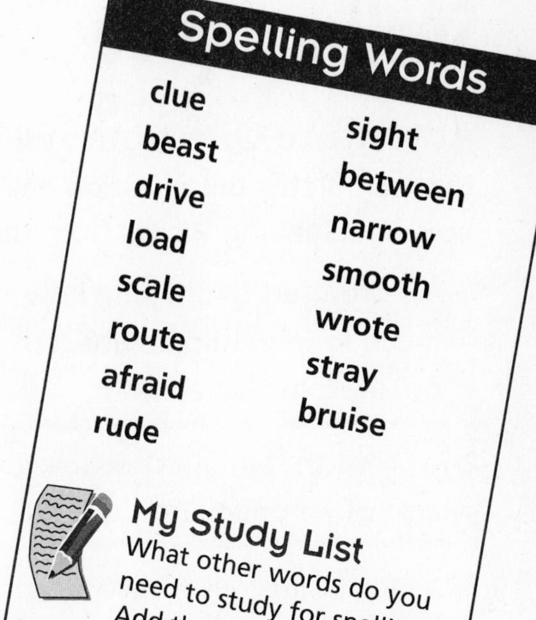

Write Spelling Words from the list on this page to answer each question.

|ā| → wake, bait, sway
|ē| → peach, speed

1–3. Which three words have the |ā| sound? Underline the patterns that spell that sound.

1 ____________________

2 ____________________

3 ____________________

4–5. Which two words have the |ē| sound? Underline the patterns that spell that sound.

4 ____________________ 5 ____________________

|ī| → prize, midnight
|ō| → froze, goal, snow

6–7. Which two words have the |ī| sound? Underline the patterns that spell that sound.

8–10. Which three words have the |ō| sound? Underline the patterns that spell that sound.

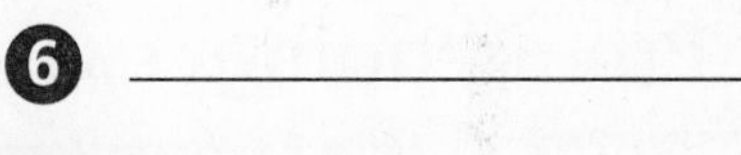

6 ____________________

7 ____________________

8 ____________________

9 ____________________

10 ____________________

|yōō| or |ōō| → huge, blue, ooze, juice, group

11–15. Which five words have the long *u* sound? Underline the patterns that spell that sound.

11 ____________________ 13 ____________________ 15 ____________________

12 ____________________ 14 ____________________

Name

Spelling Spree

Spelling Words	
because	afraid
its	it's
drive	narrow
a lot	again
smooth	between

Adventure Questions **Write the Spelling Word that completes the question next to each clue in the box. Use Spelling Words from the list on this page.**

1. a word used to describe how much food would be needed on an Arctic expedition

① What is ______________?

2. a word that might describe the size of an opening to a cave

② What is ______________?

3. a word that tells what an explorer in a car might do

③ What is ______________?

4. a word that could describe how an explorer might feel on seeing an angry lion

④ What is ______________?

5. a word an astronaut might use to describe a gentle landing on Mars

⑤ What is ______________?

Proofreading **Find and circle five misspelled Spelling Words in this farewell card. Then write each word correctly.**

Good-bye and Good Luck!

So you are off agan to explore the rain forest in Guatemala betwen Belize and Mexico. Although its sad to see you go, I know that you are excited becuse you hope to find more Mayan ruins. I know you are not afraid of any animals, but watch out for the coral snake—it's bite can be dangerous. Call me when you get back!

⑥ ______________

⑦ ______________

⑧ ______________

⑨ ______________

⑩ ______________

Mapping Your Journey With a partner, plan an adventurous journey to a real or imaginary place. On another sheet of paper, draw a map of your route. Include pictures and labels to highlight your adventures. Use Spelling Words from both Review pages in your labels.

Name

Wild Words

Words Often Misspelled Look for familiar spelling patterns to help you remember how to spell the Spelling Words on this page. Think carefully about the parts that you find hard to spell in each word.

Spelling Words

1. heard
2. your
3. you're
4. field
5. buy
6. friend
7. guess
8. cousin
9. build
10. family

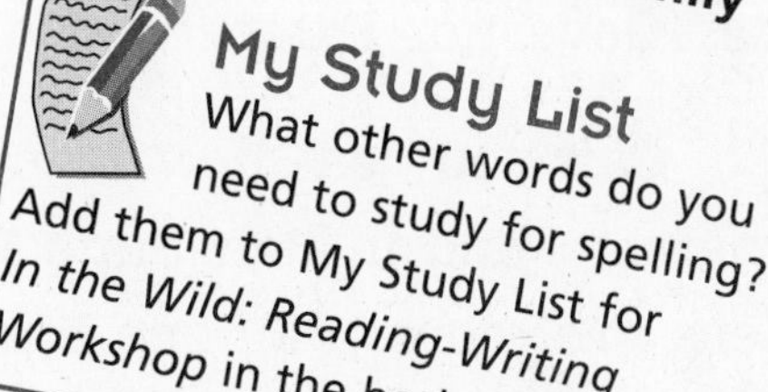

My Study List
What other words do you need to study for spelling? Add them to My Study List for *In the Wild: Reading-Writing Workshop* in the back of this book.

Write the missing letters and a missing apostrophe in the Spelling Words below.

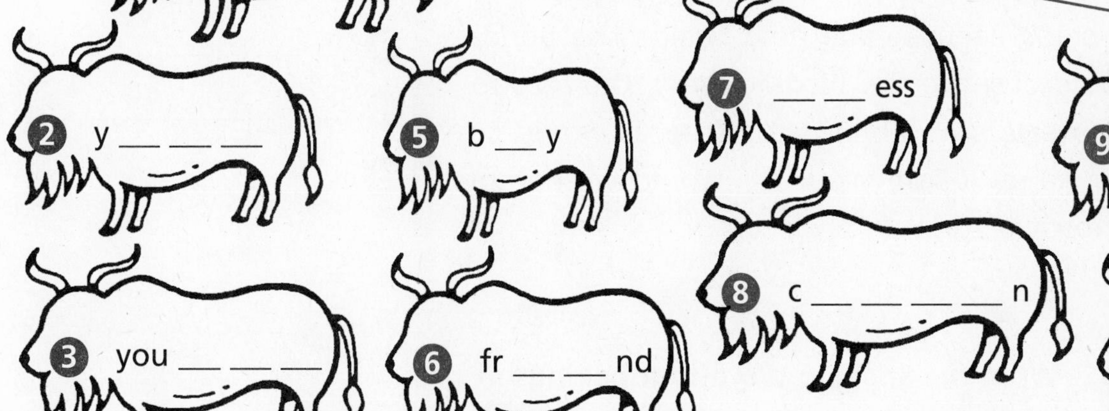

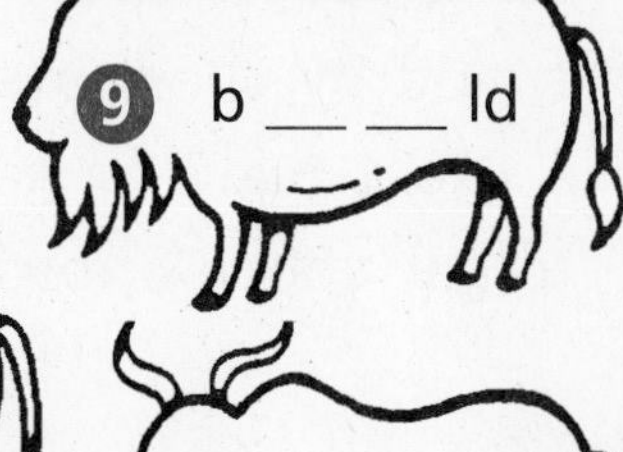

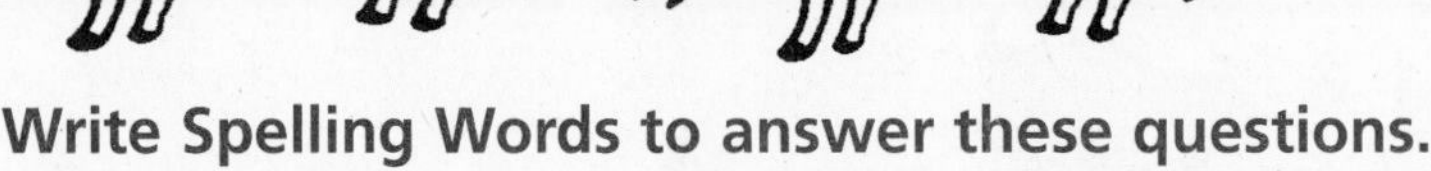

1. h __ __ __ d
2. y __ __ __
3. you __ __ __
4. f __ __ __ d
5. b __ y
6. fr __ __ nd
7. __ __ ess
8. c __ __ __ __ n
9. b __ __ ld
10. fam __ ly

Write Spelling Words to answer these questions.

11. Which word is a contraction of ***you are***?
12. Which word is the past tense form of ***hear***?
13. Which word is a homophone for ***by*** and means "to purchase"?
14. In which word is |**g**| spelled with two letters?
15. In which word is |**z**| spelled ***s***?
16. Which word has three syllables?
17. Which word shows ownership?
18. Which word has an unusual spelling for the short ***i*** sound?

19–20. Which two words have the long ***e*** or the short ***e*** sound spelled the same?

11 ________
12 ________
13 ________
14 ________
15 ________
16 ________
17 ________
18 ________
19 ________
20 ________

Name

Spelling Spree

Spelling Words	
1. heard	6. friend
2. your	7. guess
3. you're	8. cousin
4. field	9. build
5. buy	10. family

Proofreading Find and circle five misspelled Spelling Words in this part of a letter to the governor. Then write each word correctly.

Dear Governor Patchet:

Can you gess how many kinds of birds visit Emerald Pond in Bow State Park each year? Usually there are more than one hundred. United Birdwatchers would like to put a blind, a shelter where we could watch without being seen, in the field beside the pond. Then people could observe the birds closely. Our group would by the materials and bild it for free. It would be a great place to go on a famly outing. Would we be able to get youre approval for this project?

1 ______
2 ______
3 ______
4 ______
5 ______

Word Groups Write the Spelling Word that belongs in each group.

6. aunt, uncle, _____
7. they're, we're, _____
8. neighbor, classmate, _____
9. meadow, woods, _____
10. touched, smelled, _____

6 ______
7 ______
8 ______
9 ______
10 ______

A Fond Farewell Suppose that you helped a park ranger care for an injured bird. Now the bird is well, and it is time to set it free. On another sheet of paper, write a farewell message to it. Explain what it meant to you and tell about your hopes for its future. Use Spelling Words from the list.

Name

Spelling Review

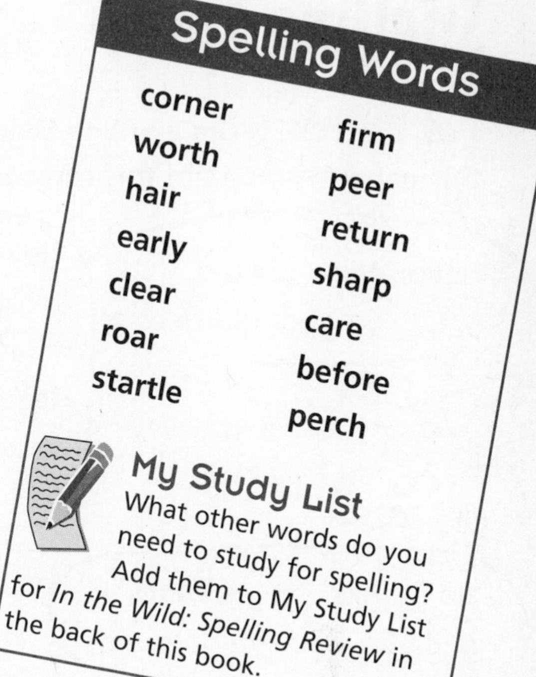

Spelling Words

corner
worth
hair
early
clear
roar
startle
firm
peer
return
sharp
care
before
perch

My Study List
What other words do you need to study for spelling? Add them to My Study List for *In the Wild: Spelling Review* in the back of this book.

Write Spelling Words from the list on this page to answer each question.

/âr/ → bare, pair
/är/ → apart

1–2. Which two words have the /âr/ sounds? Underline the patterns that spell these sounds.

3–4. Which two words have the /är/ sounds? Underline the pattern that spells these sounds.

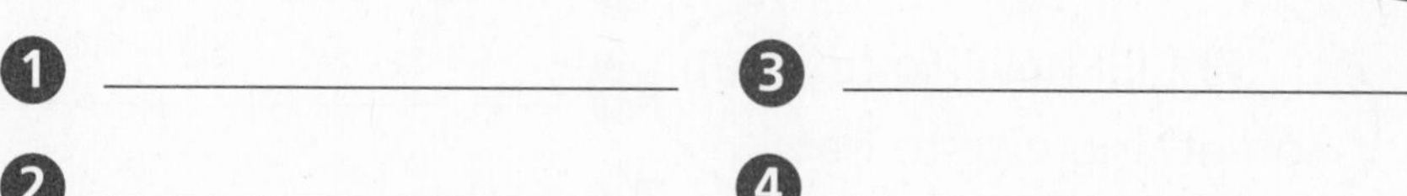

1 ____________ 3 ____________

2 ____________ 4 ____________

/îr/ → fear, steer
/ôr/ → force, soar, more

5–6. Which two words have the /îr/ sounds? Underline the patterns that spell these sounds.

7–9. Which three words have the /ôr/ sounds? Underline the patterns that spell these sounds.

5 ____________
6 ____________
7 ____________
8 ____________
9 ____________

/ûr/ → prefer, bird, hurt, learn, world

10–14. Which five words have the /ûr/ sounds? Underline the patterns that spell these sounds.

10 ____________ 12 ____________ 14 ____________

11 ____________ 13 ____________

Name

Spelling Spree

Spelling Words

- heard
- startle
- care
- corner
- guess
- roar
- early
- pair
- family
- you're
- friend

Pal Patter Write Spelling Words from the list on this page to complete this cartoon.

Hello, Wiley, my old __(1)__! I __(2)__ you got married.

Hey, Monty! Gee, __(3)__ looking well-fed! Yes, now I have a wife and __(4)__ to feed and __(5)__ for. I wonder . . . would you like to come for dinner?

No thanks! I think I'll go to bed __(6)__. See you around!

I __(7)__ I'll have to hunt up something else to eat.

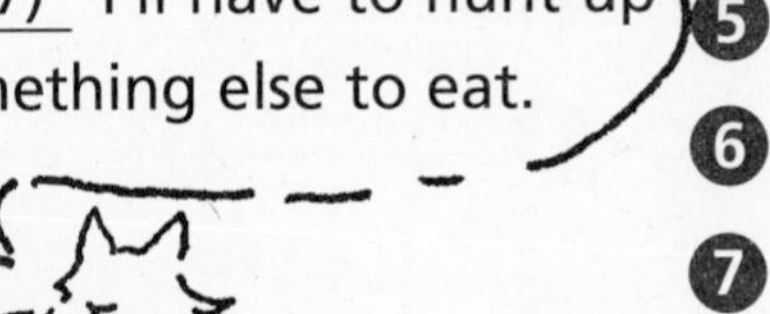

1 ____________
2 ____________
3 ____________
4 ____________
5 ____________
6 ____________
7 ____________

Proofreading Find and circle five misspelled Spelling Words in this ranger's report. Then write each word correctly.

Today I toured the far corrner of the park. I saw a pare of giraffes nibbling on some leaves. Something about the legs of one giraffe looked odd. I inched closer, not wanting to startel the animals. Then I realized a giraffe calf was hidden behind its mother! I gess it was only hours old. I let out a roare of joy. Now we have a giraffe family!

8 ____________
9 ____________
10 ____________
11 ____________
12 ____________

Conversation Challenge Work with one or more classmates to create conversations. One person writes a sentence, using a Spelling Word, to open a conversation. The next person writes the second sentence, using a Spelling Word. Take turns writing sentences, using Spelling Words from the lists on both Review pages.

Name

Grin and Spell It

Words Often Misspelled Look for familiar spelling patterns to help you remember how to spell the Spelling Words on this page. Think carefully about the parts that you find hard to spell in each word.

Spelling Words

1. enough
2. caught
3. brought
4. thought
5. every
6. ninety
7. their
8. they're
9. there
10. there's

My Study List
What other words do you need to study for spelling? Add them to My Study List for *Try to See It My Way: Reading-Writing Workshop* in the back of this book.

Write the missing letters in the Spelling Words below.

1. en __ __ __ __
2. c __ __ __ __ t
3. br __ __ __ __ t
4. th __ __ __ __ t
5. ev __ ry
6. nin __ ty
7. th __ __ r
8. th __ __ __ re
9. th __ r __
10. th __ __ __ __ s

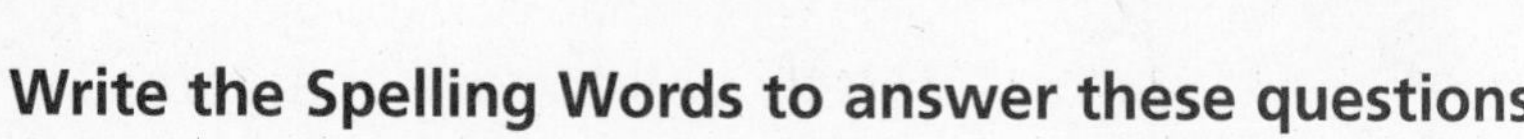

Write the Spelling Words to answer these questions.

11. Which word is a contraction of ***there is***?
12. Which word is a contraction of ***they are***?
13. In which word is the short ***u*** sound spelled ***ou***?
14. Which word shows ownership?
15. Which word means the opposite of ***here***?
16–17. Which two words include one of these words: ***nine*** or ***ever***?
18–20. Which three words have the /ô/ sound as in ***fought***?

11. ____________
12. ____________
13. ____________
14. ____________
15. ____________
16. ____________
17. ____________
18. ____________
19. ____________
20. ____________

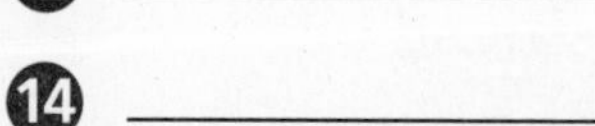

Name

Spelling Spree

Spelling Words

1. enough
2. caught
3. brought
4. thought
5. every
6. ninety
7. their
8. they're
9. there
10. there's

Proofreading Find and circle five misspelled Spelling Words in this description. Then write each word correctly.

Our house has two new things in it. They are alike in some ways, but theyr'e different in other ways. My parents braught them home from the hospital a month ago. They have four lungs that often seem like ninety. One blanket in thair room is pink, and the other is blue. In each bed theres a stuffed animal. They never seem to get enough milk, but they grow a little evry day. Can you guess what I'm describing?

1. ____________
2. ____________
3. ____________
4. ____________
5. ____________

Question Clues Write the Spelling Word that answers each question.

6. When you point at something that is not here, where is it?
It's ____________.

7. What did you do when you came up with a new idea?
You ____________.

8. How many points will beat a score of eighty-nine?
____________ points

9. What did the outfielder do to the fly ball to save the game?
She ____________ it.

10. If you have as much of something as you need, how much do you have?
You have ____________.

It's Debatable Choose a topic that you and a friend could debate. For example, perhaps you love camping, but your friend hates it. Then, on another sheet of paper, make a list of the points you would make in the debate. Use Spelling Words from the list.

Name

Spelling Review

Write Spelling Words from the list on this page to answer each question.

Spelling Words

flavor
signal
straw
feather
example
grate
shout
wall
sugar
frown
level
bother
great
fault

My Study List
What other words do you need to study for spelling? Add them to My Study List for *Try to See It My Way: Spelling Review* in the back of this book.

|ou| → counter, allow
|ô| → dawn, pause, although

1–2. Which two words have the |**ou**| sound? Underline the patterns that spell this sound.

1 ______
2 ______

3–5. Which three words have the |**ô**| sound? Underline the patterns that spell this sound.

3 ______
4 ______
5 ______

|ər| → quarter, color, collar

6–9. Which four words have the final |**ər**| sounds? Underline the patterns that spell these sounds.

6 ______
7 ______
8 ______
9 ______

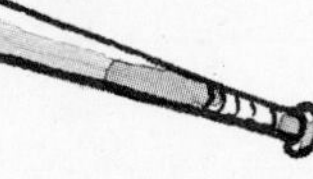

|əl| or |l| → double, towel, normal

10–12. Which three words have the final |**əl**| sounds? Underline the patterns that spell these sounds.

10 ______
11 ______
12 ______

Homophones are words that sound alike but have different spellings and meanings.

13–14. Which two words are homophones?

13 ______
14 ______

Name

Spelling Spree

Spelling Words

every	seen
spider	their
scene	although
there's	special
allow	they're
thought	

Proofreading Find and circle five misspelled Spelling Words in this post card message. Then write each word correctly.

We are having a great time here in India, althogh it is very hot. I had thawht I would not like the spicy food, but it is really special! In many restaurants, ther'es no beef on the menu. The Hindus believe that thier cows are sacred. They do not alow these animals to be killed. It's so interesting to learn about other cultures!

1 ____________________ 3 ____________________ 5 ____________________

2 ____________________ 4 ____________________

Viewers' Views Write Spelling Words to complete these movie reviews. Use Spelling Words from the list on this page.

Last week I saw a great flick at the Bijou. The movie, called *Losing It*, is one of the best films I've ever __(6)__. There are many __(7)__ effects, and __(8)__ all amazing. If I were voting, __(9)__ actor would get an award.

The new film *Losing It* is a real loser. I never __(10)__ a movie could be this bad! One __(11)__ in the film involves a giant __(12)__ that gives new meaning to the term "Worldwide Web." Do yourself a favor and skip this one!

6 ____________________

7 ____________________

8 ____________________

9 ____________________

10 ____________________

11 ____________________

12 ____________________

What Am I? With a partner, take turns asking a riddle about a Spelling Word and trying to guess the word and spell it correctly. Use Spelling Words from the lists on both Review pages.

I am a synonym for *captured*. (caught)

I can be white or brown, but I am always sweet. (sugar)

Name ....

Word Explosion!

Words Often Misspelled Look for familiar spelling patterns to help you remember how to spell the Spelling Words on this page. Think carefully about the parts that you find hard to spell in each word.

Spelling Words

1. while
2. whole
3. anyway
4. anyone
5. anything
6. favorite
7. once
8. suppose
9. everybody
10. everyone

My Study List
What other words do you need to study for spelling? Add them to My Study List for *Catastrophe!: Reading-Writing Workshop* in the back of this book.

Write the missing letters in the Spelling Words below.

1. ___ ___ ile
2. ___ ___ ole
3. ___ ___ ___ way
4. ___ n ___ one
5. ___ n ___ thing
6. favor ___ ___ ___
7. on ___ ___
8. su ___ ___ ose
9. ev ___ ___ ___ body
10. ev ___ ___ ___ one

Write the Spelling Words to answer these questions.

11. Which word has the final |ĭt| sounds?
12. Which word has a double consonant?
13. In which word is the final |s| sound spelled *ce*?
14. Which word begins with the |w| sound spelled *wh*?
15. Which word is a homophone for ***hole*** and means "complete"?
16–18. Which three words are compound words with *any*?
19–20. Which two words are compound words with *every*?

11 ______________________
12 ______________________
13 ______________________
14 ______________________
15 ______________________
16 ______________________
17 ______________________
18 ______________________
19 ______________________
20 ______________________

Name

Spelling Spree

Spelling Words

1. while
2. whole
3. anyway
4. anyone
5. anything
6. favorite
7. once
8. suppose
9. everybody
10. everyone

Catastrophe Quotations

For each imaginary quotation from a catastrophe survivor, write a Spelling Word to replace the underlined word or words.

1. "The entire crew of the ship deserve awards for getting all the passengers safely into the lifeboats."
2. "We may have lost our preferred above all others things in the fire, but we still have each other."
3. "It may take a period of time to rebuild after the volcanic eruption, but we will do it!"
4. "Do you assume there are others in the flood zone who need help getting off their roofs?"
5. "We may never face another hurricane, but I think we should build a brick house just the same."

1 ____________
2 ____________
3 ____________
4 ____________
5 ____________

Proofreading

Find and circle five misspelled Spelling Words in this part of a research report. Then write each word correctly.

Pompeii was onece a bustling city in southern Italy. On August 24, in the year 79, everbody was busy doing the things he or she did every day. The 20,000 inhabitants did not know that Mt. Vesuvius was about to erupt. Because it happened so suddenly, not evryone was able to escape. The whole city, including thousands of people, was buried under hot, wet ashes. Afterward there wasn't ennything left to show that enyone had ever lived at that spot.

6 ____________
7 ____________
8 ____________
9 ____________
10 ____________

Safety Tips

On a separate sheet of paper, write safety tips that people should think about in case of a natural disaster. Use Spelling Words from the list.

Name

Spelling Review

Write Spelling Words from the list on this page to answer the questions.

Spelling Words

struggle	baby-sit
everything	suffer
modern	notice
hallway	all right
control	sandwich

My Study List
What other words do you need to study for spelling? Add them to My Study List for *Catastrophe!: Spelling Review* in the back of this book.

A **compound word** can be written as one word, as a hyphenated word, or as separate words.

1–2. Which two compound words are written as one word?
3. Which compound word is written as a hyphenated word?
4. Which compound word is written as separate words?

1 ____________ 3 ____________
2 ____________ 4 ____________

VC|CV	V|CV	VC|V
sur|face	to|tal	sol|id

5–7. Which three words have the VCCV or VCV pattern? Draw a line to divide the syllables in each word.

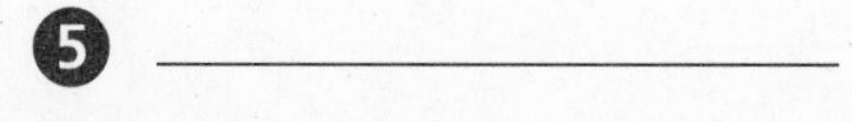
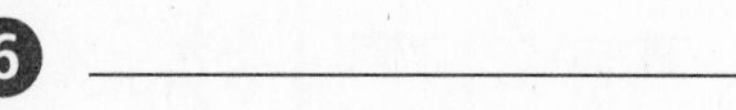

5 ____________ 6 ____________ 7 ____________

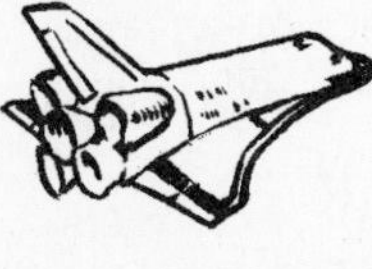

VC|CCV	VCC|CV
ex|press	emp|ty

8–10. Which three words that are **not** compound words have the VCCCV pattern? Draw a line to divide the syllables in each word.

8 ____________  9 ____________  10 ____________

Name

Spelling Spree

Spelling Words

- instant
- while
- everybody
- already
- once
- solid
- favorite
- damage
- farther
- whole

Proofreading Find and circle five misspelled Spelling Words in this news broadcast. Then write each word correctly.

Attention!

Hurricane Helga is nearing the coast! Helga's winds have all ready reached 120 miles per hour. The whole city is in danger of receiving heavy damadge. If your home is within a half mile of the Squeegee River, you should go to an emergency shelter at onse. Do not take time to collect faverite belongings. We want everybody who is in the flood zone to leave NOW wile there is still time.

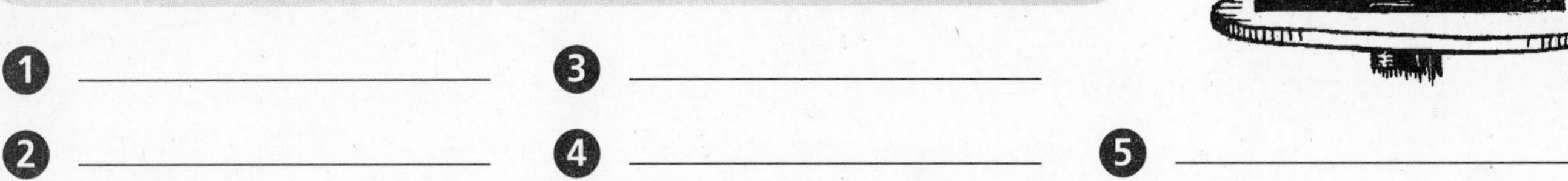

Save the Words Write the Spelling Word that is a synonym or an antonym of each clue. Then write **S** if it is a synonym. Write **A** if it is an antonym. Use Spelling Words from the list on this page.

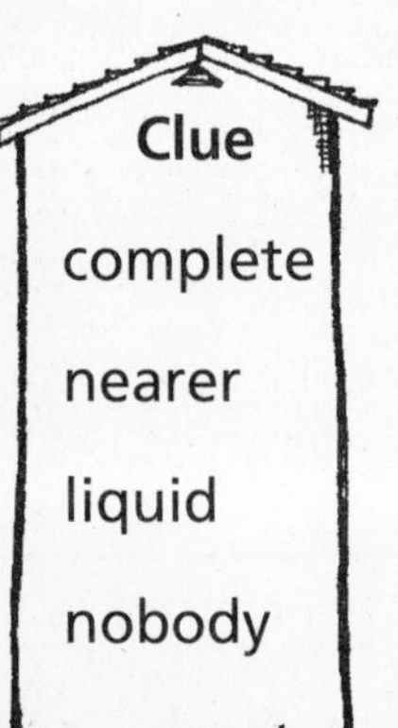

Hurricane ABC's The names of hurricanes are chosen in alphabetical order. Write the Spelling Words in the lists on both Review pages in alphabetical order. Then think of a hurricane name that begins with the first letter of each Spelling Word. Write a sentence using that name and as many Spelling Words as you can that begin with that same letter. **Example:** Hurricane **Alyssa** has **already** hit the Florida Keys, but everyone is **all right**.

Name ....

Corral Those Words!

Words Often Misspelled Look for familiar spelling patterns to help you remember how to spell the Spelling Words on this page. Think carefully about the parts that you find hard to spell in each word.

Spelling Words

1. **would**
2. **wouldn't**
3. **clothes**
4. **happened**
5. **someone**
6. **sometimes**
7. **different**
8. **another**
9. **weird**
10. **eighth**

My Study List
What other words do you need to study for spelling? Add them to My Study List for *From the Prairie to the Sea: Reading-Writing Workshop* in the back of this book.

Write the missing letters in the Spelling Words below.

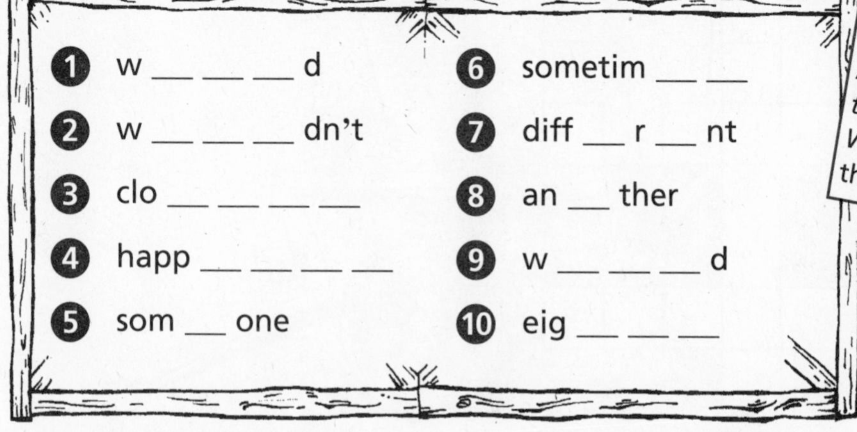

1. w ___ ___ ___ d
2. w ___ ___ ___ dn't
3. clo ___ ___ ___ ___
4. happ ___ ___ ___ ___
5. som ___ one
6. sometim ___ ___
7. diff ___ r ___ nt
8. an ___ ther
9. w ___ ___ ___ d
10. eig ___ ___ ___

Write the Spelling Words to answer these questions.

11. Which word includes the word ***eight***?
12. Which word is related to the word ***cloth***?
13. Which word rhymes with ***should***?
14. Which word is the past tense form of ***happen***?
15. Which word has the vowel + /r/ sounds spelled with two vowels + ***r***?
16. Which word has the suffix ***-ent***?
17. Which compound word includes the word ***other***?
18. Which word is a contraction of ***would not***?

19–20. Which two words are compound words with ***some***?

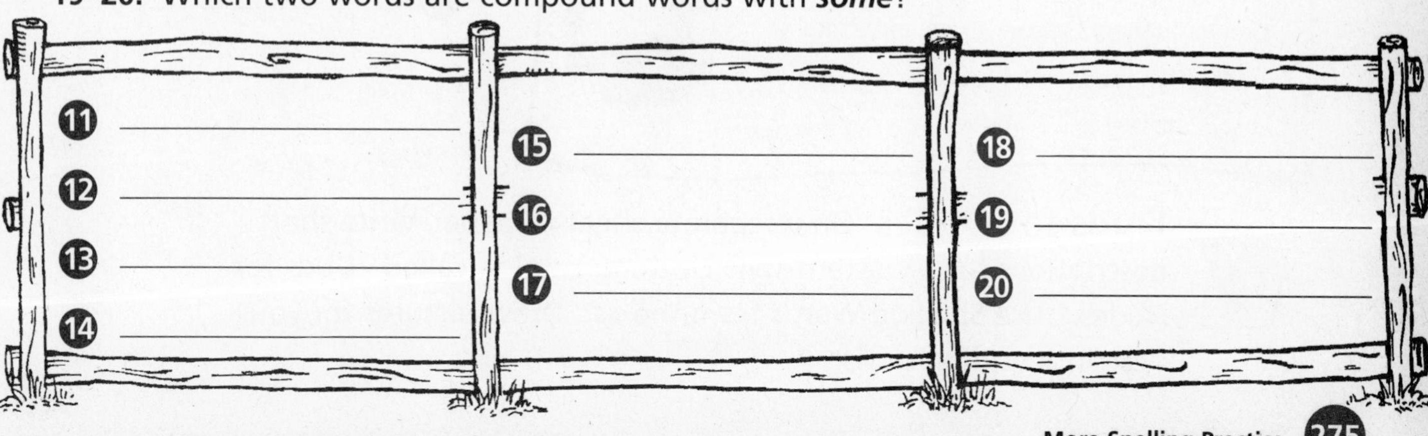

11 ______________
12 ______________
13 ______________
14 ______________
15 ______________
16 ______________
17 ______________
18 ______________
19 ______________
20 ______________

Name

Spelling Spree

Spelling Words

1. would
2. wouldn't
3. clothes
4. happened
5. someone
6. sometimes
7. different
8. another
9. weird
10. eighth

Conestoga Crossword

Complete the puzzle by writing the Spelling Word that fits each clue.

Across

3. an additional one
4. coming after the seventh
5. some person

Down

1. now and then
2. strange

Proofreading

Find and circle five misspelled Spelling Words in this personal narrative. Then write each word correctly.

In our small town in Nevada we sometimes see critters that people in big cities woud see only in zoos. The other day I took a diffarent way home from school. Suddenly a rattlesnake happenned to cross my path! I hoped that it woudn't strike at me. Luckily, it slithered off into some bushes. I raced home, sweating so badly with fear that I had to change into dry closthes!

6 __________
7 __________
8 __________
9 __________
10 __________

Duds for Dudes

On a separate sheet of paper, write short descriptions for a western-style clothing catalog called "Duds for Dudes." Use Spelling Words from the list. Draw pictures for your descriptions, if you wish.

Name

Spelling Review

Write Spelling Words from the list on this page to answer the questions.

Spelling Words

possession
slipping
enemies
healing
narrate
staring
possess
friendliness
narration
offered

My Study List

What other words do you need to study for spelling? Add them to My Study List for *From the Prairie to the Sea: Spelling Review* in the back of this book.

cheat + ing = cheating
decide – e + ed = decided
plan + n + ing = planning
number + ed = numbered

1. Which word was formed by adding ***-ed*** or ***-ing*** to a base word ending with ***e***?
2. Which word was formed by doubling the final consonant before adding ***-ed*** or ***-ing*** to the base word?
3–4. Which two words were formed by adding ***-ed*** or ***-ing*** to a base word with no other spelling changes?

1 ____________ 3 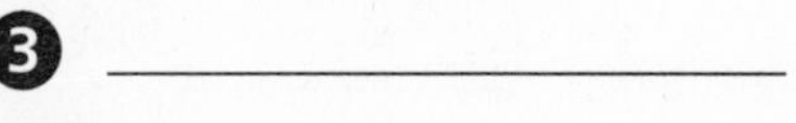

2 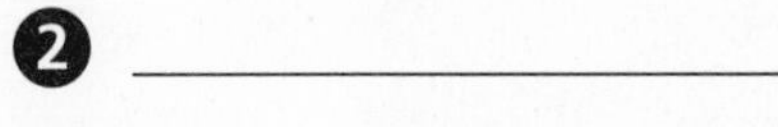 4 

If a base word ends with a consonant and ***y***, change the ***y*** to ***i*** when adding an ending or a suffix.

5–6. Which two words were formed by adding ***-es, -ed, -er, -est,*** or ***-ness*** to a base word that ends with a consonant and ***y***? Underline the letter that changed from ***y*** when the ending or suffix was added.

5 ____________

6 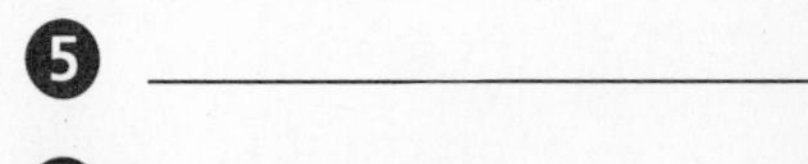

direct + ion = direction
create – e + ion = creation

7–8. Which word pair contains a verb and a related noun formed by adding ***-ion*** with no other spelling changes?
9–10. Which word pair contains a verb and a related noun formed by dropping the final ***e*** of the verb and adding ***-ion***?

7 ____________

8 ____________

9 ____________

10 ____________

Name ________________________

Spelling Spree

First Lines **Write Spelling Words from the list on this page to complete these first lines for some new Old West ballads.**

1. "Who in the nation would buy that newfangled _____?"
2. "My dog died of mange. His bones are _____ across the range."
3. "I _____ rather lasso a twister than call you Sir or Mister."
4. "I _____ think of my brother Will, who's buried on Boot Hill."
5. "Sweet Sue dumped me for Harry. Then she _____ for the lone prairie."
6. "The _____ critter I ever saw was the mule that bit me and then said, 'Hee Haw.'"

1 ________________ 4 ________________

2 ________________ 5 ________________

3 ________________ 6 ________________

Proofreading **Find and circle four misspelled Spelling Words in this poem. Then write each word correctly.**

Sometimes I think of a wierd Forty-Niner
Who herried out West to be a gold miner.
It hapend he struck gold,
But anuther, quite bold,
Stole his claim, leaving the Niner a whiner.

7 ________________ 9 ________________

8 ________________ 10 ________________

Last Words An epitaph is a short statement written in memory of a dead person. On a separate sheet of paper, write epitaphs for gravestones in the Old West. Use Spelling Words from the lists on both Review pages. **Example:** Here lies Herman the Hermit. He had neither friends nor **enemies**.

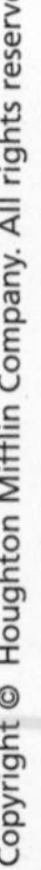

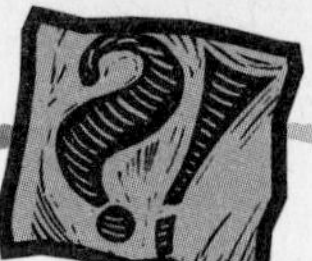

Name ....

Missing Letters

Words Often Misspelled Look for familiar spelling patterns to help you remember how to spell the Spelling Words on this page. Think carefully about the parts that you find hard to spell in each word.

Write the missing letters in the Spelling Words below.

Spelling Words

1. happily
2. minute
3. beautiful
4. usually
5. instead
6. stretch
7. lying
8. excite
9. millimeter
10. divide

My Study List

What other words do you need to study for spelling? Add them to My Study List for *Do You Believe This??: Reading-Writing Workshop* in the back of this book.

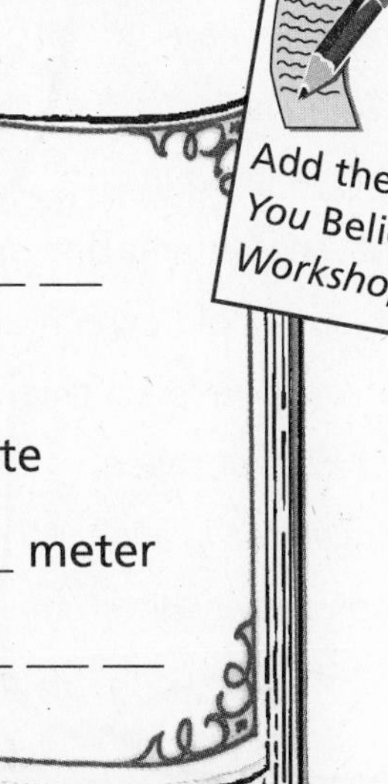

1. happ ___ ly
2. min ___ ___ ___
3. b ___ ___ ___ t ___ ful
4. usua ___ ___ y
5. inst ___ ___ d
6. stre ___ ___ ___
7. l ___ ing
8. e ___ ___ ite
9. mil ___ ___ meter
10. d ___ v ___ ___ ___

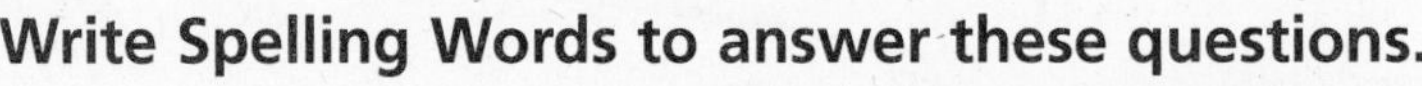

Write Spelling Words to answer these questions.

11. In which word is the final |**ch**| sound spelled with three letters?

12. In which word is the |**s**| sound spelled ***c***?

13. In which word is the long ***i*** sound spelled ***y***?

14. In which word is the short ***e*** sound spelled ***ea***?

15. Which word begins with the same word part as ***milligram***?

16–17. Which two words have two syllables and the VCV pattern?

18–20. Which three words end with suffixes?

11. ______________________
12. ______________________
13. ______________________
14. ______________________
15. ______________________
16. ______________________
17. ______________________
18. ______________________
19. ______________________
20. ______________________

Name

Spelling Spree

Proofreading Find and circle five misspelled Spelling Words in this story beginning. Then write each word correctly.

Spelling Words	
1. happily	6. stretch
2. minute	7. lying
3. beautiful	8. excite
4. usually	9. millimeter
5. instead	10. divide

Once there was a cat named Pat and a flea named Bea. Bea, who was only one milimeter long, lived cozily in Pat's thick fur. Although she usually spent her days lieing in the sun and snoozing happyly, Pat was an amazing cat. When something would exsite her, Pat would strech and grow until she was as big as a horse! Bea loved this because she could jump off onto tall bookcases, into high kitchen cupboards, or onto tree branches. Bea could see the world from a completely different point of view.

1 ____________
2 ____________
3 ____________
4 ____________
5 ____________

How Do They *Do* That? Write a Spelling Word to complete each response to seeing an amazing trick.

6. "It looked as though he was able to _____ a woman in half and put her back together!"
7. "Look at the _____ white dove he pulled from his sleeve!"
8. "How did he untie the rope around his hands and escape from a tank of water in one _____ ?"
9. "How did he make the rabbit _____ of the mouse pop out of the hat?"
10. "I don't _____ like card tricks, but that was a good one."

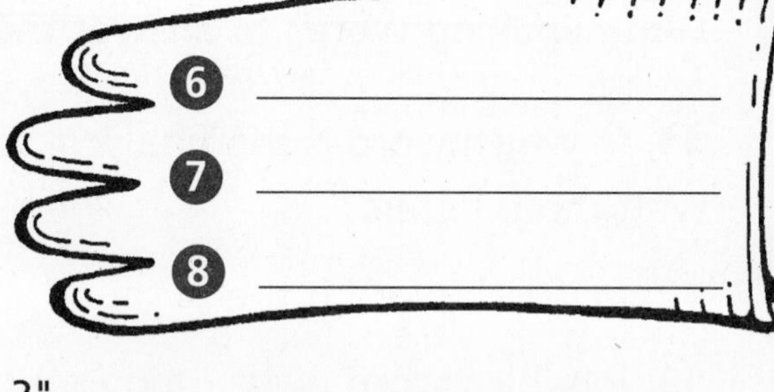

It's Amazing! On another sheet of paper, write a one-paragraph plot summary for a fantasy story. Use Spelling Words from the list.

Name

Spelling Review

Spelling Words

report
government
impolite
permit
compete
brightness
propose
untangle
inhale
mouthful
prefix
sleepless
conduct
disagree
finally

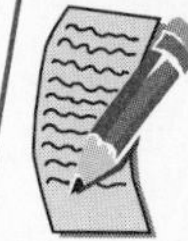

My Study List
What other words do you need to study for spelling? Add them to My Study List for *Do You Believe This??: Spelling Review* in the back of this book.

Write Spelling Words from the list on this page to answer each question.

in + tent = intent
im + press = impress
con + fuse = confuse
com + mand = command

1–2. Which two words were made by adding the prefix ***in-*** to a base word or a word root? Underline the prefix in each word.

3–4. Which two words were made by adding the prefix ***con-*** to a base word or a word root? Underline the prefix in each word.

Words with prefixes
unclear discomfort remind

5–7. Which three words were made by adding ***un-, dis-,*** or ***re-*** to a base word or a word root? Underline the prefixes.

Words with suffixes
exactly wonderful kindness
countless excitement

8–12. Which five words were made by adding ***-ly, -ful, -ness, -less,*** or ***-ment*** to a base word? Underline the suffixes.

Words with prefixes
prevent perfect pronoun

13–15. Which three words were made by adding the prefix ***pre-, per-,*** or ***pro-*** to a base word or a word root? Underline the prefixes.

1 ______
2 ______
3 ______
4 ______
5 ______
6 ______
7 ______
8 ______
9 ______
10 ______
11 ______
12 ______

 13 ______  14 ______  15 ______

Name

Spelling Spree

Spelling Words

project	excitement
lying	happily
instead	divide
distant	connect
immediate	beautiful

Unbelievable News Write the Spelling Word that means the opposite of the underlined word in each headline. Begin each word with a capital letter. Use Spelling Words from the list on this page.

1. Inventors Foresee Flying Cars in Near Future
2. Scientists Issue Delayed Response to Reported Dinosaur Sighting
3. Farmers Sadly Announce Record-Breaking Harvests
4. Local Artists Exhibit Ugly Pictures
5. Storyteller Claims He Wasn't Truthful

1 ________ 3 ________ 5 ________

2 ________ 4 ________

Proofreading Find and circle five misspelled Spelling Words in this news article. Then write each word correctly.

Students Set World Record

There was much excitment at Beauclerc Elementary School in Jacksonville, Florida, when the students learned their popcorn projict was going to be listed in the *Guinness Book of World Records*. Over six days in 1994, the students popped enough corn to fill a container 39 feet $11\frac{1}{2}$ inches long, 20 feet $8\frac{1}{2}$ inches wide, and 8 feet high.

Each class had to conect the popcorn experiment to learning. For example, one boy learned to multiply and divid by figuring out how full the box was at certain times.

Do you imagine the whole school happily munching on popcorn all day long? Not so. Most of it was given to charities insted.

6 ________

7 ________

8 ________

9 ________

10 ________

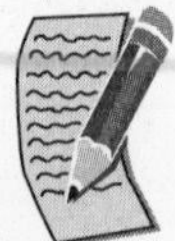

Create a Clue Write clues for five Spelling Words chosen from both Review pages. Then find a partner. Take turns asking a clue and answering it by spelling the correct Spelling Word.

Example: **What word might be a homework assignment? (report)**

Name

Whose Pet Is It?

More Homophones You know that homophones are words that have the same pronunciation but different spellings and meanings.

poll |pōl| a survey
pole |pōl| a long, slender rod

Help each pet find its owner. Write the Spelling Word that matches each meaning. Then draw lines to connect the homophone pairs.

1. to make well

______

2. to injure or damage by beating
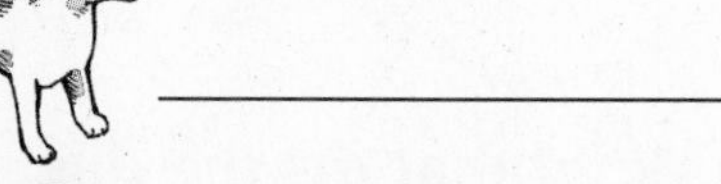
______

3. a long, slender rod

______

4. to take without permission

______

5. a device for slowing or stopping
______

6. to crack or split

______

7. a shopping center

______

8. a metal made from iron and carbon

______

9. the back part of the foot

______

10. a survey

______

Take-Home Word Lists

More Homophones

Homophones are words that have the same pronunciation but different spellings and meanings.

Spelling Words

1. poll
2. pole
3. heal
4. heel
5. steal
6. steel
7. mall
8. maul
9. break
10. brake

Challenge Words

1. presents
2. presence
3. cereal
4. serial

My Study List

Add your own spelling words on the back. →

Take-Home Word Lists

Name

My Study List

1. ____________
2. ____________
3. ____________
4. ____________
5. ____________
6. ____________
7. ____________
8. ____________
9. ____________
10. ____________

Additional Spelling Words

1. weather
2. whether
3. pedal
4. peddle

How to Study a Word

LOOK at the word.
SAY the word.
THINK about the word.
WRITE the word.
CHECK the spelling.

Name

Spelling Spree

Spelling Words	
1. poll	6. steel
2. pole	7. mall
3. heal	8. maul
4. heel	9. break
5. steal	10. brake

Proofreading Find and circle five misspelled Spelling Words in this questionnaire. Then write each word correctly.

Q.: Does your dog chew or braike things? Y / N
Q.: Does your dog steal food from your plate? Y / N
Q.: Has your dog ever had an injury that would not heel? Y / N
Q.: Does your dog sniff every tree and poal it passes? Y / N
Q.: Does your dog have nerves of stele? Y / N
Q.: Does your dog mall stuffed toys? Y / N

1. ____________
2. ____________
3. ____________
4. ____________
5. ____________

Hink Pinks Write the Spelling Word that fits the clue and rhymes with the word in dark print.

Example: a pit for a long rod a ____ **hole** *pole*

6. a terrific bargain a **real** ____
7. a shopping center in a skyscraper a **tall** ____
8. a reptile's device for stopping a **snake** ____
9. a survey of imaginary dwarfs or giants a **troll** ____
10. a folk dance done on the backs of the feet a ____ **reel**

6. ____________
7. ____________
8. ____________
9. ____________
10. ____________

Training Tips On another sheet of paper, write tips for training a dog to behave well. Use Spelling Words from the list.

Name ....

Which One?

Words Often Confused Is a corner an angle or an angel? Do you hike on a trial or a trail? It is easy to confuse words that have similar spellings and pronunciations even though the meanings are different. The Spelling Words in each pair are often confused. Pay attention to their pronunciations, spellings, and meanings.

Write the missing letters in each word on the shells to make a Spelling Word that matches the definition. Then write the Spelling Words.

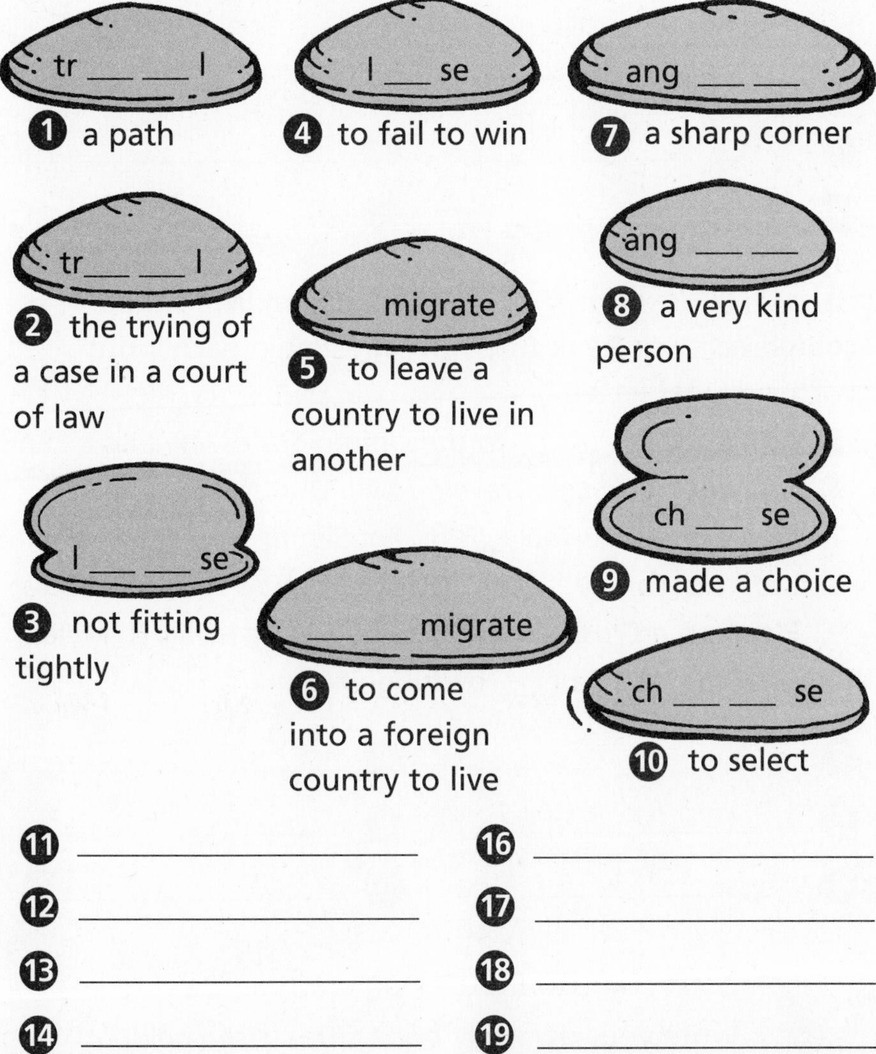

1. a path
2. the trying of a case in a court of law
3. not fitting tightly
4. to fail to win
5. to leave a country to live in another
6. to come into a foreign country to live
7. a sharp corner
8. a very kind person
9. made a choice
10. to select

11. ____________________ 16. ____________________
12. ____________________ 17. ____________________
13. ____________________ 18. ____________________
14. ____________________ 19. ____________________
15. ____________________ 20. ____________________

Words Often Confused

Some words with similar spellings are often confused. Think about their spellings, pronunciations, and meanings.

Spelling Words

1. loose
2. lose
3. choose
4. chose
5. angle
6. angel
7. trial
8. trail
9. immigrate
10. emigrate

Challenge Words

1. desert
2. dessert
3. except
4. accept

My Study List

Add your own spelling words on the back. →

Take-Home Word Lists

Name ______

My Study List

1. ______
2. ______
3. ______
4. ______
5. ______
6. ______
7. ______
8. ______
9. ______
10. ______

Additional Spelling Words

1. quit
2. quiet
3. quite
4. since
5. sense

How to Study a Word

LOOK at the word.
SAY the word.
THINK about the word.
WRITE the word.
CHECK the spelling.

Name ______

Spelling Spree

Spelling Words	
1. loose	6. angel
2. lose	7. trial
3. choose	8. trail
4. chose	9. immigrate
5. angle	10. emigrate

Proofreading Find and circle four misspelled Spelling Words in this part of a report. Then write each word correctly.

I would not chuse to meet a sawfish in the ocean. This fish's long, flat snout sticks out from its head. Set at a right angol to each edge of the snout are many razor-sharp teeth like those on a saw. Because of these teeth, a sawfish will rarely loze a battle. It swims into a school of fish, slashes its saw back and forth, and leaves a trail of stunned or dead fish behind. The sawfish is no angele.

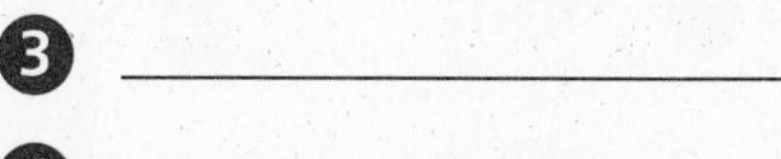

1 ______ 3 ______

2 ______ 4 ______

Silly Book Titles Write the Spelling Word that completes each book title correctly. Begin each word with a capital letter.

5. *Do You Want to ___ to the United States?* by Ellis I. Land
6. *I ___ the Road Less Traveled* by I. Duit Myway
7. *My Clothes Are Too ___!* by Jim Slimm
8. *Did Your Family ___ from Mexico?* by A. Jeannie Ologist
9. *Planning a Cross-Country Hiking ___* by Myles N. Myles
10. *How to Get a Fair ___* by Judge Ment

5 ______ 8 ______

6 ______ 9 ______

7 ______ 10 ______

Silly Book Titles On another sheet of paper, write your own silly book titles. Use Spelling Words from the list.

Name ....

Words in Lights

Words Often Mispronounced When you say ***library***, do you pronounce both ***r***'s? If not, you may have trouble spelling ***library*** correctly.

library |lī' brĕr' ē|

Look up the pronunciation of each Spelling Word in a dictionary. Are you pronouncing all of the sounds correctly?

Write the missing letters to complete the Spelling Words on the theater sign. Then write each word.

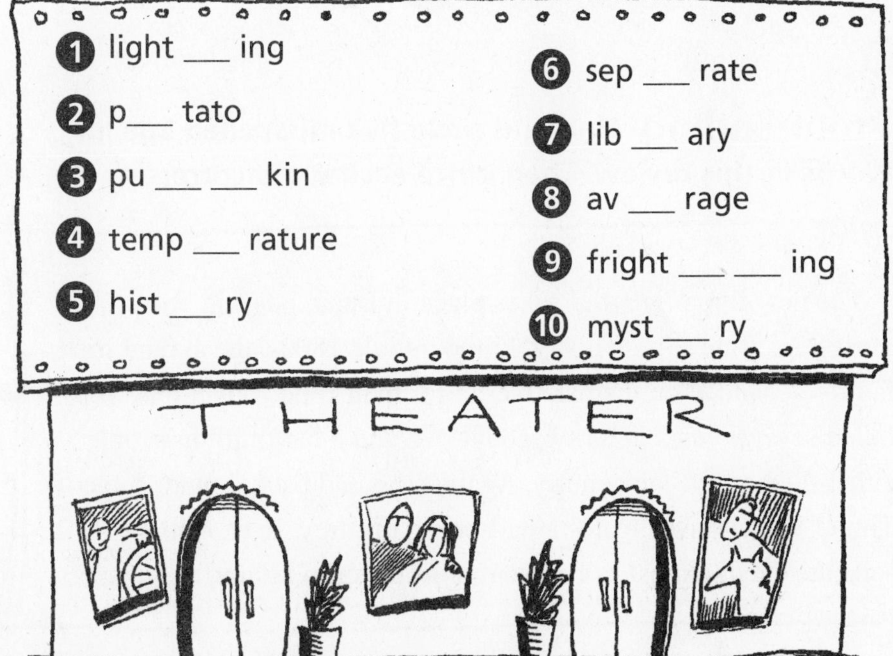

11 ____________________ 16 ____________________

12 ____________________ 17 ____________________

13 ____________________ 18 ____________________

14 ____________________ 19 ____________________

15 ____________________ 20 ____________________

Take-Home Word Lists

Words Often Mispronounced

Pronouncing words correctly will help you spell them correctly.

Spelling Words

1. library
2. lightning
3. frightening
4. pumpkin
5. mystery
6. history
7. temperature
8. separate
9. average
10. potato

Challenge Words

1. mathematics
2. veterinarian
3. restaurant
4. environment
5. prescription

My Study List

Add your own spelling words on the back. →

Name

My Study List

1. ____________________
2. ____________________
3. ____________________
4. ____________________
5. ____________________
6. ____________________
7. ____________________
8. ____________________
9. ____________________
10. ____________________

Additional Spelling Words

1. governor
2. cabinet
3. sherbet
4. victory
5. width

How to Study a Word

LOOK at the word.
SAY the word.
THINK about the word.
WRITE the word.
CHECK the spelling.

Name

Spelling Spree

Spelling Words	
1. library	6. history
2. lightning	7. temperature
3. frightening	8. separate
4. pumpkin	9. average
5. mystery	10. potato

Analogies Write the Spelling Word that completes each analogy.

1. *Comedy* is to *funny* as *horror movie* is to ____.
2. *Red* is to *tomato* as *orange* is to ____.
3. *Scale* is to *weight* as *thermometer* is to ____.
4. *Rumble* is to *thunder* as *flash* is to ____.
5. *Food* is to *supermarket* as *book* is to ____.

1 ____________________ 4 ____________________
2 ____________________ 5 ____________________
3 ____________________

Proofreading Find and circle five misspelled Spelling Words in this review. Then write each word correctly.

The new film *Shamrock* takes place in Ireland during one of the most tragic times in its histry. In the middle 1800s, the avrage Irish family depended on the patato crop for their food. When this crop failed several years in a row, about two and a half million people either died or left the country. Against this sad background, detective Tim O'Malley investigates a nail-biting mystrey. It leads to a seperate event almost as frightening as the crop failure.

6 ____________________ 9 ____________________
7 ____________________ 10 ____________________
8 ____________________

Be a Critic On another sheet of paper, create an ad for a movie. Write some "critics' opinions" about the movie. Use Spelling Words from the list.

Name

Syllable Beat

Three-Syllable Words Each Spelling Word has one stressed syllable and two syllables with less stress. To help you spell the word, divide it into syllables. Note the spelling of the syllables with less stress.

va | ca | tion |vā **kā'** shən| **av | e | nue** |**ăv'** ə nōō'|

The music shows only the stressed syllables in each Spelling Word. Write the two syllables that have less stress. Then write each word.

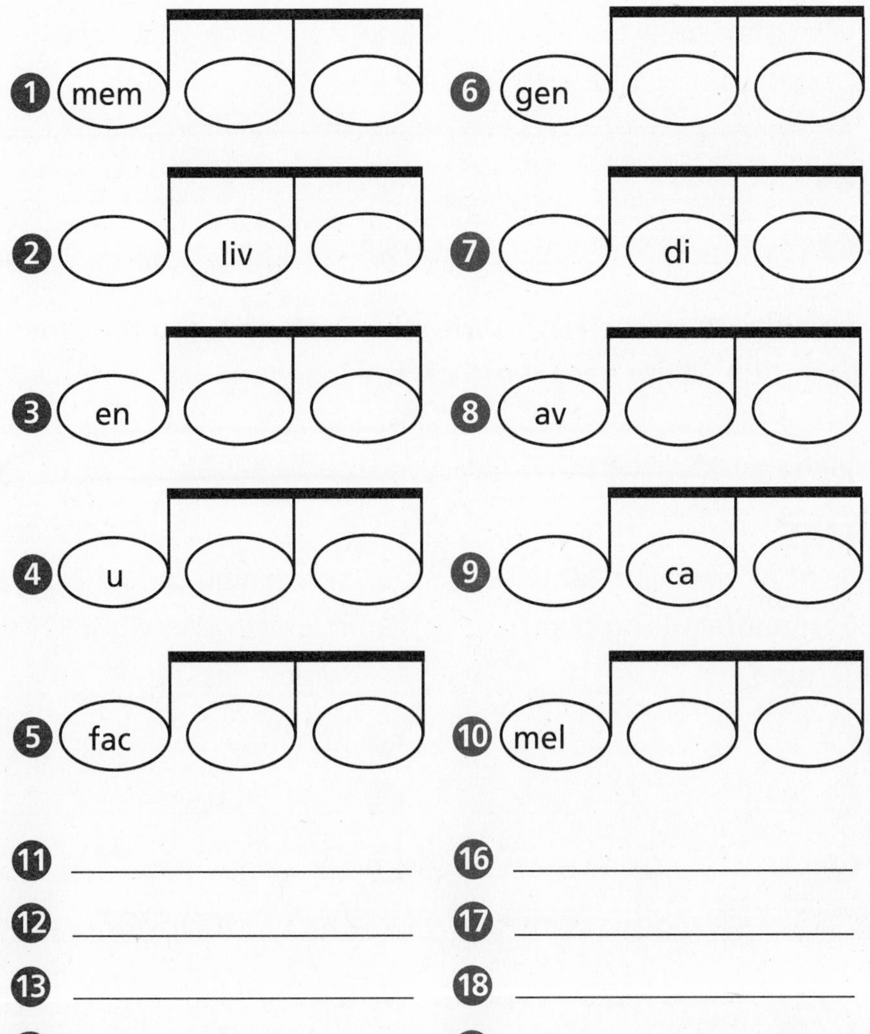

11 ______
12 ______
13 ______
14 ______
15 ______
16 ______
17 ______
18 ______
19 ______
20 ______

Take-Home Word Lists

Three-Syllable Words
Note carefully the spelling of the two syllables with less stress in three-syllable words.

Spelling Words

1. vacation
2. avenue
3. energy
4. uniform
5. general
6. condition
7. deliver
8. memory
9. melody
10. factory

Challenge Words

1. satellite
2. diagram
3. parallel
4. recipe
5. courtesy

My Study List

Add your own spelling words on the back.

Take-Home Word Lists

Name

My Study List

1.
2.
3.
4.
5.
6.
7.
8.
9.
10.

Additional Spelling Words

1. alphabet
2. educate
3. celery
4. icicle
5. citizen

How to Study a Word

LOOK at the word.
SAY the word.
THINK about the word.
WRITE the word.
CHECK the spelling.

Name

Spelling Spree

Spelling Words	
1. vacation	6. condition
2. avenue	7. deliver
3. energy	8. memory
4. uniform	9. melody
5. general	10. factory

Proofreading Find and circle four misspelled Spelling Words in this notice. Then write each word correctly.

Band Practice Tomorrow!

Band practice will be held at 4:00 P.M. tomorrow. Please be ready to play every melody we worked on before last week's vacaition. Make sure that your instrument is in good condision. Also, anyone whose unaform needs cleaning before Sunday's parade should delivver it to the bandmaster tomorrow.

1 ______ 3 ______

2 ______ 4 ______

Jukebox Jammin' Write the Spelling Word that fits each clue. Write each word on the jukebox.

5. of or involving all
6. manufacturing plant
7. tune
8. something remembered
9. strength and vigor
10. wide street

5 ______ 8 ______

6 ______ 9 ______

7 ______ 10 ______

Workers' Words Write your own song titles, using Spelling Words from the list, on another sheet of paper. Capitalize all important words.

Spelling**Relay**

How to play

Players 2 teams of 2 or more players and a caller

You need

- list of Spelling Words
- paper
- pencil

Teams of students try to spell words correctly to earn points.

1. The caller reads a word to Team 1. The first player on Team 1 says the first letter of the word, the next player says the second letter, and so on until the word is spelled. (If there are more letters in the word than players, players may have more than one turn to say a letter.)
2. If the word is spelled correctly, Team 1 gets a point. If the word is misspelled, the caller spells it aloud correctly.
3. Teams take turns trying to spell words. The player who says the last letter begins the spelling on the team's next turn. When all of the words have been spelled, the team with the most points wins.

How to play

Players 2

You need

- list of Spelling Words
- game board from page 293
- 11 game markers for each player (Use a different color for each player.)
- blank cards
- number cube, or spinner with 6 sections (See the picture below.)
- clock or watch

Getting ready

- Write each Spelling Word on a card.
- Stack the cards facedown.

Players try to win prizes by correctly spelling words that have specific letters.

1. Player 1 chooses any letter on the wheel and puts two markers on it. Then he or she throws the number cube or spins the spinner. Leaving one marker on the letter, the player moves the second marker in alphabetical order the number of letters shown on the cube or the spinner.
2. Player 2 picks a card and reads the Spelling Word aloud. If the letters between the first and the second markers include a letter in the Spelling Word, Player 1 can try to spell the word. For example, suppose the markers are on *b* and *f*. Player 1 can try to spell the word if it contains *b, c, d, e,* or *f*. If not, the player's turn is over, and the card is placed facedown at the bottom of the stack.
3. A player who spells a word correctly puts a marker on any prize that has not already been won. If a player misspells a word, the other player shows the correct spelling and then puts the card facedown at the bottom of the stack.
4. After each turn, the player takes his or her markers off the wheel. Players take turns for ten minutes or until all prizes have been won.

Variation

For an easier game, use two number cubes or a spinner numbered 1–12.

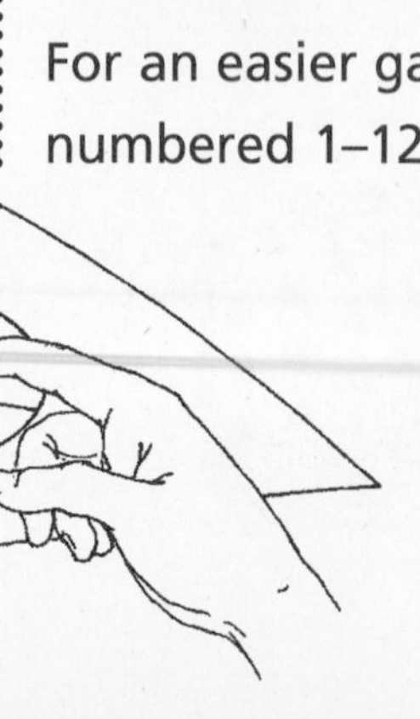

You can make a spinner, using paper, a pencil, and a paper clip.

Prize Speller

SPELLING 1-2-3-4

How to play

Players 2 or more and a caller

You need

- list of Spelling Words
- 2 pencils
- paper

Getting ready

For each player, make a game card like the one below, but leave the squares and circles blank. Each player then writes a letter in each circle on his or her card. The same letter may be used more than once but not more than three times.

HINT: Use letters that appear often in the list of Spelling Words.

Players try to write four correctly spelled words in a row by matching words with letters.

1. The caller reads a Spelling Word aloud. Players may write the word in one square that has a letter found in that word.
2. The caller continues reading words. The first player who can write four words in a row calls out "1-2-3-4!" (A row may be across, down, or from corner to corner.)
3. The caller checks the spelling of the four words. If any words in the row are spelled wrong, the player erases them and the game continues.
4. If all four words are correct, each player gets one point for each correctly spelled word, and the winner gets ten extra points.

e	r	s	o
a	e *bother*	c	s
o	s	e	r *sugar*
a	o	r	t *quarter*

Take Out the Trash

How to play

Players 2

You need

- list of Spelling Words
- paper
- pencil

A player tries to figure out another player's secret word by guessing letters.

1. Player 1 chooses a Spelling Word and tells Player 2 how many letters it has.
2. On a sheet of paper, Player 2 writes a dash for each letter of the word and draws a trash can.
3. Player 2 guesses a letter in the word. If the guess is correct, Player 1 writes the letter on each dash where it belongs. If the letter is not correct, Player 1 writes the letter in the trash can.
4. At any point, Player 2 may guess the whole word and spell it. A wrong guess or a misspelled word goes in the trash can, and Player 2 continues guessing letters.
5. Players take turns being the "guesser." For each new word, the guesser draws a new trash can. When each player has had three turns, the player with the fewest letters in the trash is the winner. (If there is a whole word in the trash, count each letter!)

The Wandering Speller

How to play

Players 2 or more

You need

- list of Spelling Words
- game board from page 297
- blank cards
- pencil
- nickel
- clock or watch

Getting ready

- Write a Spelling Word on each card.
- Stack the cards facedown.

Players spin a nickel, then follow directions on a game board to earn points.

1. Player 1 puts the nickel in the middle of the board and spins it. (See the picture and the directions below.) Player 1 then follows the directions in the space where the nickel lands.
2. If the directions tell Player 1 to spell a word or words, another player takes the correct number of cards from the stack and reads each word to Player 1. The player scores only if a word is spelled correctly. If a word is misspelled, the other player shows the correct spelling and puts that card facedown at the bottom of the stack.
3. If the nickel lands on a line but is more than halfway in one space, the player follows the directions in that space. If the nickel lands out of bounds or about equally in two or more spaces, the player spins again.
4. The player with the most points after ten minutes is the winner.

Variation

Here's a way to play without spinning the nickel. Have the player close his or her eyes. Place the nickel anywhere on the board, and put the player's finger on it. The player then slides the nickel to another position on the board and opens his or her eyes.

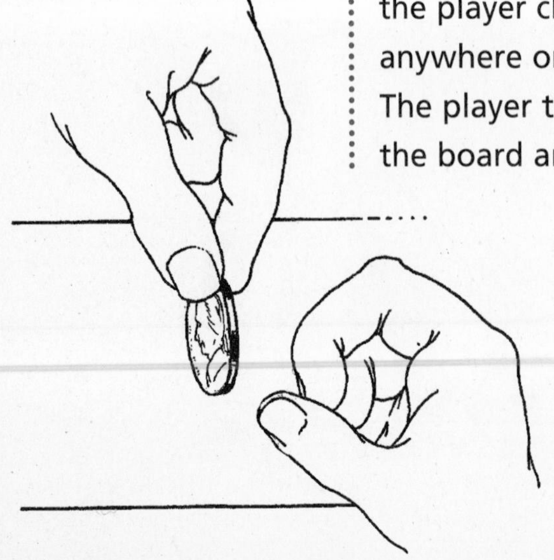

To spin the nickel, hold it with its edge on the table and flick it with another finger.

The Wandering Speller

Spell 1 word for 3 points.

Spell 2 words for 5 points.

Lose your turn to spell.

Spell 1 word, or lose all your points.

Spell 2 words for 1 point.

Spin Here

Spell 1 word for 1 point and another turn.

Spell 1 word for 1 point.

Spell 1 word for 1 point. If correct, spell another word to double your total.

Spell 1 word for 4 points, or lose your next turn.

Boardwalk

How to play

Players 2

You need

- list of Spelling Words with prefixes
- ice cream sticks or strips of sturdy paper
- pencil

Getting ready

- Use two sticks for each Spelling Word. Write the prefix on the left half of one stick. Write the rest of the word on the right half of the other stick. (See the picture below.)
- Spread the sticks facedown on a desk or a table.

Players try to build the longest "boardwalk" by matching word parts to form words.

1. Player 1 turns over two sticks, or "boards." If the word parts can form a Spelling Word from the list, Player 1 keeps them. He or she places them side by side to begin building a "boardwalk."
2. If the two boards cannot form a Spelling Word, Player 1 turns them facedown again in the same position.
3. Players take turns turning over two boards at a time. When all the boards have been taken, the player with the longest boardwalk wins.

Variations

Play the game using

★ VCCV, VCV, or VCCCV words,
★ compound words made up of two smaller words,
★ homophone pairs, or
★ words with suffixes.

un
clear
re
port

STUDENT HANDBOOK

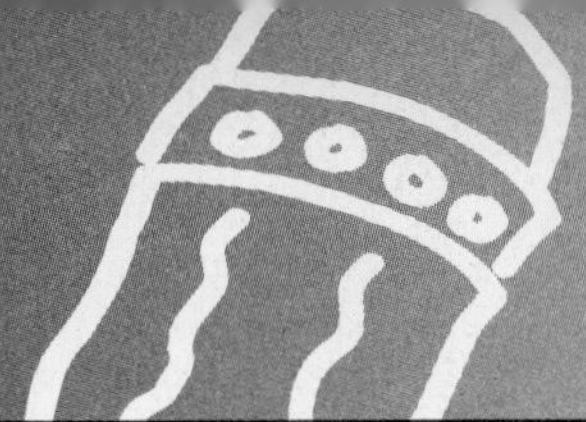

STUDENT HANDBOOK

Contents

INDEPENDENT READING LOG

Use this log to record the books or other materials you read on your own.

Date ______

Author ______

Title ______

Notes and Comments ______

______

______

______

______

Date ______

Author ______

Title ______

Notes and Comments ______

______

______

______

______

Date

Author

Title

Notes and Comments

Date

Author

Title

Notes and Comments

Date

Author

Title

Notes and Comments

Date

Author

Title

Notes and Comments

Date

Author

Title

Notes and Comments

Date

Author

Title

Notes and Comments

Date

Author

Title

Notes and Comments

Date

Author

Title

Notes and Comments

Date

Author

Title

Notes and Comments

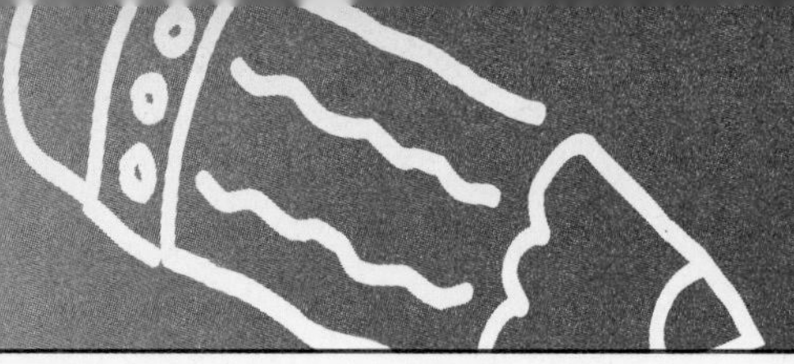

How to Study a Word

1 LOOK at the word.

- What does the word mean?
- What letters are in the word?
- Name and touch each letter.

2 SAY the word.

- Listen for the consonant sounds.
- Listen for the vowel sounds.

3 THINK about the word.

- How is each sound spelled?
- Close your eyes and picture the word.
- What familiar spelling patterns do you see?
- Do you see any prefixes, suffixes, or other word parts?

4 WRITE the word.

- Think about the sounds and the letters.
- Form the letters correctly.

5 CHECK the spelling.

- Did you spell the word the same way it is spelled in your word list?
- If you did not spell the word correctly, write the word again.

WORDS OFTEN MISSPELLED

accumulate
affectionate
again
all right
a lot
also
always
another
antique
anyone
anything
anyway
audible

beautiful
because
before
believe
benefited
brilliance
brought
build
buy

camouflage
cannot
can't
caught
clothes
coming
confidence

correspond
cousin

decent
didn't
different
divide
don't

eighth
embarrass
enough
every
everybody
everyone
everything
excellence
excite

family
fatigue
favorite
field
finally
first
friend

getting
going
guess

happened
happily
haven't
heard
height
here

I'd
I'll
instead
irresponsible
its
it's

knew
know

laboratory
lying

menace
might
millimeter
minute
morning

ninety

o'clock
once
opposite

pennant
people
pretty
probably

questionnaire

really
received
recommend
regretted
reversible
right

Saturday
scenery
school
someone
sometimes
stationary
stationery
stopped
stretch
suppose
swimming

that's
their
there
there's
they

they're
thought
through
to
tongue
tonight
too
tried
truly
two

until
usually

weird
we're
while
whole
would
wouldn't
write
writing

your
you're

Journey to Adventure!: Reading-Writing Workshop

Look for familiar spelling patterns in these words to help you remember their spellings.

Spelling Words

1. a lot
2. because
3. school
4. its
5. it's
6. tonight
7. might
8. right
9. write
10. again

Challenge Words

1. opposite
2. pennant
3. questionnaire
4. excellence
5. scenery

My Study List

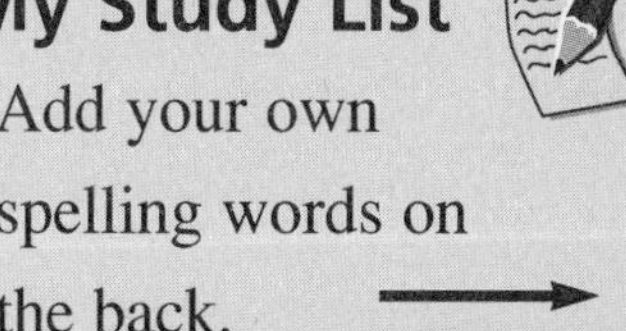

Add your own spelling words on the back. →

Arctic Explorer: The Story of Matthew Henson

Spelling Long *i* and Long *o*

|ī| → drive, sight

|ō| → froze, goal, snow

Spelling Words

1. snow
2. goal
3. froze
4. sight
5. drive
6. wrote
7. load
8. midnight
9. prize
10. narrow

Challenge Words

1. highway
2. dynamite
3. realize
4. twilight
5. cocoa

My Study List

Add your own spelling words on the back. →

James and the Giant Peach

Spelling Long *a* and Long *e*

|ā| → wake, bait, sway

|ē| → peach, between

Spelling Words

1. peach
2. bait
3. beast
4. between
5. afraid
6. wake
7. sway
8. scale
9. speed
10. stray

Challenge Words

1. seagull
2. explain
3. appeal
4. dismay
5. succeed

My Study List

Add your own spelling words on the back. →

Name ____________________

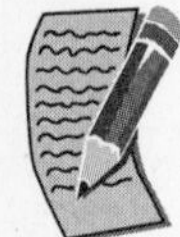

My Study List

1. ____________________
2. ____________________
3. ____________________
4. ____________________
5. ____________________
6. ____________________
7. ____________________
8. ____________________
9. ____________________
10. ____________________

Additional Spelling Words

1. brain
2. greet
3. gray
4. leash
5. crease

How to Study a Word

LOOK at the word.
SAY the word.
THINK about the word.
WRITE the word.
CHECK the spelling.

Name ____________________

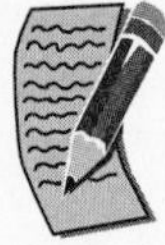

My Study List

1. ____________________
2. ____________________
3. ____________________
4. ____________________
5. ____________________
6. ____________________
7. ____________________
8. ____________________
9. ____________________
10. ____________________

Additional Spelling Words

1. borrow
2. stroke
3. shallow
4. slight
5. boast

How to Study a Word

LOOK at the word.
SAY the word.
THINK about the word.
WRITE the word.
CHECK the spelling.

Name ____________________

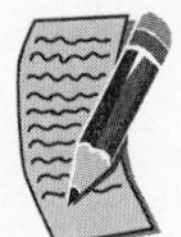

My Study List

1. ____________________
2. ____________________
3. ____________________
4. ____________________
5. ____________________
6. ____________________
7. ____________________
8. ____________________
9. ____________________
10. ____________________

Additional Spelling Words

1. to
2. too
3. two
4. they
5. that's

How to Study a Word

LOOK at the word.
SAY the word.
THINK about the word.
WRITE the word.
CHECK the spelling.

Take-Home Word Lists

Wolves

Vowel + *r* Sounds

|âr| → bare, hair

|är| → sharp

Spelling Words

1. sharp
2. bark
3. hair
4. bare
5. startle
6. pair
7. care
8. share
9. apart
10. stare

Challenge Words

1. marvelous
2. arctic
3. scarce
4. argument
5. hierarchy

My Study List

Add your own spelling words on the back. →

Take-Home Word Lists

Journey to Adventure!: Spelling Review

Spelling Words

1. clue
2. beast
3. drive
4. load
5. scale
6. route
7. afraid
8. rude
9. sight
10. between
11. narrow
12. smooth
13. wrote
14. stray
15. bruise
16. because
17. its
18. a lot
19. it's
20. again

See the back for **Challenge Words**.

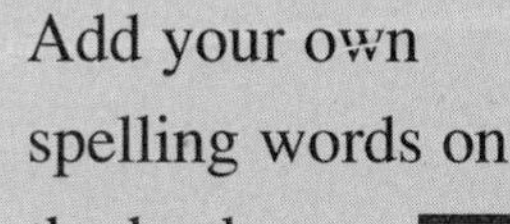

My Study List

Add your own spelling words on the back. →

Take-Home Word Lists

Voyager: An Adventure to the Edge of the Solar System

Spelling long *u*

|yo͞o| or |o͞o| → huge, blue, smooth, juice, group

Spelling Words

1. huge
2. blue
3. smooth
4. clue
5. ooze
6. group
7. juice
8. route
9. rude
10. bruise

Challenge Words

1. continue
2. through
3. include
4. pursue
5. attitude

My Study List

Add your own spelling words on the back. →

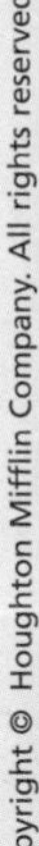

Name ____________

My Study List

1. ____________
2. ____________
3. ____________
4. ____________
5. ____________
6. ____________
7. ____________
8. ____________
9. ____________
10. ____________

Additional Spelling Words

1. bloom
2. flute
3. proof
4. youth
5. cruise

How to Study a Word

LOOK at the word.
SAY the word.
THINK about the word.
WRITE the word.
CHECK the spelling.

Name ____________

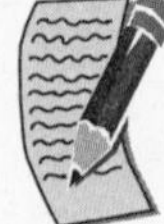

My Study List

1. ____________
2. ____________
3. ____________
4. ____________
5. ____________
6. ____________
7. ____________
8. ____________
9. ____________
10. ____________

Challenge Words

1. explain
2. through
3. continue
4. attitude
5. realize
6. opposite
7. scenery
8. highway
9. succeed
10. questionnaire

How to Study a Word

LOOK at the word.
SAY the word.
THINK about the word.
WRITE the word.
CHECK the spelling.

Name ____________

My Study List

1. ____________
2. ____________
3. ____________
4. ____________
5. ____________
6. ____________
7. ____________
8. ____________
9. ____________
10. ____________

Additional Spelling Words

1. harsh
2. spare
3. carve
4. flair
5. flare

How to Study a Word

LOOK at the word.
SAY the word.
THINK about the word.
WRITE the word.
CHECK the spelling.

Adiós falcón/Good-bye, Falcon

The Vowel + *r* Sounds in *bird*

/ûr/ → perch, bird, return, learn, world

Spelling Words

1. bird
2. perch
3. return
4. learn
5. hurt
6. world
7. prefer
8. firm
9. worth
10. early

Challenge Words

1. perfume
2. murmur
3. emergency
4. interpret
5. universe

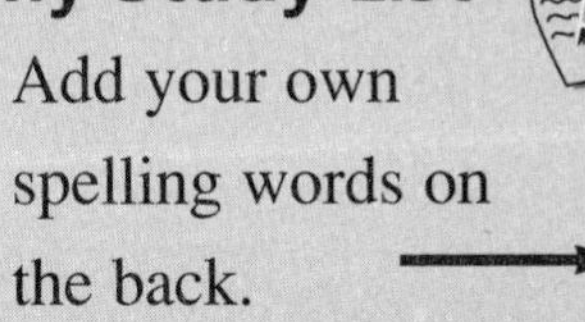

My Study List

Add your own spelling words on the back. →

Take-Home Word Lists

In the Wild: Reading-Writing Workshop

Look for familiar spelling patterns in these words to help you remember their spellings.

Spelling Words

1. heard
2. your
3. you're
4. field
5. buy
6. friend
7. guess
8. cousin
9. build
10. family

Challenge Words

1. truly
2. benefited
3. height
4. believe
5. received

My Study List

Add your own spelling words on the back. →

Take-Home Word Lists

The Midnight Fox

More Vowel + *r* Sounds

/ôr/ → porch, before, roar

/îr/ → peer, fear

Spelling Words

1. fear
2. before
3. porch
4. force
5. clear
6. corner
7. roar
8. peer
9. soar
10. steer

Challenge Words

1. orchard
2. forward
3. ordeal
4. disappear
5. volunteer

My Study List

Add your own spelling words on the back. →

Name ______________________

My Study List

1. ______________________
2. ______________________
3. ______________________
4. ______________________
5. ______________________
6. ______________________
7. ______________________
8. ______________________
9. ______________________
10. ______________________

Additional Spelling Words

1. tore
2. board
3. smear
4. scorn
5. sheer

How to Study a Word

LOOK at the word.
SAY the word.
THINK about the word.
WRITE the word.
CHECK the spelling.

Take-Home Word Lists

Name ______________________

My Study List

1. ______________________
2. ______________________
3. ______________________
4. ______________________
5. ______________________
6. ______________________
7. ______________________
8. ______________________
9. ______________________
10. ______________________

Additional Spelling Words

1. can't
2. cannot
3. didn't
4. haven't
5. don't

How to Study a Word

LOOK at the word.
SAY the word.
THINK about the word.
WRITE the word.
CHECK the spelling.

Take-Home Word Lists

Name ______________________

My Study List

1. ______________________
2. ______________________
3. ______________________
4. ______________________
5. ______________________
6. ______________________
7. ______________________
8. ______________________
9. ______________________
10. ______________________

Additional Spelling Words

1. germ
2. whirl
3. search
4. worst
5. blur

How to Study a Word

LOOK at the word.
SAY the word.
THINK about the word.
WRITE the word.
CHECK the spelling.

Try to See It My Way: Reading-Writing Workshop

Look for familiar spelling patterns in these words to help you remember their spellings.

Spelling Words

1. enough
2. caught
3. brought
4. thought
5. every
6. ninety
7. their
8. they're
9. there
10. there's

Challenge Words

1. decent
2. stationery
3. stationary
4. correspond
5. reversible

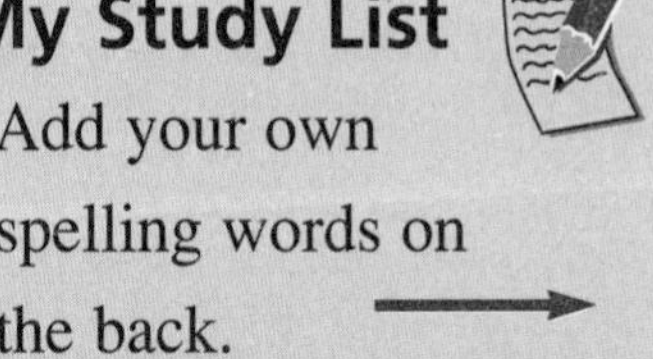

My Study List
Add your own spelling words on the back. →

In the Year of the Boar and Jackie Robinson

The Vowel Sounds in *shout* and *wall*

/ou/ → sh**ou**t, all**ow**

/ô/ → d**aw**n, f**au**lt, w**a**ll

Spelling Words

1. shout
2. wall
3. allow
4. counter
5. although
6. fault
7. frown
8. pause
9. dawn
10. straw

Challenge Words

1. announce
2. throughout
3. eyebrows
4. awkward
5. autumn

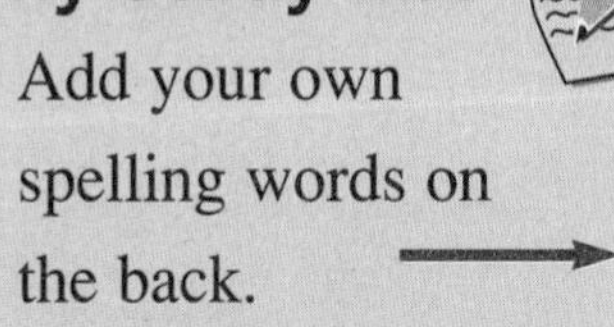

My Study List
Add your own spelling words on the back. →

In the Wild: Spelling Review

Spelling Words

1. corner
2. worth
3. hair
4. early
5. clear
6. roar
7. startle
8. firm
9. peer
10. return
11. sharp
12. care
13. before
14. perch
15. heard
16. guess
17. pair
18. family
19. you're
20. friend

See the back for **Challenge Words.**

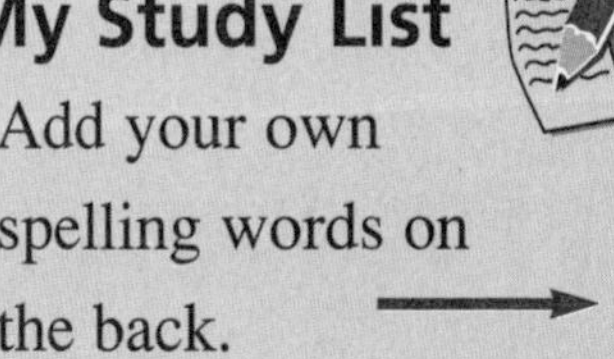

My Study List
Add your own spelling words on the back. →

Name ______________________

My Study List

1. ______________________
2. ______________________
3. ______________________
4. ______________________
5. ______________________
6. ______________________
7. ______________________
8. ______________________
9. ______________________
10. ______________________

Challenge Words

1. marvelous
2. disappear
3. perfume
4. volunteer
5. scarce
6. received
7. argument
8. truly
9. emergency
10. believe

How to Study a Word

LOOK at the word.
SAY the word.
THINK about the word.
WRITE the word.
CHECK the spelling.

Take-Home Word Lists

Name ______________________

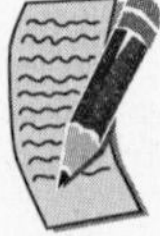

My Study List

1. ______________________
2. ______________________
3. ______________________
4. ______________________
5. ______________________
6. ______________________
7. ______________________
8. ______________________
9. ______________________
10. ______________________

Additional Spelling Words

1. coward
2. thousand
3. crawl
4. stalk
5. prowl

How to Study a Word

LOOK at the word.
SAY the word.
THINK about the word.
WRITE the word.
CHECK the spelling.

Take-Home Word Lists

Name ______________________

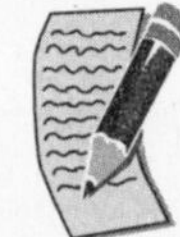

My Study List

1. ______________________
2. ______________________
3. ______________________
4. ______________________
5. ______________________
6. ______________________
7. ______________________
8. ______________________
9. ______________________
10. ______________________

Additional Spelling Words

1. know
2. knew
3. o'clock
4. we're
5. people

How to Study a Word

LOOK at the word.
SAY the word.
THINK about the word.
WRITE the word.
CHECK the spelling.

Take-Home Word Lists

Felita

Homophones

Homophones are words that sound alike but have different spellings and meanings.

Spelling Words

1. seen
2. scene
3. wear
4. where
5. bow
6. bough
7. great
8. grate
9. fair
10. fare

Challenge Words

1. raise
2. rays
3. raze
4. principal
5. principle

My Study List

Add your own spelling words on the back. →

Take-Home Word Lists

Me, Mop, and the Moondance Kid

Final Schwa + *l* Sounds

/əl/ or /l/ → eag**le**, lev**el**, speci**al**

Spelling Words

1. eagle
2. example
3. special
4. double
5. single
6. signal
7. level
8. normal
9. towel
10. model

Challenge Words

1. national
2. actual
3. duffel
4. cancel
5. natural

My Study List

Add your own spelling words on the back. →

Take-Home Word Lists

Like Jake and Me

Final Schwa + *r* Sounds

/ər/ → spid**er**, col**or**, coll**ar**

Spelling Words

1. spider
2. silver
3. color
4. feather
5. bother
6. collar
7. cover
8. quarter
9. flavor
10. sugar

Challenge Words

1. shudder
2. swagger
3. poplar
4. nectar
5. regular

My Study List

Add your own spelling words on the back. →

Take-Home Word Lists

Name ____________________

My Study List

1. ____________________
2. ____________________
3. ____________________
4. ____________________
5. ____________________
6. ____________________
7. ____________________
8. ____________________
9. ____________________
10. ____________________

Additional Spelling Words

1. humor
2. matter
3. anger
4. solar
5. tractor

How to Study a Word

LOOK at the word.
SAY the word.
THINK about the word.
WRITE the word.
CHECK the spelling.

Take-Home Word Lists

Name ____________________

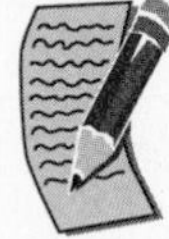

My Study List

1. ____________________
2. ____________________
3. ____________________
4. ____________________
5. ____________________
6. ____________________
7. ____________________
8. ____________________
9. ____________________
10. ____________________

Additional Spelling Words

1. fuel
2. ankle
3. squirrel
4. spiral
5. rebel

How to Study a Word

LOOK at the word.
SAY the word.
THINK about the word.
WRITE the word.
CHECK the spelling.

Take-Home Word Lists

Name ____________________

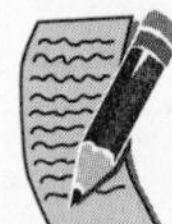

My Study List

1. ____________________
2. ____________________
3. ____________________
4. ____________________
5. ____________________
6. ____________________
7. ____________________
8. ____________________
9. ____________________
10. ____________________

Additional Spelling Words

1. coarse
2. course
3. berry
4. bury

How to Study a Word

LOOK at the word.
SAY the word.
THINK about the word.
WRITE the word.
CHECK the spelling.

Earthquakes

The VCCV and VCV Patterns

VC|CV → suf|fer
sur|face
V|CV → to|tal
VC|V → dam|age

Spelling Words

1. damage
2. surface
3. entire
4. solid
5. total
6. object
7. notice
8. suffer
9. modern
10. mirror

Challenge Words

1. tremor
2. collapse
3. occur
4. intense
5. focus

My Study List
Add your own spelling words on the back. →

Night of the Twisters

Compound Words

Compound words can be written as one word, as a hyphenated word, or as separate words.

Spelling Words

1. hallway
2. upstairs
3. flashlight
4. everything
5. driveway
6. built-in
7. first aid
8. baby-sit
9. already
10. all right

Challenge Words

1. heartbeat
2. weather station
3. freight train
4. civil defense
5. handkerchief

My Study List
Add your own spelling words on the back. →

Try to See It My Way: Spelling Review

Spelling Words

1. flavor
2. signal
3. straw
4. feather
5. example
6. grate
7. shout
8. wall
9. sugar
10. frown
11. level
12. bother
13. great
14. fault
15. every
16. spider
17. scene
18. there's
19. allow
20. thought
21. seen
22. their
23. although
24. special
25. they're

See the back for **Challenge Words**.

My Study List
Add your own spelling words on the back. →

Name ____________________

My Study List

1. ____________________
2. ____________________
3. ____________________
4. ____________________
5. ____________________
6. ____________________
7. ____________________
8. ____________________
9. ____________________
10. ____________________

Challenge Words

1. announce
2. throughout
3. national
4. shudder
5. principal
6. stationary
7. cancel
8. duffel
9. correspond
10. awkward
11. swagger
12. reversible
13. raise

How to Study a Word

LOOK at the word.
SAY the word.
THINK about the word.
WRITE the word.
CHECK the spelling.

Take-Home Word Lists

Name ____________________

My Study List

1. ____________________
2. ____________________
3. ____________________
4. ____________________
5. ____________________
6. ____________________
7. ____________________
8. ____________________
9. ____________________
10. ____________________

Additional Spelling Words

1. good-natured
2. homemade
3. eyewitness
4. salesperson
5. newscast

How to Study a Word

LOOK at the word.
SAY the word.
THINK about the word.
WRITE the word.
CHECK the spelling.

318

Take-Home Word Lists

Name ____________________

My Study List

1. ____________________
2. ____________________
3. ____________________
4. ____________________
5. ____________________
6. ____________________
7. ____________________
8. ____________________
9. ____________________
10. ____________________

Additional Spelling Words

1. pattern
2. bargain
3. repeat
4. million
5. evil

How to Study a Word

LOOK at the word.
SAY the word.
THINK about the word.
WRITE the word.
CHECK the spelling.

318

Catastrophe!: Spelling Review

Spelling Words

1. struggle
2. everything
3. modern
4. hallway
5. control
6. baby-sit
7. suffer
8. notice
9. all right
10. sandwich
11. instant
12. while
13. everybody
14. already
15. once
16. solid
17. favorite
18. damage
19. farther
20. whole

See the back for **Challenge Words.**

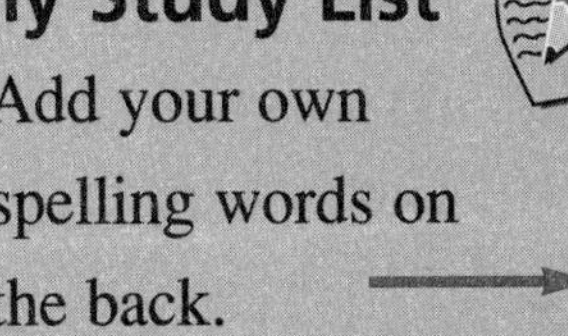

My Study List

Add your own spelling words on the back. →

Take-Home Word Lists

The Story of the Challenger *Disaster*

The VCCCV Pattern

VC|CCV → far|ther
VC|CCV → ex|plode
VCC|CV → sand|wich

Spelling Words

1. explode
2. instant
3. control
4. explore
5. address
6. struggle
7. express
8. empty
9. farther
10. sandwich

Challenge Words

1. shuttle
2. approach
3. throttle
4. exclaim
5. congress

My Study List

Add your own spelling words on the back. →

Take-Home Word Lists

Catastrophe!: Reading-Writing Workshop

Look for familiar spelling patterns in these words to help you remember their spellings.

Spelling Words

1. while
2. whole
3. anyway
4. anyone
5. anything
6. favorite
7. once
8. suppose
9. everybody
10. everyone

Challenge Words

1. embarrass
2. recommend
3. confidence
4. regretted
5. laboratory

My Study List

Add your own spelling words on the back. →

Name ______________________

My Study List

1. ______
2. ______
3. ______
4. ______
5. ______
6. ______
7. ______
8. ______
9. ______
10. ______

Additional Spelling Words

1. really
2. morning
3. also
4. always
5. first

How to Study a Word

LOOK at the word.
SAY the word.
THINK about the word.
WRITE the word.
CHECK the spelling.

Name ______________________

My Study List

1. ______
2. ______
3. ______
4. ______
5. ______
6. ______
7. ______
8. ______
9. ______
10. ______

Additional Spelling Words

1. transport
2. monster
3. orphan
4. partner
5. complex

How to Study a Word

LOOK at the word.
SAY the word.
THINK about the word.
WRITE the word.
CHECK the spelling.

Name ______________________

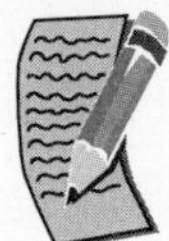

My Study List

1. ______
2. ______
3. ______
4. ______
5. ______
6. ______
7. ______
8. ______
9. ______
10. ______

Challenge Words

1. regretted
2. handkerchief
3. approach
4. tremor
5. heartbeat
6. recommend
7. collapse
8. exclaim
9. embarrass
10. focus

How to Study a Word

LOOK at the word.
SAY the word.
THINK about the word.
WRITE the word.
CHECK the spelling.

La Bamba

The Prefixes *in-* and *con-*

in- → inhale
im- → immediate
con- → confuse
com- → compete

Spelling Words

1. impress
2. confuse
3. conduct
4. inhale
5. intent
6. command
7. immediate
8. compete
9. impolite
10. connect

Challenge Words

1. confident
2. commotion
3. instrument
4. conversation
5. immigrant

My Study List
Add your own spelling words on the back. →

From the Prairie to the Sea: Spelling Review

Spelling Words

1. possession
2. slipping
3. enemies
4. healing
5. narrate
6. staring
7. possess
8. friendliness
9. narration
10. offered
11. scattered
12. nastiest
13. weird
14. creation
15. happened
16. another
17. hurried
18. would
19. departed
20. sometimes

See the back for **Challenge Words.**

My Study List
Add your own spelling words on the back. →

Pecos Bill

Adding *-ion*

act → action
create → creation

Spelling Words

1. act
2. action
3. create
4. creation
5. direct
6. direction
7. possess
8. possession
9. narrate
10. narration

Challenge Words

1. progress
2. progression
3. adopt
4. adoption

My Study List
Add your own spelling words on the back. →

Take-Home Word Lists

Name ____________________

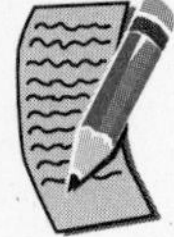

My Study List

1. ____________________
2. ____________________
3. ____________________
4. ____________________
5. ____________________
6. ____________________
7. ____________________
8. ____________________
9. ____________________
10. ____________________

Additional Spelling Words

1. correct
2. correction
3. pollute
4. pollution

How to Study a Word

LOOK at the word.
SAY the word.
THINK about the word.
WRITE the word.
CHECK the spelling.

Take-Home Word Lists

Name ____________________

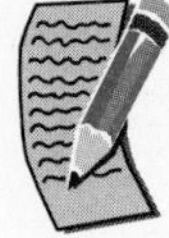

My Study List

1. ____________________
2. ____________________
3. ____________________
4. ____________________
5. ____________________
6. ____________________
7. ____________________
8. ____________________
9. ____________________
10. ____________________

Challenge Words

1. dignified
2. territories
3. satisfied
4. progress
5. drenching
6. adoption
7. irresponsible
8. altered
9. clutching
10. affectionate

How to Study a Word

LOOK at the word.
SAY the word.
THINK about the word.
WRITE the word.
CHECK the spelling.

Take-Home Word Lists

Name ____________________

My Study List

1. ____________________
2. ____________________
3. ____________________
4. ____________________
5. ____________________
6. ____________________
7. ____________________
8. ____________________
9. ____________________
10. ____________________

Additional Spelling Words

1. compose
2. improve
3. instruct
4. conform
5. immovable

How to Study a Word

LOOK at the word.
SAY the word.
THINK about the word.
WRITE the word.
CHECK the spelling.

Do You Believe This??: *Reading-Writing Workshop*

Look for familiar spelling patterns in these words to help you remember their spellings.

Spelling Words

1. happily
2. minute
3. beautiful
4. usually
5. instead
6. stretch
7. lying
8. excite
9. millimeter
10. divide

Challenge Words

1. fatigue
2. antique
3. accumulate
4. camouflage
5. tongue

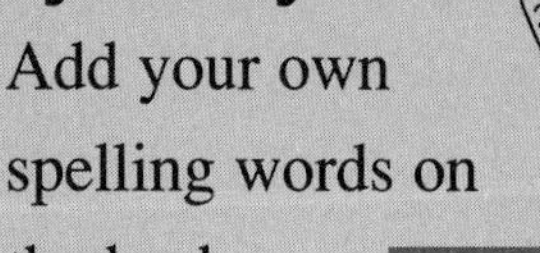

My Study List
Add your own spelling words on the back. →

Take-Home Word Lists

McBroom Tells the Truth

Words with Suffixes

-ly	→	exactly
-ful	→	wonderful
-ness	→	kindness
-less	→	countless
-ment	→	excitement

Spelling Words

1. wonderful
2. countless
3. excitement
4. exactly
5. kindness
6. sleepless
7. mouthful
8. brightness
9. finally
10. government

Challenge Words

1. positively
2. disappointment
3. gentleness
4. occasionally
5. anxiously

My Study List
Add your own spelling words on the back. →

Take-Home Word Lists

Willie Bea and the Time the Martians Landed

The Prefixes *un-*, *re-*, and *dis-*

un-	→	unclear
re-	→	remove
dis-	→	distant

Spelling Words

1. unclear
2. distant
3. untrue
4. discomfort
5. remove
6. untangle
7. unsure
8. remind
9. disagree
10. report

Challenge Words

1. unfortunate
2. disbelief
3. unnecessary
4. uneasily
5. disenchantment

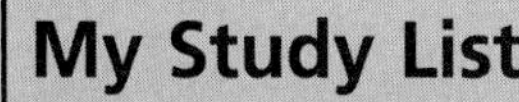

My Study List
Add your own spelling words on the back. →

Name ____________

My Study List

1. ____________
2. ____________
3. ____________
4. ____________
5. ____________
6. ____________
7. ____________
8. ____________
9. ____________
10. ____________

Additional Spelling Words

1. unable
2. refund
3. unfamiliar
4. disaster
5. rejoice

How to Study a Word

LOOK at the word.
SAY the word.
THINK about the word.
WRITE the word.
CHECK the spelling.

Name ____________

My Study List

1. ____________
2. ____________
3. ____________
4. ____________
5. ____________
6. ____________
7. ____________
8. ____________
9. ____________
10. ____________

Additional Spelling Words

1. breathless
2. paleness
3. forgetful
4. enjoyment
5. suddenly

How to Study a Word

LOOK at the word.
SAY the word.
THINK about the word.
WRITE the word.
CHECK the spelling.

Name ____________

My Study List

1. ____________
2. ____________
3. ____________
4. ____________
5. ____________
6. ____________
7. ____________
8. ____________
9. ____________
10. ____________

Additional Spelling Words

1. until
2. writing
3. tried
4. before
5. Saturday

How to Study a Word

LOOK at the word.
SAY the word.
THINK about the word.
WRITE the word.
CHECK the spelling.

Take-Home Word Lists

Do You Believe This??: *Spelling Review*

Spelling Words

1. report
2. government
3. impolite
4. permit
5. compete
6. brightness
7. propose
8. untangle
9. inhale
10. mouthful
11. prefix
12. sleepless
13. conduct
14. disagree
15. finally
16. project
17. lying
18. instead
19. distant
20. immediate
21. excitement
22. happily
23. divide
24. connect
25. beautiful

See the back for **Challenge Words.**

My Study List
Add your own spelling words on the back. →

Take-Home Word Lists

Trapped in Tar: Fossils from the Ice Age

The Prefixes *pre-*, *per-*, and *pro-*

pre- → **pre**serve
per- → **per**fect
pro- → **pro**tect

Spelling Words

1. preserve
2. protect
3. project
4. present
5. prevent
6. perfect
7. propose
8. permit
9. prefix
10. pronoun

Challenge Words

1. precise
2. procedure
3. persuade
4. prohibit
5. perspective

My Study List
Add your own spelling words on the back. →

Take-Home Word Lists

Name ____________________

My Study List

1. ____________________
2. ____________________
3. ____________________
4. ____________________
5. ____________________
6. ____________________
7. ____________________
8. ____________________
9. ____________________
10. ____________________

Additional Spelling Words

1. perhaps
2. produce
3. prospect
4. profile
5. pretend

How to Study a Word

LOOK at the word.
SAY the word.
THINK about the word.
WRITE the word.
CHECK the spelling.

Take-Home Word Lists

Name ____________________

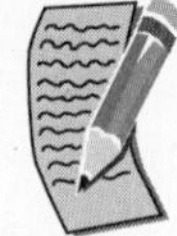

My Study List

1. ____________________
2. ____________________
3. ____________________
4. ____________________
5. ____________________
6. ____________________
7. ____________________
8. ____________________
9. ____________________
10. ____________________

Challenge Words

1. occasionally
2. confident
3. unnecessary
4. tongue
5. accumulate
6. persuade
7. procedure
8. unfortunate
9. gentleness
10. uneasily
11. antique
12. immigrant
13. disappointment

How to Study a Word

LOOK at the word.
SAY the word.
THINK about the word.
WRITE the word.
CHECK the spelling.

328

SPELLING GUIDELINES

Short Vowel Patterns

1. A short vowel sound is usually spelled *a, e, i, o,* or *u* and is followed by a consonant sound.	ask next mix	lock shut
2. The short *e* sound can be spelled with the pattern *ea.*	meant	
3. The short *u* sound can be spelled with the pattern *ou* or *o.*	touch	nothing

Long Vowel Sounds

4. The long *a* sound can be spelled with the pattern *a*-consonant-*e, ai, ay*, or *ea.*	wake bait	sway great
5. The long *e* sound is often spelled with the pattern *e*-consonant-*e*, *ea,* or *ee.*	these peach	speed
6. The long *e* sound at the end of a word may be spelled *y.*	penny	funny
7. The long *i* sound can be spelled with the pattern *i*-consonant-*e, igh,* or *ie.*	drive sight	tie
8. The long *i* sound at the end of a word may be spelled *y.*	cry	reply
9. The long *o* sound can be spelled with the pattern *o*-consonant-*e*, *oa,* or *ow.*	froze goal	snow
10. The long *u* sound |yōō| or |ōō| may be spelled with the pattern *u*-consonant-*e, ew, ue, oo, ou,* or *ui.*	huge grew blue	ooze group juice

Other Vowel Sounds

11. The sound |ou| is often spelled with the pattern *ow* or *ou.*	frown	counter
12. The sound |oi| is spelled with the pattern *oi* or *oy.*	noise	enjoy

Other Vowel Sounds (continued)

Guideline	Examples	
13. The vowel sound in *walk* can be spelled with the pattern *a* before *l, aw, au, ough,* or *augh.*	**al**though d**aw**n p**au**se	th**ough**t c**augh**t
14. The vowel sound in *cook* may be spelled with the pattern *oo* or *u.*	w**oo**ds	p**u**ll

Vowel + *r* Sounds

Guideline	Examples	
15. The vowel + **r** sounds you hear in *sharp* can be spelled with the pattern *ar.*	st**ar**tle	
16. The vowel + **r** sounds you hear in *hair* can be spelled with the pattern *are* or *air.*	sh**are**	p**air**
17. The vowel + **r** sounds you hear in *peer* can be spelled with the pattern *ear* or *eer.*	f**ear**	st**eer**
18. The vowel + **r** sounds you hear in *roar* can be spelled with the patterns *or, ore,* and *oar.*	p**or**ch bef**ore**	s**oar**
19. The vowel + *r* sounds you hear in *perch* can be spelled with the pattern *er, ir, ur, ear,* or *or.*	pref**er** b**ir**d ret**ur**n	l**ear**n w**or**ld

Consonant Sounds

Guideline	Examples	
20. The |s| sound you hear in *city* may be spelled *c* when the *c* is followed by *i* or *e*. The |s| sound at the end of a word is often spelled with the pattern *ce*.	**c**ity **c**ircle	on**ce** sli**ce**
21. The |j| sound you hear in *just* can be spelled with the consonant *j,* the pattern *dge,* or with the consonant *g* followed by *e*.	**j**ust **j**am e**dge**	lar**ge** a**ge**

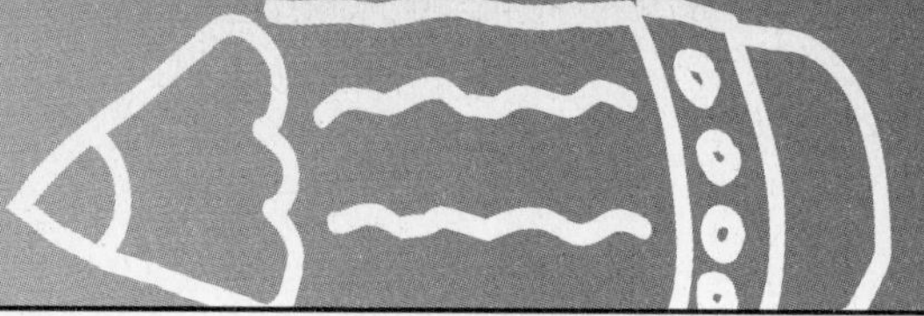

Syllable Patterns

22. The schwa + *r* sounds that you hear in *spider* are often spelled with the pattern *er, or,* or *ar.*

feath**er** coll**ar** flav**or**

23. The schwa + *l* sounds that you hear in *double* can be spelled with the pattern *al, il, le,* or *el.*

sign**al** eag**le** gerb**il** tow**el**

24. Some two-syllable words have the vowel-consonant-vowel pattern (VCV), and begin with the short vowel pattern. Divide a word with this pattern after the consonant to find the syllables. Look for spelling patterns you have learned. Spell the word by syllables.

dam | age
sol | id

25. Some two-syllable words have the vowel-consonant-vowel pattern (VCV), and the first syllable ends with a vowel sound. Divide a word with this pattern before the consonant to find the syllables. Look for spelling patterns you have learned. Spell the word by syllables.

to | tal
no | tice

26. Some two-syllable words have the vowel-consonant-consonant-vowel pattern (VCCV). Divide a word with this pattern between the two consonants to find the syllables. Look for spelling patterns you have learned. Spell the word by syllables.

sur | face
mir | ror

27. Some two-syllable words have the vowel-consonant-consonant-consonant-vowel (VCCCV) pattern. In these words, when two different consonants spell one sound, as in *farther*, or form a cluster, as in *control*, divide these words into syllables before or after those two consonants. Look for spelling patterns you have learned. Spell the word by syllables.

VC|CCV	VCC|CV
in | stant	sand | wich
ex | plore	emp | ty

SPELLING GUIDELINES

Word Endings

28. If a base word ends with *e*, drop the *e* before adding the ending *-ed* or *-ing*.

decide-decid**ed**
stare-star**ing**

29. If a base word ends with a vowel and a single consonant, double the consonant before adding *-ed* or *-ing*.

knit-knit**ted**
sli**p**-slip**ping**

30. If a base word ends with a double consonant, don't change the spelling of the base word when adding *-ed* or *-ing*.

fo**ld**-fold**ed**
ru**sh**-rush**ed**

31. When *-ed* or *-ing* is added to a two-syllable word, the consonant is usually not doubled.

depart-depart**ed**
scatter-scatter**ed**

32. When a base word ends with a consonant and *y*, change the *y* to *i* before adding *-es, -ed, -er, -est,* or *-ness*.

countr**y**-countr**ies**
suppl**y**-suppl**ied**
angr**y**-angr**ier**
tin**y**-tin**iest**
happ**y**-happ**iness**

33. Add *s* to most words to name more than one. Add *es* to words that end with *s, x, sh,* or *ch* to name more than one thing.

trip**s**	wi<u>sh</u>**es**
bu<u>s</u>**es**	pea<u>ch</u>**es**
bo<u>x</u>**es**	

Prefixes and Suffixes

34. A **prefix** is a word part added to the beginning of a base word or word root.

reread	**con**fuse
unfair	**com**pete
dislike	**pre**serve
inhale	**per**fect
immediate	**pro**tect

35. A **suffix** is a word part added to the end of a base word or word root.

thought**ful**	home**less**
soft**ly**	good**ness**
writ**er**	excite**ment**

Special Spellings

36. **Homophones** are words that sound alike but have different meanings and spellings.

    bough-bow
    seen-scene

37. In **contractions**, an apostrophe takes the place of the letters that are dropped.

    have not-haven't
    should not-shouldn't

38. A **compound word** is made up of two or more smaller words. It can be written as one word, as two words joined by a hyphen, or as two separate words.

    sunlight pen pal
    great-aunt

39. **Silent consonants** are consonants that are not pronounced.

    wrong i**s**land
    pa**l**m of**t**en
    honest **k**new
    knee ha**l**f
    clim**b** ans**w**er

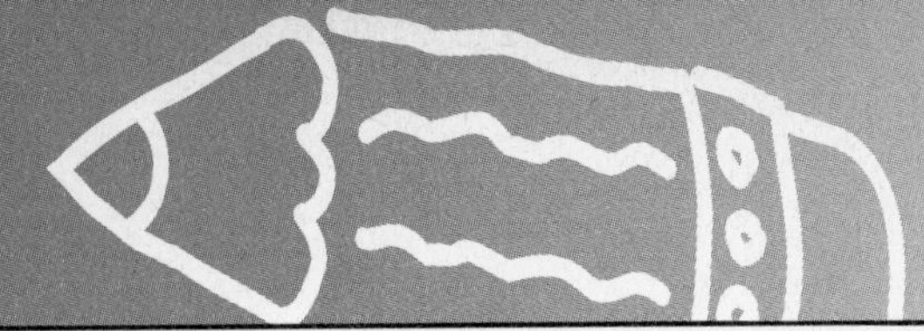

GRAMMAR GUIDE

SENTENCES

Definition

A **sentence** is a group of words that expresses a complete thought. It has a subject (who or what) and a predicate (what the subject does or is). A sentence begins with a capital letter.

Lightning flashed in the sky. **T**he alert ranger spotted the fire.

- A group of words that does not express a complete thought is called a **sentence fragment.** A fragment is not a sentence. A fragment is missing a subject, a predicate, or both.

Flashed in the sky. The alert ranger.
During the storm. When the tree fell.

Kinds of Sentences

There are four kinds of sentences.

- A **declarative sentence** tells something. It ends with a period.

  Deserts are dry**.**

- An **interrogative sentence** asks something. It ends with a question mark.

  Do you like deserts**?**

- An **imperative sentence** gives an order. It ends with a period.

  Always carry water**.**

- An **exclamatory sentence** expresses strong feeling. It ends with an exclamation point.

  How hot it was**!** **I**t was so hot**!**

Subjects and Predicates

Every sentence has a **subject** and a **predicate.**

- The **subject** tells whom or what the sentence is about. The **complete subject** includes all the words in the subject. It may be either one word or more than one word.

  The pilots of the plane waved. **They** were preparing for take-off.

- The **simple subject** is the main word or words in the complete subject.

  The pilots of the plane waved. **South America** is their destination.

- In an imperative sentence the subject *you* is understood.

  (You) Please bring your camera.

- The **predicate** tells what the subject is or does. The **complete predicate** includes all the words in the predicate. It may be either one word or more than one word.

  Captain Ortega **is a good pilot.** The large jet **landed.**

- The **simple predicate** is the main word or words in the complete predicate.

  Two helicopters **landed there.** They **have landed there before.**

Run-on Sentences

A **run-on sentence** is two or more sentences that are run together incorrectly.

- Correct a run-on sentence by writing each complete thought as a separate sentence.

  RUN-ON: Electricians often wear rubber gloves electricity cannot go through rubber.

  CORRECTED: Electricians often wear rubber gloves. Electricity cannot go through rubber.

- Correct a run-on sentence by making it into a compound sentence (using *and, but,* or *or*). In a compound sentence, the two parts should be related.

  RUN-ON: Some jobs require special clothing these clothes provide protection.

  CORRECTED: Some jobs require special clothing**, and** these clothes provide protection.

Run-on Sentences (continued)

- Correct a run-on that has three parts by dividing it into one compound sentence and one short sentence.

  RUN-ON: Some firefighters wear flameproof suits the suits are coated with metal they totally cover the firefighter.

  CORRECTED: Some firefighters wear flameproof suits. (*short*) The suits are coated with metal**, and** they totally cover the firefighter. (*compound*)

NOUNS

Definition

A **noun** names a person, a place, a thing, or an idea.

Nouns		
Persons	boy student	writer Li Chen
Places	lake Fenway Park	Olympia mountain
Things	boat calendar	sweater *Little Women*
Ideas	truth freedom	belief happiness

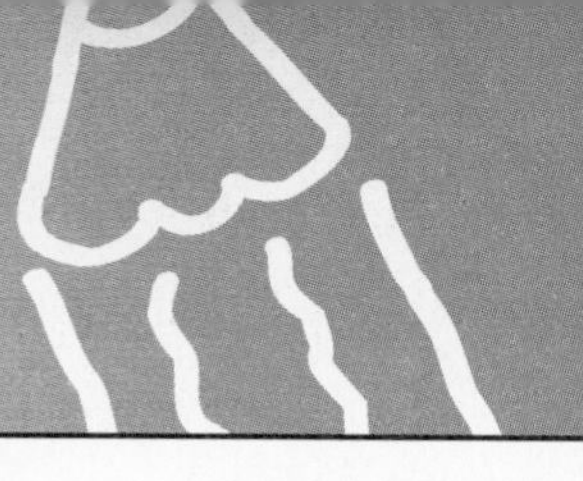

Common and Proper Nouns

A **common noun** names any person, place, or thing. A **proper noun** names a particular person, place, or thing. Capitalize proper nouns. Capitalize each important word in proper nouns of more than one word.

Common and Proper Nouns

Common nouns	Proper nouns	Common nouns	Proper nouns
street	North Drive	river	Hudson River
city	Vancouver	building	White House
state	Maryland	law	Bill of Rights
continent	Asia	author	Walter Dean Myers
ocean	Arctic Ocean	holiday	Fourth of July
mountain	Mt. McKinley	month	November
lake	Great Salt Lake	day	Monday

Singular and Plural Nouns

Singular nouns name one person, place, or thing,

The **farmer** drove to the **market** with the **box**.

Plural nouns name more than one person, place, or thing.

The **farmers** drove to the **markets** with the **boxes**.

- Form the plural of most nouns by adding *s* or *es*. Look at the ending of a singular noun to decide how to form the plural. Some nouns have special plural forms. (See chart on the next page.)

Singular and Plural Nouns (continued)

Rules for Forming Plural Nouns

Rule	Singular	Plural
1. Most singular nouns: Add *s.*	street house	streets houses
2. Nouns ending with *s*, *x*, *ch*, or *sh*: Add *es.*	dress ax bench dish	dresses axes benches dishes
3. Nouns ending with a vowel and *y*: Add *s.*	valley joy	valleys joys
4. Nouns ending with a consonant and *y*: Change the *y* to *i* and add *es.*	city cranberry	cities cranberries
5. Nouns ending in *f* or *fe*: Change the *f* to *v* and add *es* to some nouns. Add *s* to other nouns.	life calf leaf cliff	lives calves leaves cliffs
6. Nouns ending with a vowel and *o*: Add *s.*	rodeo studio radio	rodeos studios radios
7. Nouns ending with a consonant and *o*: Add *s* to some nouns. Add *es* to other nouns.	solo piano hero echo tomato	solos pianos heroes echoes tomatoes
8. Nouns that have special plural spellings	woman mouse foot ox	women mice feet oxen
9. Nouns that remain the same in the singular and the plural	sheep moose trout deer	sheep moose trout deer

Singular and Plural Possessive Nouns

A **singular possessive noun** shows that one person, place, or thing has or owns something.

- To form the possessive of a singular noun, add an apostrophe and *s.*

  the car**'s** tires   a student**'s** papers   Rosa**'s** opinion

A **plural possessive noun** shows that more than one person, place, or thing has or owns something.

- If a plural noun ends with *s,* add only an apostrophe.

  the cars**'** horns   two students**'** books   two girls**'** ideas

- If a plural noun does not end with *s,* add an apostrophe and *s.*

  the children**'s** choice   the oxen**'s** tracks   the people**'s** cheers

Singular	Singular Possessive	Plural	Plural Possessive
girl	girl's	girls	girls'
calf	calf's	calves	calves'
pony	pony's	ponies	ponies'
child	child's	children	children's
mouse	mouse's	mice	mice's
deer	deer's	deer	deer's

VERBS

Definition

A **verb** shows action or a state of being. It is the main word in the predicate.

ACTION: The fire **burns** brightly.   BEING: It **is** warm.

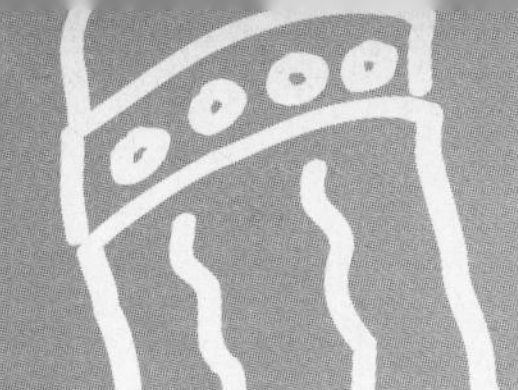

GRAMMAR GUIDE

Action Verbs and Direct Objects

An **action verb** shows what the subject does or did. Action verbs can also show action that you cannot see.

Roberta **swings** at the ball. Roberta **ran** to first base.

The coach **thought** about the players in the field.

A **direct object** is a noun or a pronoun in the predicate that receives the action of the verb.

- Direct objects follow action verbs only and answer the question *what* or *whom*

  The captain steers the big **ship**. (steers what? steers the big **ship**)

  The captain calls the **crew**. (calls whom? calls the **crew**)

- An action verb does not always have a direct object.

  The ship sails. The ship sails across the ocean.

Linking Verbs

A **linking verb** tells what the subject is or is like. It links the subject with a word or words in the predicate that name or describe the subject. If the word names the subject, it is a **predicate noun**. If it describes the subject, it is a **predicate adjective**.

PREDICATE NOUNS	PREDICATE ADJECTIVES
Anna is a **lifeguard**.	Anna is **cheerful**.
Jennifer is a **runner**.	Sue is **strong** and **fast**.
Who will be the **winner**?	The winner appears **happy**.

Linking Verbs (continued)

- A linking verb does not show action.

Common Linking Verbs					
am	is	are	was	were	will be
look	feel	taste	smell	seem	appear

- Some verbs can be either linking verbs or action verbs.

  LINKING: The soup **tastes** salty.

  ACTION: I **taste** the salt in this soup.

Main Verbs and Helping Verbs

A verb may be one word or a group of words.

The whistle **blew**.

The coach **blew** the whistle.

The runners **have started** the race.

- A **verb phrase** is made up of a main verb and a helping verb. The **main verb** shows the action. A **helping verb** works with the main verb. The helping verb comes before the main verb.

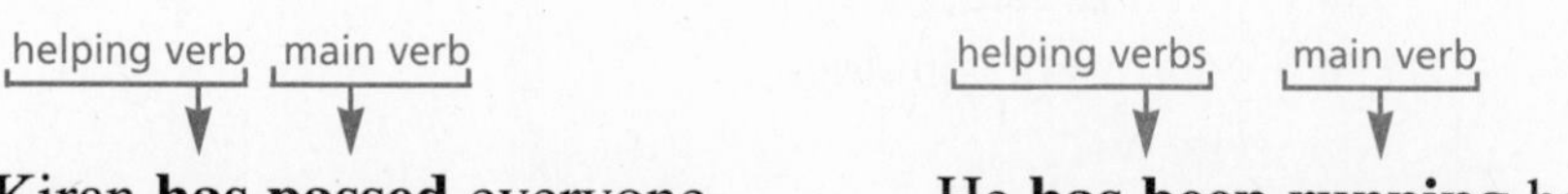

Kiran **has passed** everyone.

He **has been running** hard.

Common Helping Verbs				
am	are	were	shall	has
is	was	will	have	had

Verb Tense

The **tense** of the verb lets you know *when* something happens.

PRESENT: Bats **hunt** at night.
PAST: They **hunted** last night.
FUTURE: They **will hunt** tonight also.

Present Tense

A **present tense verb** shows action that is happening now. A present tense verb and its subject must agree in number (singular or plural).

- Add *s* or *es* to most verbs to show the present tense if the subject is singular.
- Do not add *s* or *es* if the subject is plural or is *I* or *you*.

Rules for Subject-Verb Agreement	
Singular subject: Add *s* or *es* to the verb.	The **driver trains** his dogs. **He teaches** one dog to lead. **He studies** his map.
Plural subject *I* or *you*: Do not add *s* or *es*.	The **dogs pull** the sleds. **Driver and team travel** far. **They work** together. **I like** your report on dogs. **You write** well.

Verb Tense / Present Tense (continued)

- Change the spelling of some verbs when adding *s* or *es*.

Rules for Forming the Present Tense

Most verbs: Add *s*.	get - get**s** play - play**s**
Verbs ending with *s*, *ch*, *sh*, *x*, and *z*: Add *es*.	pass - pass**es** punch - punch**es** push - push**es** mix - mix**es** fizz - fizz**es**
Verbs ending with a consonant and *y*: Change the *y* to *i* and add *es*.	try - tr**ies** empty - empt**ies**

Past Tense

A **past tense verb** shows that something already happened. Form the past tense of most verbs by adding *-ed*.

We **cooked** our dinner over a campfire last night.

- Change the spelling of some verbs when adding *-ed*.

A squirrel **hoped** for a few crumbs.

It **begged** for a peanut.

Then it **hurried** back to its nest.

(See chart on the next page.)

Verb Tense / Past Tense (continued)

Rules for Forming the Past Tense	
Most verbs: Add *-ed.*	play - play**ed** reach - reach**ed**
Verbs ending with *e*: Drop the *e* and add *-ed.*	believ**e** - believ**ed** hop**e** - hop**ed**
Verbs ending with a consonant and *y*: Change the *y* to *i* and add *-ed.*	stu**dy** - stud**ied** hur**ry** - hurr**ied**
Verbs ending with single vowel and a consonant: Double the final consonant and add *-ed.*	st**op** - sto**pped** pl**an** - pla**nned**

Future Tense

A **future tense verb** tells what is going to happen. Use the main verb with the helping verb *will* or *shall* to form the future tense.

Nori **will bring** his bird book tomorrow.
Nori and I **will look** for some nests.
Shall we **invite** Melissa?

Verb Tenses with *be* and *have*

Be and *have* have special forms in the present and past tense. Change the forms of *be* and *have* to agree with their subjects.

(See chart on the next page.)

Verb Tenses with *be* and *have* (continued)

Subject	Form of *be*		Form of *have*	
	Present	**Past**	**Present**	**Past**
Singular subjects:				
I	am	was	have	had
You	are	were	have	had
He, she, it (or singular noun)	is	was	has	had
Plural subjects:				
We	are	were	have	had
You	are	were	have	had
They	are	were	have	had

Irregular Verbs

Irregular verbs have special forms to show the past.

Irregular Verbs

Verb	Past tense	Past with helping verb
bring	brought	(has, have, had) brought
come	came	(has, have, had) come
go	went	(has, have, had) gone
make	made	(has, have, had) made
run	ran	(has, have, had) run
say	said	(has, have, had) said
take	took	(has, have, had) taken
think	thought	(has, have, had) thought
write	wrote	(has, have, had) written

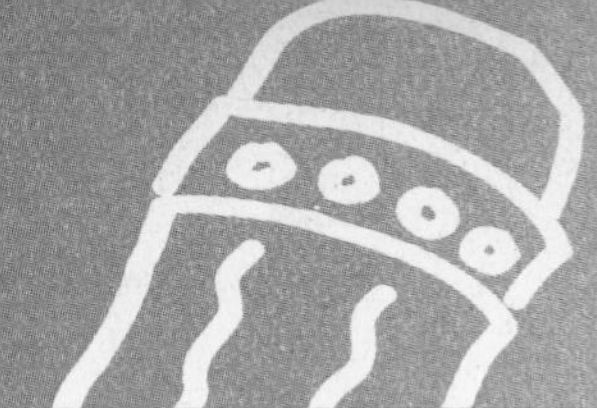

GRAMMAR GUIDE

Irregular Verbs (continued)

- Some irregular verbs follow similar patterns.

Verb	Past Tense	Past with Helping Verb
ring	rang	(has, have, had) rung
sing	sang	(has, have, had) sung
swim	swam	(has, have, had) swum
begin	began	(has, have, had) begun
tear	tore	(has, have, had) torn
wear	wore	(has, have, had) worn
break	broke	(has, have, had) broken
speak	spoke	(has, have, had) spoken
steal	stole	(has, have, had) stolen
choose	chose	(has, have, had) chosen
freeze	froze	(has, have, had) frozen
blow	blew	(has, have, had) blown
grow	grew	(has, have, had) grown
know	knew	(has, have, had) known
fly	flew	(has, have, had) flown

ADJECTIVES

Definition

An **adjective** is a word that describes a noun or a pronoun.

Powerful lions stared at us. They seemed **irritated.**

- An adjective tells what kind or how many. It can come before a noun or after a linking verb.

what kind	**Spotted** fawns were resting.	They looked **peaceful**.
how many	**Three** elephants were eating.	Monkeys did **several** tricks.

Adjectives (continued)

- When two or more adjectives are listed together, use a comma to separate them, unless one of the adjectives tells how many.

  Large, colorful parrots screeched. **Two white** geese honked loudly.

Articles

A, *an*, and *the* are special adjectives called **articles**. *A* and *an* refer to any person, place, or thing. *The* refers to a particular person, place, or thing.

Let's take **a** trip. (any) It's time for **the** trip. (particular)

Articles	
a	Use before singular words that begin with a consonant sound. **a** jet **a** high step
an	Use before singular words that begin with a vowel sound. **an** engineer **an** hour
the	Use before singular and plural words. **the** answer **the** plans

Demonstrative Adjectives

This, that, these, and *those* are demonstrative adjectives. They tell which one.

- *This* and *these* refer to nouns close to the speaker or writer. *That* and *those* refer to nouns farther away.

  This book is my favorite. **That** book is Aja's favorite.

- *This* and *that* are used with singular nouns, *these* and *those* with plural nouns.

  These books are mine. **Those** books are Aja's

Comparing with Adjectives

To compare two people, places, or things, add *-er* to most adjectives. To compare three or more, add *-est.* Use *more* and *most*, not *-er* and *-est,* with long adjectives.

ONE PERSON: Sy is **tall**. He seems **gigantic.**

TWO PERSONS: Lu is **taller** than Sy. She seems **more gigantic** than he does.

THREE OR MORE: Carlos is **tallest** of all. He seems **most gigantic.**

- Change the spelling of some adjectives when adding *-er* and *-est.*

Rules for Comparing with Adjectives

Rule	Examples
1. **Most adjectives:** Add *-er* or *-est* to the adjective.	bright bright**er** bright**est**
2. **Adjectives ending with *e*:** Drop the *e* and add *-er* or *-est.*	safe saf**er** saf**est**
3. **Adjectives ending with a consonant and *y*:** Change the *y* to *i* and add *-er* or *-est.*	busy bus**ier** bus**iest**
4. **One-syllable adjectives that end with a single vowel and a consonant:** Double the final consonant and add *-er* or *-est.*	flat flat**ter** flat**test**
5. **Some adjectives with two or more syllables:** Use *more* or *most* instead of *-er* or *-est.*	careful **more** careful **most** careful

Comparing with Adjectives (continued)

The adjectives *good* and *bad* have special forms for making comparisons.

- Use *better* and *worse* to compare two. Use *best* and *worst* to compare more than two.

ONE:	The dress rehearsal of our play was **good**.	No one made a **bad** mistake.
TWO:	Our first performance was **better**.	Our next one was **worse**.
THREE OR MORE:	Our last performance was **best**.	The third one was **worst**.

Comparing with *good* and *bad*		
Describing one person, place, or thing	good	bad
Describing two persons, places, or things	better	worse
Describing three or more persons, places, or things	best	worst

Proper Adjectives

A proper adjective is formed from a proper noun. A proper adjective begins with a capital letter. When a proper adjective is two words, capitalize both words.

Proper Noun	Proper Adjective
Italy	**Italian** cooking
Mexico	**Mexican** rug
Switzerland	**Swiss** watch
South America	**South American** bird

GRAMMAR GUIDE

ADVERBS

Definition

An **adverb** is a word that describes a verb and tells *how, when,* or *where.*

HOW: The plane landed **smoothly** at the airport.

WHEN: **Soon** Jeff would see his grandparents at the gate.

WHERE: They were waiting for him **there**.

How	When	Where
fast	tomorrow	here
hard	later	inside
together	again	far
happily	often	upstairs
quietly	first	downtown
secretly	next	somewhere
slowly	then	forward

Comparing with Adverbs

Use special forms of adverbs to compare actions.

Rules for Comparing with Adverbs		
Most short adverbs: Add *-er* or *-est* to the adverb.	late lat**er** lat**est**	earl**y** earli**er** earli**est**
Long adverbs and most adverbs that end with *-ly*: Use *more* or *most* with the adverb.	often **more** often **most** often	quickly **more** quickly **most** quickly

Comparing with Adverbs (continued)

ONE ACTION:	Amy will finish the book **soon.**
	She will return the book **promptly.**
TWO ACTIONS:	Amy will finish **sooner** than Jessie will.
	She will return the book **more promptly** than Jessie will.
THREE OR MORE:	Amy will finish **soonest** of all.
	She will return the book **most promptly** of all.

PRONOUNS

Definition

A **pronoun** is a word that takes the place of a noun.

Carl watches the swimmers.	**He** watches **them**.
The swimmers listen for the whistle.	**They** listen for **it**.
Mary held Mary's blue ribbon.	**She** held **her** blue ribbon.
Mr. Jones and I clapped loudly.	**We** clapped loudly.

Subject Pronouns

There are seven **subject pronouns**. Some are singular, and some are plural.

Subject Pronouns	
Singular	**Plural**
I you he, she, it	we you they

Bill, will **you** keep time?

Li and Andy, will **you** hand out towels?

Tania and I will record the times. **We** know what to do.

Carlton and Amy will cheer the team. **They** are very loud.

Subject Pronouns (continued)

- Use **subject pronouns** as subjects of sentences.

  I want to compete in a swim meet. **You** offered some tips.
  They have helped improve my speed.

- Use **subject pronouns** after forms of the verb *be*.

  The first swimmer into the water was **I**.
  Did Tina and Angelo win? Yes, the winners were **they**.

- When using *I* with another noun or subject pronoun, always name yourself last.

  Mel and I go to every swim meet. The time keepers at the last one were **Al and I**.

Object Pronouns

There are seven **object pronouns**. Some are singular, and some are plural. (Note that *it* and *you* may be subject or object pronouns.)

Object Pronouns	
Singular	**Plural**
me	us
you	you
him, her, it	them

Jeremy took Lupe and Carlos on a hike. He took **them** to Crystal Falls.
Dad gave the compass to Rebecca. Dad gave **it** to **her** last night.
Jeremy asked Leroy and me to carry the lunches. He gave **us** a pack.

- Use **object pronouns** after action verbs.

  Dad helped **her** build a campfire. They built **it** inside a circle of stones.

- Use **object pronouns** after words such as *to, for, about, between,* and *after.*

  Will Jeremy cook dinner for **us**? Arlyn will do the dishes with **me**.

- When using *me* with another noun or object pronoun, always name yourself last.

  Dad showed **Jeremy and me** how to fish.
  The fish weren't biting for **him and me**.

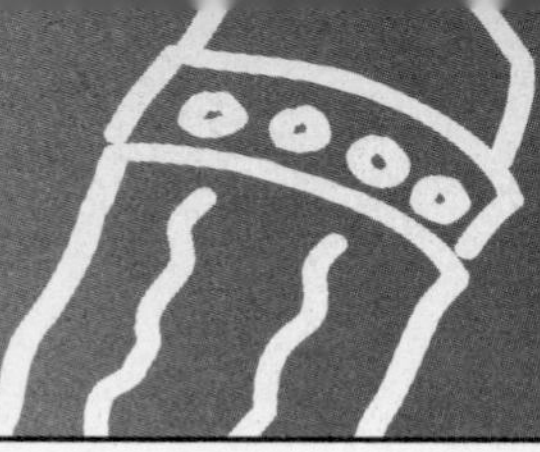

GRAMMAR GUIDE

Possessive Pronouns

A **possessive pronoun** shows ownership. It replaces a possessive noun.

Paul's pen is black. He keeps it in **his** pocket.

The blue notebook is Kate's. The pencil is also **hers**.

- There are two kinds of possessive pronouns. Some possessive pronouns appear before nouns. Other possessive pronouns stand alone.

Two Kinds of Possessive Pronouns			
Possessive pronouns used with nouns		Possessive pronouns that stand alone	
my	**My** book is green.	mine	The green book is **mine**.
your	Clean **your** desk.	yours	**Yours** is messy.
his	**His** bike is blue.	his	The red bike is **his**.
her	This is **her** house.	hers	**Hers** is the gray house.
its	**Its** coat is shaggy.	its	**Its** is the shaggy coat.
our	Those are **our** pens.	ours	Those pens are **ours**.
your	Take **your** sweaters.	yours	Leave **yours** here.
their	**Their** hats are red.	theirs	Those hats are **theirs**.

Contractions with Pronouns

You can combine pronouns with the verbs *am, is, are, will, would, have, has,* and *had* to form contractions. A contraction is a shortened form of two words.

- Use an apostrophe (') to replace any letters dropped from the second word.

Pronoun + Verb	Contraction	Pronoun + Verb	Contraction
I am	I'm	I have	I've
he is	he's	he has	he's
it is	it's	it has	it's
you are	you're	you have	you've
they are	they're	they have	they've
I will	I'll	I had	I'd
you will	you'll	you had	you'd
we would	we'd	we had	we'd

- Do not confuse possessive pronouns with contractions that sound the same. To decide which one to use, think about the meaning of the word.

Possessive pronouns	Contractions with pronouns
your = belonging to you	you're = you are
its = belonging to it	it's = it is

Your new dog is really cute. **You're** very lucky.
Its body is long and low. **It's** a dachshund.

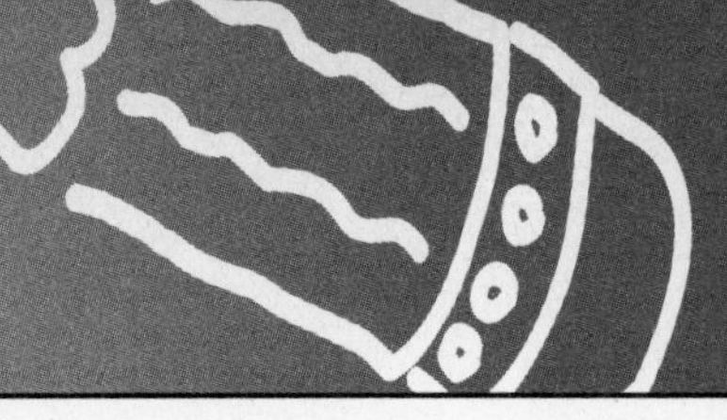

Double Subjects

Do not use a noun and a pronoun to name the same person, place, or thing.

INCORRECT	CORRECT
Mary she is my sister	**Mary** is my sister.
	She is my sister.
Her hat it is pretty	Her **hat** is pretty.
	It is pretty.

PREPOSITIONS AND PREPOSITIONAL PHRASES

Definition

A **preposition** relates the noun or the pronoun that follows it to another word in the sentence.

I liked the book with the blue cover. Sula gave it to me.

Common Prepositions

about	before	except	of	through
above	behind	for	off	to
across	below	from	on	under
after	beside	in	out	until
along	by	inside	outside	up
around	down	into	over	with
at	during	near	past	without

GRAMMAR GUIDE

Prepositional Phrases

A **prepositional phrase** is made up of a preposition, its object, and all the words in between.

We packed the fruit in our knapsacks.

The **object of the preposition** is the noun or the pronoun that follows the preposition.

I liked the book with (prep.) the blue **cover** (obj. of prep.).   Sula gave it to (prep.) **me** (obj. of prep.).

- The object of the preposition can be a compound object.

  We took enough oranges for Manuel and Anita.

- Check the pronoun in a compound object by removing the other object.

  Jim sat with Ann and **me**. (*Think:* Jim sat with **me**.)

  E-Ling waved to Alonso and us. (*Think:* E-Ling waved to **us**.)

- A prepositional phrase can be at the beginning, in the middle, or at the end of a sentence.

  At dawn we began our walk.   The map of the area helped us.

  The path went by a forest and a large lake.

ABBREVIATIONS

Abbreviations are shortened forms of words. Most abbreviations begin with a capital letter and end with a period. Use abbreviations only in special kinds of writing, such as addresses and lists.

• Titles

Mr. *(Mister)* Mr. Pedro Arupe
Mrs. *(Mistress)* Mrs. Jane Chang
Ms. Carla Tower
Sr. *(Senior)* James Morton, Sr.
Jr. *(Junior)* James Morton, Jr.
Dr. *(Doctor)* Dr. Ellen Masters

Note: *Miss* is not an abbreviation and does not end with a period.

• Words Used in Addresses

St. *(Street)*
Rd. *(Road)*
Ave. *(Avenue)*
Dr. *(Drive)*
Blvd. *(Boulevard)*
Rte. *(Route)*
Apt. *(Apartment)*
Pkwy. *(Parkway)*
Mt. *(Mount* or *Mountain)*
Expy. *(Expressway)*

• Words Used in Business

Co. *(Company)*
Corp. *(Corporation)*
Inc. *(Incorporated)*
Ltd. *(Limited)*

• Other Abbreviations

Some abbreviations are written in all capital letters, with a letter standing for each important word.

P.D. *(Police Department)*
J.P. *(Justice of the Peace)*
P.O. *(Post Office)*
R.N. *(Registered Nurse)*

ABBREVIATIONS (continued)

- **States**

The United States Postal Service uses two capital letters and no period in each of its state abbreviations.

AL *(Alabama)*
AK *(Alaska)*
AZ *(Arizona)*
AR *(Arkansas)*
CA *(California)*
CO *(Colorado)*
CT *(Connecticut)*
DE *(Delaware)*
FL *(Florida)*
GA *(Georgia)*
HI *(Hawaii)*
ID *(Idaho)*
IL *(Illinois)*
IN *(Indiana)*
IA *(Iowa)*
KS *(Kansas)*
KY *(Kentucky)*
LA *(Louisiana)*
ME *(Maine)*
MD *(Maryland)*
MA *(Massachusetts)*
MI *(Michigan)*
MN *(Minnesota)*
MS *(Mississippi)*
MO *(Missouri)*
MT *(Montana)*
NE *(Nebraska)*
NV *(Nevada)*
NH *(New Hampshire)*
NJ *(New Jersey)*
NM *(New Mexico)*
NY *(New York)*
NC *(North Carolina)*
ND *(North Dakota)*
OH *(Ohio)*
OK *(Oklahoma)*
OR *(Oregon)*
PA *(Pennsylvania)*
RI *(Rhode Island)*
SC *(South Carolina)*
SD *(South Dakota)*
TN *(Tennessee)*
TX *(Texas)*
UT *(Utah)*
VT *(Vermont)*
VA *(Virginia)*
WA *(Washington)*
WV *(West Virginia)*
WI *(Wisconsin)*
WY *(Wyoming)*

- **Initials**

Initials are abbreviations that stand for a person's first or middle name. Some names have both a first and a middle initial.

E.B. White *(Elwyn Brooks White)*
T. James Carey *(Thomas James Carey)*
Mr. John M. Gordon *(Mister John Morris Gordon)*

TITLES

Underlining

The important words and the first and last words in a title are capitalized. Titles of books, magazines, TV shows, movies, and newspapers are underlined.

The Call of the Wild (book) Cricket (magazine) Nova (TV show)
Treasure Island (movie) The Phoenix Express (newspaper)

Computer Tip: Use italic type for these kinds of titles instead of underlining.

Quotation Marks with Titles

Titles of short stories, songs, articles, book chapters, and most poems are set off by quotation marks (“ ”).

“The Necklace” (short story) “Home on the Range” (song)
“Three Days in the Sahara” (article) “The Human Brain” (chapter)
“Deer at Dusk” (poem)

QUOTATIONS

Quotation Marks with Commas and Periods

Quotation marks are used to set off a speaker’s exact words. The first word of a quotation begins with a capital letter. Punctuation belongs *inside* the closing quotation marks. Commas separate a quotation from the rest of the sentence.

“Where,” asked the stranger, “is the post office?”
“Please put away your books now,” said Mr. Emory.
Linda whispered, “What time is it?”
“It’s late,” replied Bill. “Let’s go!”

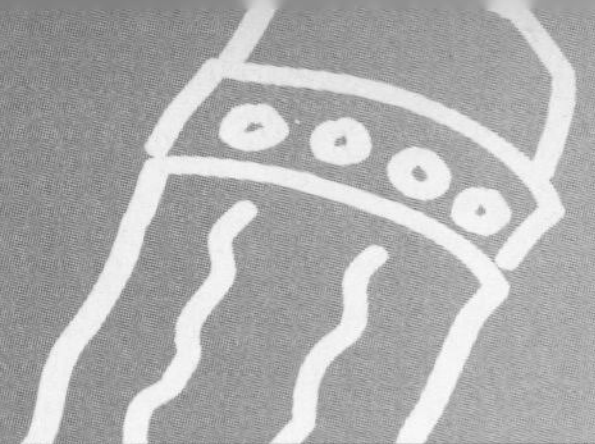

GRAMMAR GUIDE

Writing a Conversation

Begin a new paragraph each time a new person begins speaking.

"Are you going to drive all the way to Columbus in one day?" asked my Uncle Ben.

"I really haven't decided," said my father. "I was hoping that you would share the driving with me."

CAPITALIZATION

1. Capitalize the first word of every sentence.

What a wonderful day this is!

2. Capitalize the pronoun *I*.

What can I do this afternoon?

3. Capitalize proper nouns. If a proper noun is made up of more than one word, capitalize each important word.

Emily G. Messe District of Columbia Lincoln Memorial

4. Capitalize titles or their abbreviations when used with a person's name.

Governor Bradford Senator Smith Dr. Ling

5. Capitalize family titles when they are used as names or as part of names.

We called Aunt Leslie. May we leave now, Grandpa?

6. Capitalize proper adjectives.

We ate at a French restaurant. That is a North American custom.
She is French.

7. Capitalize the names of days, months, and holidays.

The meeting is on the first Tuesday in May.
We watched the parade on the Fourth of July.

Capitalization (continued)

8. Capitalize the names of groups.

Aspen Mountain Club International League

9. Capitalize the names of buildings and companies.

Empire State Building Able Supply Company Central School

10. Capitalize the first, last, and all important words in a title. Do not capitalize words such as *a, in, and, of,* and *the* unless they begin or end a title.

Secrets of a Wildlife Watcher "Growing Up"
The Los Angeles Times

11. Capitalize the first word in the greeting and the closing of a letter.

Dear Marcia, Sincerely yours,

12. Capitalize the first word of each main topic and subtopic in an outline.

I. Types of fire departments
  A. Full-time departments
  B. Volunteer departments

PUNCTUATION

End Marks

There are three end marks. A *period* (**.**) ends a declarative or imperative sentence. A *question mark* (**?**) follows an interrogative sentence. An *exclamation point* (**!**) follows an exclamatory sentence.

The notebook is on the shelf. *(declarative)*
Watch that program at eight tonight. *(imperative)*
Where does the trail end? *(interrogative)*
This is your best poem so far! *(exclamatory)*

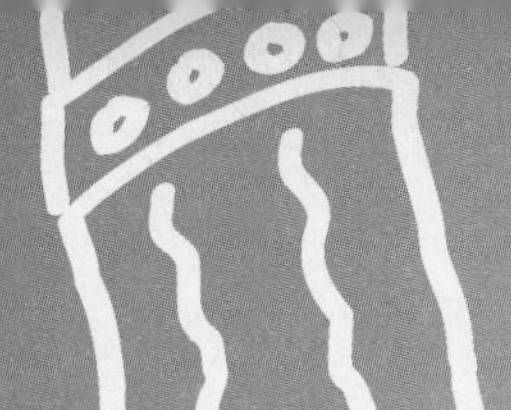

GRAMMAR GUIDE

Apostrophe

To form the possessive of a singular noun, add an apostrophe and *s*.

doctor's grandfather's James's community's

For a plural noun that ends in *s,* add only an apostrophe.

sisters' families' Boltons' hound dogs'

For a plural noun that does not end in *s,* add an apostrophe and *s* to form the plural possessive.

geese's children's men's mice's

Use an apostrophe in contractions in place of dropped letters. Do not use contractions in formal writing.

isn't *(is not)*	I'm *(I am)*
can't *(cannot)*	they've *(they have)*
won't *(will not)*	they'll *(they will)*
wasn't *(was not)*	could've *(could have)*
we're *(we are)*	would've *(would have)*
it's *(it is)*	should've *(should have)*

Colon

Use a colon after the greeting in a business letter.

Dear Mrs. Trimby: Dear Realty Homes:

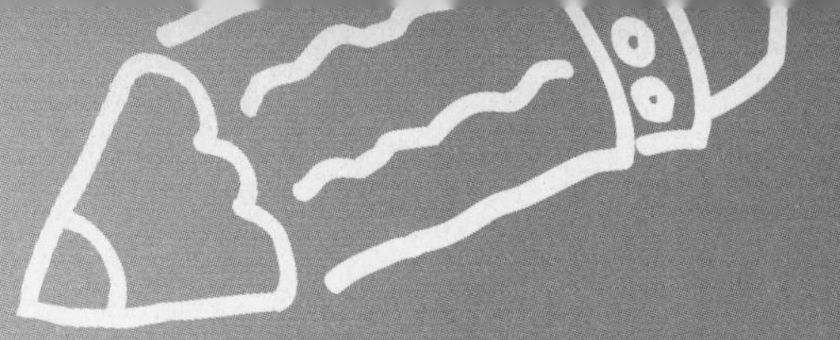

Comma

A comma (,) tells your reader where to pause.

1. For words in a series, put a comma after each item except the last. Do not use a comma if only two items are listed.

   We made a salad of lettuce, peppers, and tomatoes.

2. Use commas to separate two or more adjectives that are listed together unless one adjective tells how many.

   The fresh, ripe fruit was placed in a bowl.
   One red apple was especially shiny.

3. Use a comma before the conjunctions *and, but,* and *or* in a compound sentence.

   Some students were at lunch, but others were studying.

4. Use commas after introductory words such as *yes, no, oh,* and *well* when they begin a sentence.

   Yes, it's a perfect day for a picnic. Well, I'll make dessert.

5. Use a comma to separate a noun in direct address.

   Gloria, hold this light for me.
   How was the movie, Grandma?
   Can you see, Joe, where I left my glasses?

6. Use a comma to separate the month and the day from the year.

   I celebrated my birthday on July 3, 1992.

7. Use a comma between the names of a city and a state.

   Denver, Colorado Miami, Florida

8. Use a comma after the greeting in a friendly letter.

   Dear Tayo, Dear Aunt Claudia,

9. Use a comma after the closing in a letter.

   Your friend, Yours truly,

Quotation Marks See Quotations, p. 309.

GRAMMAR GUIDE

PROBLEM WORDS

Words	Rules	Examples
can may	*Can* means "to be able to do something." *May* means "to be allowed or permitted."	Nellie can read quickly. May I borrow your book?
good well	*Good* is an adjective. *Well* is usually an adverb. It is an adjective only when it refers to health.	The weather looks good. She sings well. Do you feel well?
its it's	*Its* is a possessive pronoun. *It's* is a contraction of *it is*.	The dog wagged its tail. It's cold today.
let leave	*Let* means "to permit or allow." *Leave* means "to go away from" or "to let remain in a place."	Please let me go swimming. I will leave soon. Leave it on my desk.
sit set	*Sit* means "to rest in one place." *Set* means "to place or put."	Please sit in this chair. Set the vase on the table.
teach learn	*Teach* means "to give instruction. *Learn* means "to receive instruction.	He teaches us how to dance. I learned about history.
their there they're	*Their* is a possessive pronoun. *There* is an adverb. It may also begin a sentence. *They're* is a contraction of *they are*.	Their coats are on the bed. Is Carlos there? There is my book. They're going to the store.
two to too	*Two* is a number. *To* means "in the direction of." *Too* means "more than enough" and "also."	I bought two shirts. A squirrel ran to the tree. Can we go too?
your you're	*Your* is a possessive pronoun. *You're* is a contraction for *you are*.	Are these your glasses? You're late again!

ADJECTIVE AND ADVERB USAGE

Double Comparisons

Never combine *-er* with the word *more*. Do not combine *-est* with the word *most*.

You are a better (not *more better*) artist than I.
The fourth question is the easiest one (not *most easiest*).

Negatives

A negative is a word that means "no" or "not." Do not use two negatives to express one negative idea.

INCORRECT: We can't do nothing.
CORRECT: We can't do anything.
CORRECT: We can do nothing.

Negative Words		
no	no one	never
none	nothing	neither
nobody	nowhere	

PRONOUN USAGE

Agreement

A pronoun must agree with the noun to which it refers.

Kee bought a newspaper. Mary read it.
Jeff and Cindy came to dinner. They enjoyed the meal.

Double Subjects

Do not use a double subject—a noun and a pronoun—to name the same person, place, or thing.

INCORRECT: The food it was delicious.
CORRECT: The food was delicious.

PROOFREADING CHECKLIST

Check your paper for mistakes. Use the questions below to help you. Correct any mistakes you find. After you have made the corrections, put a check mark in the box next to the question.

- ❑ **1.** Did I indent each paragraph?
- ❑ **2.** Did I make each sentence a complete thought?
- ❑ **3.** Are there any run-on sentences?
- ❑ **4.** Did I spell all words correctly?
- ❑ **5.** Did I use capital letters correctly?
- ❑ **6.** Did I use punctuation marks correctly?
- ❑ **7.** Did I use nouns, verbs, adjectives, and pronouns correctly?

Is there anything else you should look for? Make your own proofreading list on a separate piece of paper.

PROOFREADING MARKS

Mark	Explanation	Example
¶	Begin a new paragraph. Indent the paragraph.	¶ We went to an air show last Saturday. Eight jets flew across the sky in the shape of *V*'s, *X*'s, and diamonds.
^	Add letters, words, or sentences.	The leaves were red ^and orange.
ℓ	Take out words, sentences, and punctuation marks. Correct spelling.	The sky is bright ~~blew.~~ blue Huge clouds ~~,~~ move quickly.
/	Change a capital letter to a small letter.	The ~~F~~ireflies blinked in the dark.
≡	Change a small letter to a capital letter.	New York city is exciting.

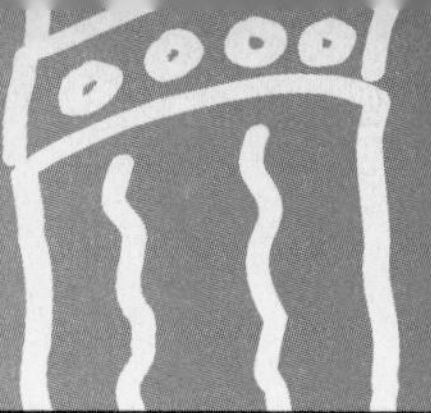

MY NOTES

MY NOTES

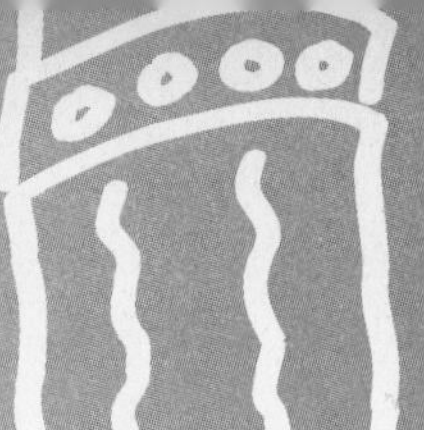

MY NOTES

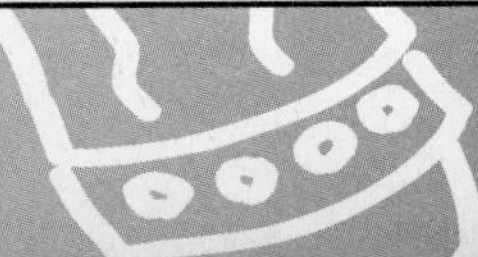

MY NOTES